Detroit's
Coming of Age

nAS 1973

Bill —

May Detroit continue to come of
age as you minister in it's Northeast
corner —

Shalom,
Howie

by Don Lochbiler

Detroit's Coming of Age
1873 to 1973

A Savoyard Book
published for The Detroit News
by Wayne State University Press
Detroit, 1973

Library of Congress Cataloging in Publication Data
Lochbiler, Don, 1908-
   Detroit's coming of age, 1873-1973
   (A Savoyard book)
   Appeared also as 52 weekly installments in The Detroit News
during its centennial year.
   1. Detroit—History.   I. Detroit News   II. Title
F574.D4L57   917.74'34'034   73-19955
ISBN 0-8143-1498-8

Contents

Foreword

In the story of urban America it would be difficult to parallel the evolution of the city of Detroit from a localized hub of Michigan and Great Lakes commerce to the 1973 sprawling giant known world wide as the birthplace of the industrial mass production.

If any portent of a larger future existed it was in the frontier enthusiasm common to Detroiters, even in 1873, a year of national depression. Their city was a crossroad of opportunity and young men of driving ambition gravitated to it and achieved beyond their greatest expectations. Here newcomers rubbed shoulders with lumbermen busy extracting more riches out of Michigan's pine forests than were taken from the California gold fields. The lumber wealth supplied ready capital for venture enterprise, and developing industry attracted a labor force with highly-specialized mechanical skills. It followed that when the world was ready for the automobile, Detroit was ready to become the Motor City.

This book is not a formal history of a Detroit century. Neither is it a sociological treatise. Rather it is an exercise in the dramatist's technique of focusing on moments of exciting action to impart the flavor of an era.

Writer Don Lochbiler invites the reader to savor the ups and downs, the comedy and pathos, the heady excitement of a city on the make through the 1873-1973 century which also encompassed the first hundred years of publication of The Detroit News.

In these pages the reader will go back for the last

performance of "The Great Houdini" at Detroit's Garrick Theatre; he will attend the funeral of Margaret Mather, a child of the streets who became a foremost Shakespearean actress, and die a bit with Socialite Maude Ledyard whose diplomat husband was to become the first Peking victim of China's Boxer Rebellion.

He will read of Detroit's lusty labor movement from the 1900 Labor Day parade through the blazing career of the late Walter Reuther. He will "be there" with the great Barney Oldfield setting automotive racing records,and get the background story of those mad "guys with buzz wagons" who were to put the world on wheels.

The selections, fifty-two of them — one for each week of The News' centennial year — are the work of a reporter-researcher whose Detroit News career (1927-1973) covered the last forty-six of The News' first one hundred years. Born in Detroit, Lochbiler started his research in 1968 as a project in anticipation of his paper's centennial observance.

For five years Lochbiler kept at it, checking back on stories which were legendary (and sometimes proved by his research to be untrue) when he was a beginning reporter. Other stories came from his own questioning. What was written on the day the first electric trolley clanged into Detroit action? When did the last horse-drawn fire engine run? What were the great fire, disaster, police and theatrical stories of the century?

The resulting illustrated series appeared in weekly installments during The News' centennial year. Beyond all else they make clear that every Detroiter can take pride in his city's colorful heritage.

Martin S. Hayden
Editor,
The Detroit News

Prelude
to a Centennial

America was growing up.

And in 1873 people all over the land were thinking about it. There was an enormous upsurge of national pride. During the spring, plans were discussed eagerly for a centennial exposition in 1876, commemorating the 100th anniversary of American independence.

The timing seemed right to flex muscles and get things done. In Detroit, two men especially were moved to set about converting their long-cherished dreams into reality.

One of them, Silas Farmer, focused his dream on the city's past. Writers everywhere were taking up projects for centennial histories of their communities. There was a lot of history in Detroit — it was 75 years older than the United States — and Farmer felt he was the one to set it down.

In 1873 Farmer was 34. He would live another 29 years, and virtually all the remainder of his life would be devoted to telling Detroit's long story.

Another Detroiter, James E. Scripps, focused his dream for the city in another way. In 1873, he was 38. He would devote the rest of his life to Detroit history, too. But Scripps would print that history as it was lived, day by day, in the newspaper he founded, The Evening News — which later became The Detroit News.

Between them, Farmer and Scripps would chronicle the story of Detroit with a thoroughness probably never achieved before their time for any city, anywhere.

James E. Scripps
He dreamed of the future

Farmer devoted several years to research before he let it be known he was working on a local history. Then he issued a prospectus with an elaborate two-color title page, "The Metropolis of Michigan. A Centennial Memorial. Detroit, illustrated, 1775-76, 1875-76."

The more he dug into the past, the more fascinated Farmer became — and the more he came and went, but no Detroit history appeared. Instead Farmer issued a new prospectus, with an added map.

In 1876 and 1877, Farmer sent letters to the citizens who had ordered his book, explaining the delay. Many subscribers were skeptical. The '70's passed, the '80's arrived, and still the promised volume failed to appear.

Farmer was too busy to worry about his subscribers. He interviewed surviving pioneers. He canvassed industries, churches and business houses. He journeyed to Quebec and to France to consult old archives.

2   At last, in 1884, the history was published — and

Silas Farmer
He focused on the past

expectations were exceeded. The book contained
more than 1,000,000 words and hundreds of drawings and many maps.

The maps fitted Farmer's talents. His father,
John Farmer, drew the first map of the government road from Detroit to the Maumee River in
northern Ohio in 1834, and the following year he
began to publish maps of the Michigan Territory.

Silas Farmer, born in 1839, joined his father's oc-
cupation and took out his first map copyright in
1869. The map trade provided a living through the
years he devoted to historical research.

His masterpiece received continuing acclaim.
New editions were printed in 1889 and 1891. A second volume of equal size, containing biographies of
prominent Detroiters, was added. The later editions
carried the subtitle, "A Chronological Cyclopedia."
It was well worth the name.

Many able historians have written about Detroit
since Farmer, but their tasks began where he left
off. For the city's growth up to the 1880's, all drew
upon his definitive material. 3

Like Farmer, Scripps had printer's ink in his veins. His father, James Mogg Scripps, was one of the leading bookbinders of England when the son, James Edmund Scripps, was born in 1835.

Nine years old when his parents came to America, young Scripps grew up on a frontier farm in Illinois. He made his way to Chicago, where he graduated from commercial college and later got a $7-a-week job on a newspaper.

By today's standards most newspapers of the period were sorry specimens. They ran to four pages and there was little local news. Also, their cost was relatively high.

Detroit's population doubled to 80,000 by 1870 but only 12,000 papers were sold daily. Scripps thought in terms of a paper that everyone could afford, with adequate coverage of local news.

Soon he was ready to test his theories. He put them before prospective readers in an editorial in his first issue, Aug. 23, 1873:

"There has been an error in leaving the field of popular journalism entirely unoccupied . . . .

"In my opinion there should be papers in which only such things are published as are of interest to the great mass of readers . . . Popularity and usefulness are our only aims, the wants of the great public our only criterion in the choice of matter for our columns."

Scripps had faith in Detroit's future but he could hardly envision that within his lifetime the city would experience a boom which would make it the fastest-growing metropolis in the land for many years. He could hardly foresee that the horse-and-buggy city in which he started his paper would put all America on wheels.

The press run of his first issue was only a thousand papers and no one knew better than Scripps how precarious his venture was. It would have been hard to imagine that when The News celebrated its own centennial in 1973 it would be the largest evening newspaper in the nation.

Scripps' efforts achieved a reality far beyond measurement. Silas Farmer's million-word account of Detroit's first century pales besides the hundreds of millions in the history of the city from 1873 to 1973, as embodied in the files of the paper's century run.

4

When Scripps and Farmer dreamed their dreams the 20th century seemed far in the future. But both lived to see it.

Farmer died in 1902. His plates and records went to another history-minded Detroiter, Clarence M. Burton, who followed in his footsteps as the city historian. Today they are part of the public treasure in the Burton Historical Collection of the Detroit Public Library.

Farmer's history was republished as recently as 1969. It remains in constant use.

Scripps died May 29, 1906. It was a time for his newspaper to look back on its founder's life. The story was told of the diary Scripps kept through his adult years — a diary in which he outlined his hopes for a newspaper 14 years before he was able to make it all come true.

The News went on with the task he set for it — recording day by day the drama and pathos, the tragedy and comedy of Detroit.

1. General Grant Remembers

"All quiet on the Potomac!"

Smiling Detroiters greeted each other happily with the phrase that had been a Civil War watchword. They were preparing for the reunion of the Army of the Potomac in their city in June, 1882, 20 years after it had fought the bloody Seven Days battles before Richmond. But Detroit was anything but quiet when Wednesday, June 14, arrived.

Flags decorated the streets and bunting covered the reviewing stand erected in the Campus Martius for the veterans' parade. James Vernor, the druggist, displayed in his show window the dressing gown of Jefferson Davis — a war trophy brought home by Sgt. Wesley D. Pond of the 4th Michigan Cavalry.

At Music Hall, where a reception was planned, the stage was set to carry out the "All quiet on the Potomac" theme. A large panorama by Robert Hopkin showed tents glistening in the moonlight. The painted tents were flanked with real cannons and stacked muskets.

A big crowd gathered at the Michigan Central Depot, where 1,500 visitors arrived by 8;30 a.m. Four more special trains were expected shortly. The most eager throng in town, however, jammed Woodward Avenue in front of the Russell House. They were waiting for a glimpse of America's greatest living hero, Gen. Ulysses S. Grant, the former President.

The ex-President and his wife had arrived by Canada Southern late Tuesday night, and few had seen them as they were driven to the hotel in a carriage put at their disposal by Mayor William G. Thompson. When they finally appeared after a late breakfast, the general hardly seemed to hear the cheers. It was not to the Music Hall that Grant ordered the carriage, but to an old mansion on Fort Street where Mrs. Letitia Chandler, the widow of an old friend, lived alone. And if the Grants talked on the way about the days 33 years before when they first came to Detroit, it was a strange story they remembered.

They were a newlywed couple then. Tripping gaily off the steamer from Buffalo at the Shelby Street wharf in the spring of 1849, both Grant and his bride, the former Julia Dent, were delighted to reach Detroit. Grant's orders had kept him in the snowbound village of Sackett's Harbor, New York, all winter. He pulled strings furiously for a transfer to his old regiment, the 4th Infantry, at the Detroit Barracks.

The northern weather was hard on Julia. She was a Missouri girl. Grant had married her the previous summer, on his first leave after the Mexican War. On the ride to the Campus Martius in the National Hotel bus, they glanced eagerly at the sights of Detroit. A thriving city of 20,000 it was a metropolis compared with Sackett's Harbor. Looking forward to a shopping spree, Julia gave special note to the big dry goods emporium of Z. Chandler & Co., on Jefferson near Woodward.

At the National Hotel, the room assigned to them by their host, the suave J. M. Barstow, was small. Nothing was elaborate at the two-story, brick-fronted National.

It didn't really matter. The Grants needed the room only until the more comfortable quarters Grant had found for them would be ready. He had arranged for them to have a white cottage on east Fort, between Russell and Rivard, that rented for $250 a year. This was a bit steep for the lieutenant, even though his allowances brought his base pay of $30 up to $69.50 a month, but it wasn't far from the Detroit Barracks.

They moved in and toasted the new home, along with Grant's 27th birthday, on April 27. There was no basement in the cottage and no furnace, but a   7

Ulysses S. Grant

kitchen stove and two fireplaces made it cozy.
Warming pans were a necessity in the unheated
bedrooms.

Julia soon was a belle of the 4th Regiment's social
affairs. Her husband, who found most of his simple
duties as regimental quartermaster were performed by an efficient sergeant, bought a race
horse. The favorite course was along Jefferson
from Third to 12th. Grant competed with some success against the Campaus, the Forsythes, the Ci-
cottes and others. Sometimes, too, he entered
longer races ending up at Ten Eyck's tavern in
Dearborn.

Michigan's first state fair was held that summer
on the outskirts of Detroit north of Grand Circus
Park. The Grants enjoyed it. A farm boy himself,
Grant took a good look at the prize livestock.

That autumn the garrison staged a military reception every Saturday night, usually in the ballroom of the Michigan Exchange Hotel. Grant never
had learned to dance, but brother officers were all
too happy to whirl Julia through the cotillions. More
to Grant's liking were the officers' weeknight gather-

Zachariah Chandler

ings in the back room of the American Bar at Jefferson and Randolph.

Julia became pregnant and stopped going to dances early in 1850. In the spring she left to give birth to the baby at her parents' home in St. Louis. Grant moved in with their friends, Capt. and Mrs. John Gore, on Jefferson at Russell. The two men often walked to a store the post sutler had opened on Jefferson near Woodward, with a back room reserved for the officers — equipped with a barrel of whisky and a tin cup.

After Julia returned with their son, Frederick Dent Grant, much of her time was taken up with baby. Grant spent many evenings in the sutler's back room. On a night in January, 1851, he slipped on the icy sidewalk outside Zachariah Chandler's residence at Jefferson and St. Antoine. Grant sent the doctor's bill for treating his injured ankle to Chandler, and when Chandler refused to pay, Grant brought suit. The merchant demanded a jury trial and conducted his own case. Admitting failure to clear his sidewalk, he denounced Grant, Gore, and the military stationed in Detroit generally.

"Soldiers are but idle loafers living off the tax paying community," he declared. "And, Lt. Grant, if you soldiers would only stay sober, perhaps you wouldn't fall on people's sidewalks."

Grant won, but the jury awarded him only 5 cents in damages. Chandler was ordered to pay court costs.

Chandler had considerable political influence, and he may have used it. At any rate, a few months later the War Department closed the Detroit Barracks — and sent Grant back to Sackett's Harbor. Interestingly enough, Grant joined a chapter of the Sons of Temperance there.

Soon Chandler was elected mayor of Detroit. He was the leader of Michigan abolitionists and helped finance the "Underground Railroad," aiding fugitive slaves to reach haven in Canada. In 1852, Chandler was the unsuccessful Whig candidate for governor. Grant was promoted to captain that year. In 1854, Chandler and other former Whigs formed a new political organization, the Republican Party, to fight slavery. For Grant, 1854 was a sad year — he was virtually forced to resign his commission because of heavy drinking.

Not until the Civil War brought him back to the Army did Grant's star rise again, but by 1857 the Republicans were strong enough to elect many candidates — among them Chandler as U.S. senator from Michigan. When the two principals in the Detroit icy sidewalk suit met in wartime Washington, both could smile at the past. Chandler was the big man of the all-important Congressional Committee on the Conduct of the War. Grant was President Abraham Lincoln's best general.

Both men were destined to rise even higher. When Grant became President he named Chandler to his Cabinet as secretary of the interior. And in America's turbulent centennial year, Chandler emerged as the political mastermind who put Grant's successor in the White House in the nation's most disputed election.

The 1882 visit of the Grants was a welcome one for Letitia Chandler. Since the death of her husband in 1879, her life had revolved around mementos and memories.

Grant never saw Detroit again. He died three

Gen. Grant's old home on Fort St.

years later, and the cottage on Fort Street was draped in black.

On the 100th anniversary of his birth, in 1922, patriotic societies dedicated a flagpole there. In 1936 the house was to be torn down. But a history-minded citizen, P.W.A. Fitzsimmons, stepped in to save it.

Today it stands restored on the State Fair grounds — white picket fence, warming pans and all.

2. "Year of a Hundred Years"

The poet Henry W. Longfellow called 1876 the "Year of a Hundred Years" in the verses he wrote for America's centennial.

In Detroit the long-awaited celebration began well before midnight Monday, July 3. Rain started to fall at dusk, and by 11 p.m. decorations that had been put up all over town looked in sad shape. But the downpour let up toward 12 o'clock, and within a few minutes the downtown streets were alive with merrymakers.

As the City Hall bell struck 12, guns reverberated throughout the city. Church bells struck up a patriotic clangor. The sky was illumined with rockets and Roman candles set off from the top of the City Hall tower.

Rain came down, too, from 10 to noon the morning of the Fourth, the hours of the grand procession up Woodward Avenue — decorated for the occasion from the ferry dock to Grand Circus Park. But nothing could dampen the spirits of the crowd which gathered at the City Hall itself.

Of all the buildings in town that day, Detroiters were proudest of their new City Hall. They would have been as shocked to think it would not last a hundred years as if they had been told that America itself would never complete a second century. But time was to run out for the beloved City Hall before the end of a century run.

It was dedicated on an earlier Fourth of July, in 1871, and there is no mystery about what Detroit's

City Hall as it appeared in the beginning

80,000 inhabitants did that day, of all days. Almost to a man, they spent it marveling at the new edifice.

Young fry explored every turret, tower and balcony. Hardly any citizen was too old to climb the iron stairways to the top of the main tower. Silas Farmer, of course, was among the climbers, and he described the details for use in the history he was planning — it was 13 steps from the sidewalk to the entrance door, 67 to the stairway, 143 to the clock and 213 to the tower.

The view from the top, as Farmer wrote, was

magnificent: "The usually clean streets look still cleaner in the distance. The grove of shade trees, the elegant residences, the river and its shipping, the Canadian shore and Belle Isle, all unite to form a panorama not often excelled."

Another reward of the climb was a closeup view of the 14-foot stone maidens on the cornices of the first section of the tower. They represented Justice, Industry, Art and Commerce.

But the top attraction was the tower clock. The largest in America, dedication-day orators boasted. At noon, the pendulum weighing 125 pounds was set in motion. The clock began its appointed task — so the speakers confidently said — of ticking off the centuries.

One of the nation's foremost clockmakers, W. A. Hendrie of Chicago created the clock especially for Detroit. He regarded it as his masterpiece.

Some citizens looked upon Hendrie's bill as something of a masterpiece, too. It was $2,850, and there were scandalized cries against spending that much of the taxpayers' money on a mere timepiece, however huge. But once the City Hall was finished only a few curmudgeons could continue to grumble. Each of the four dials was eight feet, three inches in diameter, and every night illumination was provided so citizens could tell the time from across the street.

Everyone admired the clock's intricate machinery. A city engineer of a later era described it as "massive and durable as a tractor." Even more massive than the machinery was the bell. It weighed 7,670 pounds and cost $2,782.

Children especially liked the six cast-iron deer which graced the City Hall lawn. The era was one in which inanimate wildlife was considered to add eclat to the urban scene, and stone lions guarded the grounds of numerous fine mansions on Jefferson, Fort and Woodward.

In all, Detroit spent $600,000 on the showplace City Hall. A big outlay admittedly, but the citizens felt it was worth the money.

Three years after the building was completed there was another big Fourth of July. That was when two formidable watchdogs of the peace were added to its adornments. These were cannons captured by Commodore Oliver Hazard Perry from the British at the Battle of Lake Erie, which sealed American victory in the War of 1812.

Niches provided for statues on the east and west sides of the City Hall were left unoccupied until 1884. In that year sculptures of Antoine Cadillac, Fr. Gabriel Richard, Fr. Jacques Marquette and Sieur de LaSalle, were added.

Commissioned by a leading citizen, Bela Hubbard, they were carved by the foremost Detroit sculptor of the period, Julius Theodore Melchers. A native of Prussia, Melchers came to Detroit in 1885 after working on the Crystal Palace in London.

The Detroit Business Pioneers instituted a rite of washing the faces of the City Hall clock once a year. The ceremony was on July 24, the anniversary of Detroit's founding. The town's most dignified and venerable business leaders gladly took their turns as steeplejack clock-washers.

If the clock told time for the people, the City Hall itself told their mood — in good times or bad. It was gala with flags and bunting when the 20th century arrived, or when such dignitaries visited the city as Adm. George Dewey, hero of the Spanish-American War, or President Theodore Roosevelt.

It was somber with wreaths when a favorite son like Gov. Hazen S. Pingree died in England and the city counted the days of his long journey home.

Every summer flowers spelled out a big "welcome" sign on the lawn for visitors. In 1944, the lawn gave way to a municipal Victory Garden, planted with vegetables, in a wartime campaign to raise more foodstuffs

In 1946, after 75 years' accumulated grime had darkened the structure dirty gray, John C. Lodge, dean of the City Council, moved to restore it to its pristine beauty. Sandblasting operations were authorized. Much dust was raised. The building emerged with its creamy yellow sandstone gleaming to the eye. But it was the last blaze of glory.

With the completion of the City-County Building in 1957, old City Hall's days were numbered. Many protested when Mayor Louis C. Miriani announced that razing of the building for an underground garage was being studied. It was urged that it *15* should be preserved as a downtown tourist center. Old-timers like George W. Stark, city historiographer, and Pingree's daughter, Mrs. Wilson W. Mills, president of the Detroit Historical Society, led a valiant fight. Legal maneuvers kept the landmark in being past its 90th birthday in 1961.

But that September it fell before the wrecker's ball.

3. The Day of Jubilee

Thanksgiving was the keynote. Detroiters also had a strong sense of history that day.

For the first time in America, white men and black marched together as equals under the Constitution.

The beat of marching feet on April 7, 1870, marked the successful termination of a long and bitter struggle — a struggle to determine, as Abraham Lincoln underscored at Gettysburg, whether the nation could long endure.

His wartime Emancipation Proclamation was followed by the 13th Amendment, abolishing slavery. It was not enough. In many states, blacks were still prevented from voting.

But in the spring of 1870, three-fourths of the states ratified the 15th Amendment, which declared:

"The right of the citizens of the United States to vote shall not be denied or abridged by the United States or by any state on account of race, color, or previous condition of servitude."

Detroit was quick to take action when, on March 31, the secretary of state in Washington certified the amendment to be the law of the land. April 7 was set as the date for a civic celebration here.

The morning dawned bright and clear. Strong winds dried out the woodblock streets, washed by mud in heavy rains earlier in the week.

Downtown, the buildings were decked with flags and bunting. At 11 a.m. artillerymen from Fort

Governor Henry P. Baldwin

Wayne detonated a salute from a cannon set up in the Campus Martius.

Reverberations carried to the far limits of the city. In 1870, they were nowhere more than a couple of miles from the Detroit River.

At the signal, troopers of the First Michigan Cavalry, in Union blue, started their mounts from the marshaling area around East Lafayette and Beaubien. The color guard at their head bore the regiment's wartime honors with the flags.

War veterans of the Loyal League fell in behind the troopers. Following them came most of the city's black citizens, more than 1,000 marchers. They had assembled in nearby churches.

Banners along the line of march honored Lincoln and Ulysses S. Grant. In 1870 Grant was serving his first term as President.

Other banners honored leaders, black and white, who won places in the forefront of the fight for

Frederick Douglass

human equality — Frederick Douglass, William Lloyd Garrison, John Brown, Carl Schurz.

The parade swung over numerous streets — Congress, Hastings, Larned, Rivard, Jefferson, Woodward, Fort, Griswold.

Out toward the north end of town, the marchers circled Grand Circus Park, then bore down Woodward to the Campus Martius. There were many memories for them at the Campus.

Here the Phalanx, Detroit's own black regiment, marched off to receive many battle honors in the war. Here the citizens assembled to pay their tribute to the Great Emancipator after Lincoln was assassinated in 1865.

The paraders of 1870 broke ranks at the Campus to enter the Detroit Opera House, its facade bedecked with flags. The program called for five hours of speechmaking.

Behind the rostrum on the stage were 32 young

women of the African Baptist and Methodist churches. All were dressed in white.

They represented the 32 states whose ordinances of ratification put the 15th Amendment into effect.

In the center of the group, two tall and slender girls, also dressed completely in white, held torches high. They portrayed the goddesses of Truth and Liberty.

As the audience stood at attention, the Detroit Light Guard band played "The Star-Spangled Banner." The Rev. W. R. G. Mellen offered prayers.

After speeches by D. Bethune Duffield, William A. Howard and other civic leaders, the chairman, William Lambert, introduced the foremost dignitary present, Gov. Henry P. Baldwin of Michigan.

Gov. Baldwin turned the thoughts of the assemblage back to the years of bondage. He recalled the patient chants of workers in the cotton fields of the South about a longed-for "day of jubilee."

Now at long last, he said, the day of jubilee had come. It belonged by right to Detroit's black citizens.

Applause for the governor was prolonged. The tailor, William Lambert, presiding over the day of jubilee in the Opera House, took up the theme started by the state's chief magistrate.

Only a few weeks before, he pointed out, America observed the centennial of the Boston Massacre of March 5, 1770.

And the first blood shed in the massacre had been that of a black slave, Crispus Attucks.

Lambert continued with his own memories of the night of March 12, 1859, when John Brown, the fiery liberationist, brought 14 fugitives seeking their freedom to Detroit.

Brown had freed them in raids into slave territory. He brought them north by way of the "Underground Railroad," as the network of clandestine sympathizers all along the routes to liberty was called.

Detroit veterans of the "railroad" — Lambert among them — met with John Brown that night. Lambert remembered vividly the desperate urgency which characterized "John Brown of Ossawatomie," as he was called after the scene of a suc-

William Lambert
He continued the Jubilee

cessful defense against proslavery forces in Kansas. Before the year was out, his raid on Harper's Ferry led to Brown's death by hanging.

Yet within a few years after that time of desperation, all the slaves in America were free, Lambert declared.

Other speakers who had spent most of their lives in bondage pieced out the epic story. They told of journeys made while hidden in the hay of farmers' wagons, of nights huddled in outbuildings and caves in the quest for freedom.

There were those in the Opera House on the day of jubilee who would never forget spending their first hours in Detroit in a secret loft of the Finney House barn at State and Griswold, while their host, Seymour Finney, suavely persuaded the slave-catchers from the South who put up at his hotel a block away, that their quarry must already have reached Canada.

Others found shelter in Lambert's frame home at 497 East Larned, or in the house at 293 East Jefferson where George DeBaptiste operated his catering service for well-to-do Detroiters.

Outside, the shadows were lengthening across Campus Martius by the time Lambert turned over the rostrum in the Opera House to DeBaptiste, whose leadership in the underground no longer was a secret.

Smiling, DeBaptiste told the throng he was resigning as superintendent and chief engineer of the mythical railroad to freedom. Its work was done.

"We don't need it any more," he said.

The crowd roared agreement.

At the end the auditorium was silenced. Softly out of the hush came the first cadences of the "Battle Hymn of the Republic."

"Mine eyes have seen the glory of the coming of the Lord,
He is trampling out the vintage where the grapes of wrath are stored" . . .

Slowly the chorus swelled in power, rang loud at last in climax:

"Glory, glory, hallelujah! His Truth is marching on."

4. A Centennial Prodigy

No Detroiter who went to the Centennial Exposition in Philadelphia in 1876 gained more from it than 18-year-old Julius Rolshoven.

It was the first time he had been that far from Detroit on his own. In his boyhood he had been given the nickname Jules, and a pun may have been intended. His father owned the biggest jewelry store in town.

At 15, he went to work in the store. Within three years he was an expert jewelry designer. Well pleased with their son, Frederick and Theresa Rolshoven let him go to the exposition for a holiday — and to "broaden his mind."

Afterward, some people at home said the exposition must have turned his head. At any rate, new horizons called Jules. He went to New York and found work with a jewelry firm. And he enrolled as a student — of all things — with a sculptor.

Before long, the sculptor wrote to the Rolshovens. Their son had great talent, he said, and more study — abroad — was recommended.

Eventually, they agreed. At 19 Jules was off to Duesseldorf, Germany's greatest art center. He enrolled at the academy there, and studied later in Munich, in Italy and in Paris.

Detroiters shook their heads. How long were his foolish parents going to indulge him in this folly?

But the news of young Rolshoven took quite a turn. He began teaching art classes — first in Paris, then London, then Florence. Soon he was exhibiting

Julius Rolshoven, *Courtesy of the Detroit Institute of Arts.*

paintings in major European cities. The critics praised his work and he was honored with numerous awards and medals.

Detroit began to boast about Julius Rolshoven. The city had turned out an authentic artist. It was surprising how many folks said they had known he had it in him all the time.

In 1884, Jules returned to give the first home town exhibition of his work — and he received an ovation. While here he did a much admired portrait of his sister, Mrs. E. C. Bolton. Also, he received commissions to paint many other prominent Detroit women.

Even before there was a Detroit art museum, one of his canvases went on permanent public display here. It came about because the painting caught the fancy of Charles Churchill, whose chop house on Woodward, north of Campus Martius, was the city's most sumptuous tavern in the 1880's.

The work was a beautiful nude, called "LaVenera Bruna," produced in pastel during Rolshoven's early days in Paris. The first pastel exhibition in London awarded it the place of honor.

Churchill gave the nude a place of honor, too. It was displayed for years on the back wall above his bar. Its fame spread.

Rolshoven also traveled afar, seeking fresh inspiration for his work. He became a world citizen of art. He made his home in an Italian Renaissance palace he restored in Florence. But World War I proved to be a blessing in disguise for him — he returned to America for several years and discovered New Mexico.

Just as the Philadelphia Exposition did in 1876, the rugged scenery and brilliant sunlight of the Southwest brought about an expansion of the mind of Rolshoven.

"I have traveled all over in search of atmosphere, but nowhere else have I seen nature provide everything it does here," he said.

His greatest inspiration came from the Pueblo Indians. He visited their ancient homesites, studied their religion and shared their dances, feasts and festivities. A spate of paintings resulted which modern critics term his best. They bear titles like "Taos Indian Maiden," "Summer Deer" and "Taos War Chief."

The climax was a canvas measuring 12 by 16 feet, called "To the Land of Sip'ophe"—The Land of the Sunset. It shows a cavalcade of warriors riding to the shadow world which, according to the myth of the Pueblos, is the dwelling place of the ancients, toward which all humanity is bound.

The Detroit Institute of Arts owns five paintings by Rolshoven, including two given to the museum by his widow in 1955, a celebrated portrait for which she posed called "La Tosca" and a self-portrait. The Detroit Athletic Club has "The Masquerade," a painting which Rolshoven worked on intermittently for 14 years, and the nude from Churchill's — acquired when prohibition closed the bar.

La Tosca, a painting by Julius Rolshoven. It now hangs in the Detroit Institute of Arts. The painting was given to the Institute in 1955 by his widow, who was the model.

Rolshoven's portrait of his sister went to the home of her son, Frederick R. Bolton, Detroit attorney. A painting of Rolshoven's father, who died in 1906, was given by Bolton to the Harmonie Club. Many of the Pueblo canvases, including "To the Land of Sip'ophe" are displayed in the Rolshoven Collection of the University of New Mexico, at Albuquerque.

Wherever his art took him, Rolshoven unfailingly came back to Detroit each Christmas for a reunion with his widowed mother. He was the eldest of five and throughout their mother's long lifetime all of the children usually made the annual pilgrimage.

In 1930, the artist was 72 and his mother 92. With his wife, he embarked for America on the liner Roma from Genoa for the holiday. He was taken ill on the ship.

When the Roma docked in New York an ambulance was waiting to take him to St. Luke's Hospital. He died at 2 a.m. on Dec. 7. At that hour his mother, who had talked hopefully about the planned reunion the night before, was sleeping peacefully in her home on East Grand Boulevard.

Mrs. Rolshoven died in her sleep, three hours after her son. Joint funeral services followed.

In death as in life, mother and son kept their Christmas rendezvous.

5. The Boys of Holy Trinity

From Antoine de la Mothe Cadillac on, practical men and visionaries as well saw his former frontier outpost at the Straits as a place of unique opportunity.

Both kinds of men were included among Cadillac's voyageurs. There were plenty of both, too, among the English and the Americans whose flags succeeded his fleur-de-lis atop the community's fort.

It remained for Irish and Germans to begin, in the 19th century, another outpouring of people from European homelands. They perceived in Detroit a Mecca where both opportunity to earn a living and freedom to enjoy life could be the capstones of a new home in America.

In the later years of that century, Corktown to the west of the central business section and Germantown to the northeast emerged as visible symbols of such aspirations. And they were among the liveliest places in town.

While old St. Anne's Church continued Detroit's original French Catholic tradition, Corktown grew up under the cross of Holy Trinity Church, at Sixth and Porter. On tree-lined streets for blocks around were the cottages of the Irish.

Germantown was more diverse. Its religious centers included Trinity German Evangelical Lutheran Church, at Gratiot and Rivard, in addition to St. Joseph's at Orleans and Jay. Germantown boasted a goodly leaven of free thinkers as well, to spice the

Early sketch of Holy Trinity Church, built for Detroit's second Catholic parish, from the *History of Detroit and Wayne County and Early Michigan* by Silas Farmer

arguments in the beer halls and in the German language newspapers.

Many of the youngsters raised in Corktown would become lawyers, judges and civic leaders around the turn of the century. In 1880, however, their emigrant fathers mostly were just getting started up the economic ladder.

Escape from the city's midsummer heat was not easy for the acolytes at Holy Trinity. The annual outings arranged for them by Fr. A. F. Bleyenbergh, the pastor, were awaited eagerly.

Fr. Bleyenbergh persuaded the operators of the steam yacht Mamie to donate it one day each July for the altar boys. Oridinarily the vessel was rented to charter parties through the season.

Boarding the Mamie on the morning of Thursday, July 22, 1880 was a happy group. There were 26 altar boys, all anxious for a fun filled day.

Six adults accompanied them. In addition to the pastor, there were Thomas Kelly, sexton of Holy Trinity, and his brother John, Elizabeth Murphy, Fr. Bleyenbergh's housekeeper Mary Hahn; a domestic for the sisters of Holy Trinity School, and Mrs. Mary Martin, whose husband, Fred, was engineer of the Mamie.

The boys kept their skylarking within bounds as the Mamie sped downriver. But they let off steam when the yacht docked at Monroe, where they ate lunch and saw the sights of the town.

They were particularly excited about seeing the home of Gen. George A. Custer. His last stand at the Little Big Horn four years before was a tragedy fresh in the minds of all Americans.

On the return trip, the Mamie's progress against the current was slower. She did not reach the mouth of the Detroit River until 9 p.m., and darkness settled on the water.

The Mamie's enclosed deck cabin was entered from the rear. Worn out by a strenuous day, most of the boys were glad to stretch out inside.

Soon a number of them were asleep. The evening was so mild that the cabin door was propped open for ventilation.

At 9 o'clock, the new steamer Garland was just leaving the Detroit Stove Works' wharf at the foot of Adair, on Detroit's east side.

The Garland had been taken over for a cruise down the river by the Molders' Union, and 1,200 excursionists crowded on board.

Another chartered ferry, the Fortunes, took on overflow left on the wharf and followed the Garland.

The Mamie was opposite Wyandotte when Fr. Bleyenbergh first saw the lights of the Garland and the Fortune. He was seated on deck near the bow, chatting with Elizabeth Dusseau, a church worker, who joined the cruise party at Monroe.

"They seemed to be racing," the pastor remarked.

The steamers presented a colorful sight as they neared the Mamie. The Garland, it could be seen now, was well in the lead.

On board the Garland, James P. Murtagh, an employe of The Evening News, was seated on the main deck, near the bow, chatting with a friend, Henry Meridan.

"We saw the yacht coming upstream, headed for the Garland," he related later. "The two boats got closer and closer. We began to feel uneasy.

"The yacht gave a short whistle. It was answered by a whistle from the Garland and I heard the bell to stop the Garland's engine.

"The Mamie continued straight ahead until she was 50 or 60 feet away. I heard some one on board her shout 'Hard to port.'

"Then, instead of passing by on our starboard side, the Mamie suddenly swerved directly across our bow."

Murtagh heard what he described as "a terrible crunching, grinding sound" as the bow of the Garland struck the Mamie just back of the wheelhouse. The Mamie crushed like an eggshell as the steamer rode over her amidships.

Fr. Bleyenbergh and Miss Dusseau grabbed ropes from the Garland and were pulled on board. Capt. Will Hoffman of the Mamie and the engineer, Fred Martin, leaped to the deck of the Garland.

For a few moments the Mamie's bow was pressed under water by the weight of the Garland, her stern tilted above the surface. A rush of steam from a broken pipe on the Mamie enveloped the scene.

And as the ships separated, cries for help were heard from the black void.

John Quirk, a Garland passenger, was a good swimmer. He jumped into the water, found a boy struggling against the waves, and brought him back to the steamer.

Murtagh, Meridan and others threw life preservers into the river, and three more boys clinging to them were picked up by the Garland.

All the rest — 12 altar boys and the five adults

Commemorative plaque. This bronze plaque in Holy Trinity Church is in memory of the twelve acolytes and five church members who died in a Detroit River accident on July 22, 1880.

who had accompanied the pastor that morning —were dead.

Much controversy would arise about the cause of the disaster, but on Tuesday, July 27, Detroit was still too dazed to assess blame.

On that day, a shocked congregation filled Holy Trinity. On a catafalque before the altar were 17 coffins. Twelve were white for the boys, five were black for the adults.

Clergy assembled from all over the diocese. As Fr. Bleyenbergh chanted the requiem mass, 48 priests were in the sanctuary.

"It was a massacre of the innocents," the pastor said.

All Detroit agreed. Contributions from those of every faith poured in for a memorial plaque to be placed in the church.

Corktown and Germantown are gone now, their populations — like those of many later ethnic enclaves which enriched the life and culture of Detroit — absorbed into the mainstream of a polyglot city. But the spires of Holy Trinity and St. Joseph remain as of old.

St. Joseph's has been restored and is as much admired as when it was dedicated in 1873. The original cost was $200,000, a huge sum when the average wage of skilled workmen was $1 a day, but the parishioners built the edifice in large part with their own hands. Many of the city's best woodcarvers and stone masons belonged to the congregation.

The church was hailed as one of the most beautiful Gothic Revival structures in America.

The richly carved main altar came from Munich, Germany, as did the stained windows of the apse.

Another large window representing the death of St. Joseph was imported from Innsbruck, Austria.

The parishioners were fond of statues, and the church overflows with them. There are over 60 sculptures, including a large Pieta and 14 Stations of the Cross in deep relief.

Holy Trinity is not so ornate, but it, too, is worth a a visit. The gem is the plaque to the altar boys, with this inscription:

"He pleased God, and was beloved, and lying among sinners he was translated. He was taken away lest wickedness should alter his understanding, or deceit."

6. The Skyscrapers That Vanished

Detroit lost a landmark when the home of James Abbott, onetime postmaster, was torn down.

Long before, Abbott had come to the conclusion that increasing commercialism was making his neighborhood too noisy, and decided to move to a more relaxed atmosphere. Abbott was well in the van of the trend to suburbia. He made his move in 1835.

Griswold Street was opened that year as far north as State, and Abbott found what he wanted. Quitting his place on lower Woodward, he selected a choice lot on the southeast corner of Griswold and Fort. He didn't know it, but he also was picking out the site of Detroit's first skyscraper.

Abbott wasn't just an officeholder. He also was agent for the American Fur Co., a post lucrative enough for him to do much entertaining.

Soon the carriages of Little Old Detroit's elite found the way out Griswold through his Greek Revival doorway, graced with rectangular transom and sidelights.

Commerce overtook Abbott's gabled retreat, and the excavation that replaced it in 1889 became the epicenter of Detroit's wave of the future.

Detroiters watched progress on the structure being built on the southeast corner of Fort and Griswold.

It was to be known as the Hammond Building. To say that a lot of ham went into the building might sound like an atrocious pun, but in a way it did — $750,000 worth.

A "wonder of the world" is what Detroiters called the Hammond
Building, completed in 1890. It was at the southeast corner of
Fort and Griswold, and at the time was one of the largest
masonry structures in the nation. George Hammond died before
it was completed. His widow carried on the project.

Majestic Building. Begun by Christopher R. Mabley, merchant
king of the 1890's, the Majestic Building at Woodward and
Michigan was completed in 1896, after his death. It displaced the
Hammond Building as Detroit's tallest structure and dominated
the skyline for years. In 1961 it was torn down to make room
for the First Federal Building.

George H. Hammond was in the dynamic tradition that became Detroit's trademark. Born in Massachusetts, he left school at the age of 10 to embark upon a business career. Coming to Detroit in 1854, he started a mattress factory. It burned down two years later. Undaunted, he began again with a butcher shop at Third and Howard. As late as 1871 the Detroit City Directory listed him as a butcher, but 15 years later he died a multimillionaire, one of the nation's industrial giants in what Mark Twain liked to call the Gilded Age.

Hammond's great idea was launched with another Detroit merchant, William Davis, who operated a fish market near the butcher shop. Davis patented an oversize icebox, big enough to bring a weekend's supply of fish for Detroit gourmets every Friday. Hammond bought the patent and adapted the invention to the shipment of fresh meat in refrigerator cars. His first carload of iced meat went to Boston in 1869. By the time of his death in 1886 he was operating 1,000 cars.

Meat packing soon centered in Chicago, and Hammond built a plant just across the Indiana state line. The city which grew around it took his name. Hammond, Ind., boomed, but Hammond himself remained a loyal Detroiter.

Harry W. J. Edbrooke, a Chicago architect, read in a newspaper that Hammond had sold his Indiana plant for $750,000 and planned to erect an office building in Detroit with the proceeds. Hoping to share in the bonanza, Edbrooke hurried to Detroit, but at this juncture Hammond died. Edbrooke was able to persuade Hammond's widow to give him the job.

Ellen Barry Hammond, who bore Hammond 11 children, achieved a proud memorial to her husband. The building was 11 stories high, one of the largest masonry structures in the nation up to that time. Detroit acclaimed it as a "wonder of the world," and to celebrate, the citizens turned out for a dedication that was capped by the 1890 equivalent of a moonwalk. To the cheers of the throng below, high-wire performer successfully strode a cable stretched from the new edifice to the City Hall tower.

George H. Hammond

Visitors came from all over the state to climb to the roof of the Hammond Building. The view, everyone agreed, was spectacular.

Detroit's leading families of the period — Joys, McMillans, and Newberrys — were represented among the first tenants. Some rode bicycles to work and a problem developed. Under strict rules at first enforced, the bikes were kept in the basement and were not allowed in the service elevator. A sort of blue-blood tenant revolt resulted, under the leadership of millionaire Henry B. Joy, and it was successful. The tenants won the right to leave their machines on the first floor.

Tenants also came to the Hammond Building on horseback, and hitching posts adorned the curbstones. Thomas A. E. Weadock, dean of the Detroit

C. R. Mabley
Detroit merchant

bar, was one of the more flamboyant equestrians.

After the turn of the century the Detroit Tigers established their downtown office in the building, and fans could look to the rooftop to see if a white flag with a blue circle was flying. It meant the Tigers would play at Bennett Park that day.

For decades Sharpe's Restaurant, in the basement, was an oasis of grace and charm. Copies of Hans Holbein paintings decorated the walls. Denizens of City Hall called Sharpe's "The Corn Beef Cave." Politicians hatched many a vote-catching nuance in its back booths.

In 1896 the Hammond Building acquired its greatest rival — and Detroiters shook their heads over it.

Christopher R. Mabley, a Detroit merchant king

in the Gay '90's, had his heart set on putting up the city's most impressive structure.

"Never mind the expense, but be sure it's higher than the Hammond Building," he told his architect, Daniel H. Burnham. Burnham was the designer of New York's Flatiron Building, in its day the world's tallest.

From the time the Hammond Building was completed, Mabley dreamed of housing his department store in a structure that would top it. And he wanted his tower to excel in quality as well.

Mabley spent $700,000 for the site, a fabulous sum then for Detroit real estate. With 161 feet of frontage on Woodward and 127 feet on Michigan, it was one of the most valuable pieces of property downtown. Proudly, Mabley put a large "M" on the capstone of his building. He placed it on almost everything else, too; even the brass knobs of the hundreds of office doors carried his initial.

But Mabley died before the tower was completed in October, 1896. Other owners finished the project, and they decided the name "Mabley" no longer was suitable.

With "M's" all over the place, they had to find a new name to match the initial. And they did— the Majestic Building. The Sunday News-Tribune of Oct. 4, hailed it as a good choice.

"It is a structure of which Detroit has good reason to be proud," the article stated. "It has few equals for elegance, size and completeness in the entire country. It gives the city an enviable prominence in this age of mammoth buildings."

Sightseers who had admired the view from the top of the Hammond now flocked to the Majestic Building. Elevators whisked them to the 14th floor. There they could pay a dime and climb a flight of stairs to a roof observatory.

As advertised, they found "a view unobstructed for 12 miles." It was a thrill to look down on the once preeminent Hammond Building. As for the City Hall, it looked like a toy.

While on the roof, people could watch U.S. Weather Bureau experts making observations of the rarefied atmosphere. There was a protective railing on all sides. Each night the roof was — blazoned with brightly colored lights.

James Abbott
Early "suburbanite"

Even the basement marked a "first" in Detroit's history. The city's first self-service restaurant was opened there. It quickly caught on, as turn-of-the century office workers learned to eat their lunches on the run and have time for midday shopping.

Instead of Mabley's department store, the first six floors of the building were occupied by an enterprising competitor, Pardridge and Blackwell. Later, when Pardridge and Blackwell expanded into a building of their own, the entire Majestic Building above the first-floor shops was devoted to offices. Many of the tenants were lawyers.

Considerable rivalry developed between tenants of the two buildings in the field of politics. If a candidate for mayor set up his headquarters in one of the skyscrapers, his opponent was sure to take a suite in the other.

41

The Majestic Building's most dramatic hour came on Oct. 7, 1916. At noon that day, a crowd of 15,000 filled the street on the Woodward side. Hundreds more were in the windows of nearby structures.

They all were waiting to watch Harry H. Gardiner, a brisk little man who liked to be called the "Human Fly," in a feat never before attempted. Gardiner was going to try to climb the 221-foot face of the building. He appeared wearing a white duck suit, white hat, white tennis shoes and rimless eyeglasses, and waved to the Pathe and Universal newsreel cameramen who were on the Majestic roof to record it all.

Gardiner's hands and feet were powerful. He started up the building hand over hand, his fingers finding crevices and holds between bricks and large blocks. Once he found a loosened stone. The Fly pulled it out and handed it to his manager, who was leaning from a window above.

The crucial test came at the 13th floor, where the windows were surmounted by arches of stone and ornamental work. Only one window, at the corner of the building, had no arch. To reach it, Gardiner was forced to pass around the bulging support of the nearest arch.

Three times he tried — and failed. On the fourth try, the climber straddled the pillarlike obstruction and got a heelhold on a solid ledge.

Edging his body downward to where he could reach the window ledge with his hands, Gardiner gripped it and let go with his heels. His body dangled in space and the spectators were sure he would fall, but the Fly began to writhe, swinging back and forth like a pendulum.

"Then suddenly the heels shot out, reached up to the windowsill and rested there, the hands moving away until the body was almost straight," The Detroit News reported in an extra about the climb.

"The body shook as if it were shot through with a powerful electric current, then with a twist rolled over the ledge. The left hand shot up and gripped the crag of stone and —

"There stood Gardiner, upright, smiling on the thousands below."

The climb took just 37 minutes.

For many years the rivalry between the two skyscrapers continued, from top to bottom. On the roofs, the weather signal flags of the Majestic competed with the Detroit Tigers' flag above the Hammond for the attention of passersby. In the basements, the eating places competed for the trade of the hungry. In between, the politicians continued their endless quest for votes.

In their greatest competition of all, however, neither building was able to complete a century run. The Hammond was demolished in 1956 to make room for the National Bank of Detroit. The Majestic was torn down five years later to be replaced by the First Federal Building.

In the longevity sweepstakes, neither skyscraper reached the three-score-and ten mark. But they set the stage for a proud skyline befitting one of the great cities of the world.

7. They Marched for Mr. Lincoln

It was America's biggest parade and Detroit was thrilled to play host.

The Grand Army of the Republic (GAR) came to town for its silver anniversary encampment in 1891 at the peak of its glory. The membership exceeded 300,000. The organization of Union veterans of the Civil War was a powerful political force in the land.

Detroit had been busy with preparations for months. By Sunday, Aug. 2, all was in readiness. The city was ablaze with flags and bunting. Four great arches had been erected over major avenues along the parade route.

The Peace Arch, at Fort and Griswold, raised a lofty inscription for the marchers to read: "Cheerily On, Courageous Friends, to Reap the Harvest of Perpetual Peace." On the opposite side, the message was "Their Prowess Brought Us Peace; Enduring Be Their Fame."

The War Arch, at Jefferson and Woodward, was shaped like a miniature Eiffel Tower. It was emblazoned with reproductions of fine battle paintings.

Insignia of every Army Corps was displayed on a third arch across Woodward at Grand Circus Park. Last on the line of march, the Triumphal Arch, at Jefferson and the railroad, displayed turrets and battlements allegorical of victory. Everyone agreed that Detroit prepared a worthy welcome for the incoming hordes of heroes.

Downtown stores entered into the spirit with vim. Fyfe's shoe shop displayed an oil painting of "The Capture of New Orleans." The J. L. Hudson Co.

stacked copies of a history of the war, to be given to every veteran buying a $10 suit. Mabley & Co. handed out GAR medals with every purchase.

Everyone enjoyed the military Sunday. Bands of incoming posts blared at depots and docks. Fife and drum corps beat out their rhythms at the hotels. Citizens turned out in holiday attire to greet the visitors. Incoming bigwigs included Secretary of War Redfield Proctor and former President Rutherford B. Hayes. The barouches of prominent Detroiters who were to entertain them met them at the railway stations.

Detroit women were entranced by the arrival of Clara Barton, heroine of wartime nursing. She had become the founder of the American Red Cross. Miss Barton arrived early Monday aboard one of two 24-car trains, decorated in the national colors, bringing a large Washington delegation. Ladies of the party were taken in carriages to the Russell House.

By nightfall, it was estimated that boat, trains and interurban cars had brought a record influx of 100,000 into the city.

Tuesday dawned clear and sunny. It was perfect for the big parade. Veterans began pouring out of the hotels at 7 a.m., resplendent in dress uniforms. At 10:45 the cannon on the USS Michigan in the river boomed the signal to march.

On a prancing black charger, the national commander-in-chief, Gen. W. C. Veazey of Vermont, was escorted by Detroit's mounted police. Troop after troop of mounted posts followed.

Chicago's umbrella brigade — pirouetting red, white and blue parasols, each with 42 stars — drew applause. So did Woolcott Post of Wisconsin, led by a pretty girl in a Goddess of Liberty costume.

A Florida post with huge seaweed hats drew chuckles. The spectators roared at Farragut Post, marching behind a big banner — "The Goose Hangs High" — followed by a stuffed goose suspended aloft. There was incessant music; of 122 bands in the parade, 38 represented Michigan. Temporary stands had been built at intervals along the three-mile line of march, with seats going for as high as $1.

The silk hats of visiting dignitaries congregated

45

The Civil War veterans in their GAR campaign uniforms parade past the Soldiers and Sailors Monument and the Russell House at Woodward and Cadillac Square. Fifty years later the only Detroiters carrying on were Augustus F. Chappell and John C. Haines.

in the main reviewing stand at the Campus Martius. After the parade they adjourned to the assembly rooms of Detroit Post, at 58 West Congress. Hospitality flowed freely here throughout the encampment. With parlors, a library and a billiard room, the post owned one of Detroit's best downtown clubs.

An exodus of sightseers began after the parade, and 25,000 left on boats and trains by Tuesday night. Yet throngs on the downtown streets seemed as massive as ever. The delegates got down to serious work Wednesday morning, with business sessions at Beecher's Hall — the main topic was pensions. But Wednesday afternoon was picnic time on Belle Isle, and by 5 p.m. it was estimated an astonishing 150,000 were there.

46

It was "a crush of humanity unequaled in Michigan," The Detroit News reported.

Most of those remained for the pretentious evening attraction, a fireworks spectacle on the river of "Perry's Victory." The four ships of Commodore Oliver Hazard Perry's gallant 1812 fleet were depicted in huge set pieces.

Built especially for the pyrotechnical display, the Excelsior grandstand, at the foot of Mt. Elliott, contained 5,000 seats and was lighted by electricity. Another 3,000 seats had been put up at the Walkerville ferry dock. The schooner Onward took off from the foot of Bates at 7:30 p.m. with 400 passengers, to cruise under the rainbow tints of the fireworks-lighted sky. Ferries of the Detroit, Belle Isle & Windsor Ferry Co., including the Sappho and the Fortune, also made special evening cruises.

Another fireworks display, "The Siege of Sevastopol," was presented Thursday night. But by that time, Detroiters and visitors alike were sated with spectacles.

Before he left for his home at Fremont, Ohio, the venerable ex-President Hayes talked with his host, Col. Frank J. Hecker, about the nation's future. Hayes said much concerning another GAR leader who had become his protege, Maj. William McKinley. Already an Ohio congressman, McKinley was planning to run for governor of his state.

He was proving an apt pupil of Hayes' political savvy, too. McKinley had become an expert at the trick, when shaking a long line of hands at a rally, of pulling forward firmly on each grasped hand. It speeded things up remarkably.

At the same time Secretary Proctor was talking politics with his host, Gen. Russell A. Alger — Detroit's most distinguished GAR leader. Before the encampment was over, Alger issued a public statement denying a report out of Washington that he would seek the Republican vice-presidential nomination in 1892.

In the whirligig of destiny, McKinley was elected President in just five years. Alger became his secretary of war.

The two led the country through another conflict, one that brought a new generation of veterans to center stage. The Spanish-American War, however,

Augustus F. Chappell

only emphasized an inevitable trend for the men of the GAR.

By 1899, the attrition of death and old age considerably reduced the membership rosters. Posts in Detroit maintained separate meeting places, but as their ranks dwindled they began to think about combining forces. In short, they needed a citadel.

A public subscription campaign by Fairbanks Post No. 17 and Farquhar Post No. 163 raised $6,-000, then languished. The city stepped in, agreeing to pay an additional $35,000 needed to erect a suitable structure on an available city-owned site and lease it to the veterans.

The available site was a triangle bounded by

John C. Haines

Grand River, Cass and Adams. Once it had been a part of the Lewis Cass farm, but under the will of Gen. Cass it was donated to the city on condition that a marketplace be maintained there.

So it was, that when the building first called Memorial Hall rose on the triangle, with crenellated towers and the general aspect of a military installation, the 30-year lease to the GAR had a provision that the ground floor be operated as a market. The provision was given a liberal interpretation, and the veterans rented rooms for stores and even for a bank. Fourteen affiliated organizations shared its meeting halls and offices on the upper floors, and it was one of the busiest places in town.

But old rivalries still ran high. For many years, Detroit Post refused to have anything to do with the hall.

Detroit Post still considered itself something special. Members of other posts called it, with a touch of envy, "the millionaires' post." Actually, there were not enough full-fledged millionaires to form a decent-sized pedro club. But its members were prominent in business, the professions and politics.

Other posts accepted any qualified Union veteran. Their memberships in the peak period ran as high as 700. Detroit Post limited its roster to 150 and accepted only applicants who were "congenial" to the charter members.

The regulation GAR uniform was a dark blue sack coat with brass buttons, along with trousers of the same material, and the wide-rimmed hats always were black. Detroit Post dandies decided on a uniform wholly unlike the regulation — and it looked so good the departmental commander gave his consent. They wore well-tailored Prince Albert coats, with dark trousers, white bow ties and buff gloves. They put double gold cord on their GAR hats and they sported slim black canes. They carried all this finery well and they spent more time on the drill manual than any other post.

At one national encampment after another, they won high honors. At one grand parade when McKinley was President, he was so much impressed that he arranged to meet the Detroit Post members and shake hands with them individually. By virtue of the technique that Hayes taught him long before, he could still shake hands with enjoyment.

At an encampment held in Louisville, the Detroiters were studied with great care by a native son as they arrived at their hostelry, the Galt House. He sported the long gray mustache, imperial slouch hat and black string tie of the traditional Kentucky colonel.

"They may be Yankees, but they look like gentlemen!" he exclaimed.

It was also at the Louisville encampment that Confederate Gen. Simon B. Buckner got on such good terms with Detroit Post members that he ordered a 100-pound cake baked and presented it with his compliments.

50

"Your post takes the cake in everything," he said.

Not until the late 1920's, when only a handful of members remained active, did Detroit Post join the others at GAR Hall. By then, many posts outstate could hardly muster a corporal's guard. By 1933, only 33 Civil War veterans were left in Detroit, and just 19 of these were able to gather for their annual reunion.

But it was typical of the sessions for which the hall was famous down the decades, with the familiar picket lines formed around the game of seven-up and the old raillery between the infantry and cavalry breaking out once more:

"Remember," drawled Thomas Davey, 87, once of the 16th Michigan Infantry, "remember when Gen. Joe Hooker offered $500 reward to anyone who could find a dead cavalryman?"

"The cavalry was there all right," flared Augustus F. Chappell, of Fairbanks Post, who once led Sheridan's troopers across the Rapidan. "Old Joe had to eat those words."

And the cavalry was still there, in the person of Chappell, until 1941, when only two were left of all the throngs who had used the GAR Building. The other was the last commander of O.M. Poe Post No. 433, John C. Haines, an aging infantryman.

The two carried on their gentle feud until Chappell died that autumn, at 98. Haines liked to chuckle over the infantry holding the field, and on Aug. 15, 1942, he celebrated his 100th birthday.

Old-timers of the Detroit Federation of Musicians, who honored him as their oldest member, serenaded Haines at his home to celebrate the completion of his century run. A letter of congratulation came from President Franklin D. Roosevelt.

Listening to the band play "When Johnny Comes Marching Home," Haines fingered the key to old GAR Hall — his final charge. "Everything in my life is right here," he said.

In September he paid a last visit to the hall. He lifted the post commander's gavel for the final time. It was a roll call for which only his own voice — and his memories — could answer. A few weeks later Commander Haines was dead.

8. An Enduring Friendship

Ex-President Hayes and Secretary of War Red-field Proctor, who enjoyed the hospitality of the Russell A. Alger home on Fort Street during the Grand Army of the Republic's silver jubilee encampment in 1891, were not the first distinguished guests to be entertained there. Nor were they destined to be the last.

From its completion in 1885, the mansion was a Detroit showplace. For decades it was the busiest of the numerous fine Victorian residences erected in the city from wealth piled up as Michigan's vast pinelands were harvested.

Taken on a tour of the house by the Algers in 1889, Johanna Staats of The Sunday News found it replete with works of art from the four quarters of the globe. In the entrance hall she lingered over an Italian chest inlaid with pearl and silver, the wood blackened by age.

Two majolica pots filled with palms stood under the hall's vaulted marble arches. One was surmounted by an antique Venetian lamp of wrought iron, the other by a rainbow in stained glass bearing the date 1530. A highbacked bench with a Milanese coat-of-arms also interested Miss Staats, her catalog of delights grew lengthy before she was well past the entry.

"Further down the hall," she wrote, "is a great fireplace with a meditative stag's head." On the mantel were a tinted marble of St. Jerome, Benares brass from India and a carved ivory screen.

The drawing room was so full of paintings it might have been called the art gallery. Many were French, but the two portraits most admired by guests, those of Gen. Alger and his wife, were the work of a Detroit artist, Gari Melchers.

The elegance of the place emphasized the fact that a half-dozen blocks of Fort Street, west of the business district, were developing into a highly fashionable neighborhood for members of what would be called in another century Detroit's "Establishment." The friendships among residents in the area could be traced in the directorates of banks, railroads and industrial ventures important to Detroit's expansion.

Alger ranked high among them. Even in the field of transportation, his life-style still commands respect.

True, he might leave his mansion in a horse-drawn vehicle, but a two-minute trot took him to the railroad station. There, a private car awaited his pleasure.

As president of a 30-mile-long line upstate which served his lumbering interests, Alger qualified for one of America's two most exclusive gentlemen's clubs — the other being the United States Senate, which he joined later.

The nation's railway presidents gave one another the privilege of attaching their private cars, without cost, to any scheduled passenger run in the land. Alger's luxurious car, the "Michigan," was almost as well known in Washington and New York as in Detroit.

The man who moved about so pleasantly made it on his own. He was a contemporary of Horatio Alger Jr. — no relation — the scribbler whose rags-to-riches formula produced an endless series of books emulated by several generations of American boys.

Russell A. Alger outdid Horatio Alger's fictional heroes. Orphaned at 12, he worked in his native Ohio for an uncle in return for board and lodging, with a bonus of three months off each winter to go to school.

Seven years later, his wage was only $15 a month. From this he saved enough to move to the land of opportunity — Michigan. Largely on borrowed capital, he started a lumber business in Grand Rapids.

Gen. Russell A. Alger

In April, 1861, at 25, he felt he was earning enough to marry. A few days after the ceremony the bombardment of Fort Sumter in the harbor of Charleston, S.C., precipitated the Civil War.

Within a few weeks after President Lincoln's call for troops to defend the Union, Alger left his firm and his bride to enlist. Soon he was chosen as an officer of the Second Michigan Cavalry. Within six months he was a major.

Alger served in 60 battles and skirmishes. He became colonel of the regiment, part of Gen. George A. Custer's brigade. At war's end, 29 years old, he was brevetted a major general.

Setting up business anew in Detroit, he rode the Michigan lumber boom to emerge as one of the country's foremost "green gold millionaires." Pine lands acquired by his company in huge tracts at $1.25 an acre reached a valuation of $5 for each standing tree.

In 1884, Michigan Republicans nominated Alger

Gen. Henry M. Duffield

Portraits of Gen. Alger and Gen. Duffield were painted by Detroit artists. The paintings hang in the Grosse Pointe Farms home of Mr. and Mrs. Alger Shelden. Shelden is Gen. Alger's grandson. His wife, Frances, is Gen. Duffield's granddaughter.

for governor. He won despite a national sweep by the opposition which put Grover Cleveland in the White House, the first Democrat there since the war.

Alger's victory against the odds brought him widespread attention. Modestly at first, talk grew about the chances of Michigan's favorite son for the presidential nomination of his party in 1888.

No one pushed the idea harder than Alger's friend, Henry M.Duffield. He was a frequent visitor in the Fort Street mansion.

His early years were in marked contrast to Alger's. His father, Dr. George Duffield, was pastor of the First Presbyterian Church and a leader of Detroit cultural and intellectual interests.

55

In 1861, when the war crisis struck, Henry Duffield was a 21-year-old senior at Williams College. He enlisted in the Ninth Michigan Volunteers after his graduation in June. After his regiment reached Tennessee, Duffield was made its adjutant. Eventually he became assistant provost marshal-general of the Department of the Cumberland, with the rank of colonel.

Following the war he studied law and practiced in Detroit in partnership with his brother, Divie Bethune Duffield. From 1867 to 1871 he was attorney for the Board of Education. His success in a suit brought against the city to recover fines collected in municipal courts was the beginning of Detroit's public library system.

Alger and Duffield were brought together by mutual interests in the GAR and politics. Duffield served as aide to four Michigan governors — and the fourth was Alger.

The bond of friendship between them became a byword. But its most enduring result would not be manifested until another century, long after the lifetimes of both were over.

Promoting Alger's candidacy for the Republican presidential nomination in 1888, Duffield journeyed about the nation. By the time the convention met in June, the boomlet for a favorite son was a force to be reckoned with.

An endorsement of Alger just before the voting began from the famous orator of liberation, Frederick Douglass, was particularly heartening. Douglass' influence among black delegates was strong.

After the day's balloting, Duffield received an accolade from an unexpected source. This was Gen. Lew Wallace, the author of "Ben Hur," who was backing a fellow Hoosier, Benjamin Harrison, in the Chicago chariot race.

"The greatest surprise of the convention is the way Alger has loomed up," he said. "I thought he was an unknown quantity, and here's he's ahead of Harrison."

The efficacy of Duffield's preconvention spadework was evident as delegates from Massachusetts to Nevada voted for Alger. Senator John Sherman of Ohio was the leader on the first round, with 299 votes, followed by Walter Q. Gresham of Indiana with 114. Senator Chauncey M. Depew of New York received 99 votes, Alger 84 and Harrison 79.

On the second ballot Alger climbed to second place. The totals were Sherman 249, Alger 116, Gresham 108, Depew 99 and Harrison 93.

Tremendous uproar followed the third vote, when it was seen that Sherman, the front runner, dropped to 244. Gresham, with 123, and Alger, 122, were neck-and-neck. Harrison was given 94 and Depew 90.

Back-of-the-scenes deals before the next roll call were crucial, and now Harrison's managers were gleeful. The tally showed Sherman 236, Harrison 217, Alger 135, Gresham 98.

"This is the time to rally," shouted Duffield. He bounded out on the floor, pleading, arguing, gesticulating.

But the Harrison bandwagon was rumbling. He won the nomination on the eighth ballot and was elected President in November.

Never again did Alger come so close to the White House. In 1892, Harrison's renomination for a second term was uncontested, but he lost the election to Cleveland.

In 1896, another remarkable friendship, that of William McKinley and Mark Hanna, dominated the political scene. Hanna sewed up enough votes for McKinley before the Republican convention to put the nomination in the bag.

As secretary of war in McKinley's Cabinet during the crisis with Spain, Alger made a perennial GI dream come true for his own loyal friend. Duffield, who rose from private to colonel in the previous war, was brought back in the new one as a brigadier general.

In Cuba, as commander of the Second Army Corps, Duffield acted as the vital connecting link between the land forces and the fleet of Admiral William T. Sampson.

Michigan returned Alger to Washington as a senator in 1902. He died in the capital in 1907. Duffield survived him for five years.

But the story of their friendship was not finished. When Alger's body was returned to Detroit for burial in Elmwood Cemetery, a small grandson at a window of the old Fort Street mansion noted every detail of the cortege. He would remember how strange it seemed that cold January morning to see straw strewn in Fort Street, to deaden the sound of the horses' hoofs as the procession to the cemetery began.

In 1925, this grandson, Alger Shelden, met a granddaughter of Gen. Duffield, Frances Pitts Duffield, at a dance given in her honor as one of the season's debutantes. The marriage which resulted united the bloodlines of the two generals.

Today in the Shelden home in Grosse Pointe Farms, the memory of an enduring friendship remains green. On the walls are the oil portraits of Gen. and Mrs. Alger which graced the Fort Street mansion, as well as canvasses of Gen. and Mrs. Duffield from the Duffield residence.

Alger Shelden is the source for a story about the last visit of a U.S. president to the old Alger showplace. Hitherto told only within the family circle, it affords a fitting conclusion to this chapter.

Theodore Roosevelt gave Secretary of War Alger a few headaches after achieving fame as colonel of the Rough Riders at San Juan Hill in Cuba. He was still unpredictable when he visited the mansion in 1902, as President.

Alger assembled Detroit's elite to meet him. T.R. cut the introductions short, however, to inspect a prize which immediately caught his eye. This was a stuffed mountain lion, a memento of an Alger trip to the West long before.

The President studied the trophy from every angle, then asked for a tape measure. While the guests gathered around in a puzzled circle, he carefully took measurement of the big cat.

At the conclusion of this task, T.R. straightened up and flashed a triumphant grin at his host.

"Your mountain lion is three inches shorter than mine." he said.

9. Clang, Clang, Clang Went the Trolley

"Rapid transit, ahoy!"

That was the greeting in The Evening News when Detroit's first trolley car took to the streets.

At the beginning of the Gay '90's, the horsecar-riding public included just about everybody in town. Even the most enthusiastic cyclists used the cars in bad weather. Everyone was interested when the Detroit Electrical Works accepted a contract to electrify the Jefferson Avenue line of the Citizens Railway — but not everyone approved.

Some considered the whole idea of stringing naked, lightning-bearing copper wires right above the middle of the street to be outlandish and dangerous. And was it really necessary?

After all, the horsecars had served the city well since Civil War days. In nearly 30 years there had been only one day when the sturdy dobbins failed to meet the task of getting people back and forth. That was on Oct. 25, 1872, when an epidemic of that dread horse disease, the epizootic, compelled all the lines to stop running.

Poles and lines for the great experiment went in place without incident, but the two companies were cautious. In case anything went wrong, they didn't want a crowd on hand for the first test run.

The secret was well kept, but when traction officials gathered at the electrical powerhouse on St. Antoine at 7:30 a.m. on Monday, Aug. 22, 1892, it was clearly a tipoff.

59

The word spread rapidly through the neighborhood, and more than 40 people were waiting outside the works at 7:42 a.m. when F. M. Zimmerman, a company foreman, pulled a lever throwing current into the trolley system. John Cochran, the Jefferson line's best driver, gingerly maneuvered the trolley arm on car 295 to the overhead wire. In a shower of sparks, he quickly climbed aboard to watch how Zimmerman operated the controls.

With a whirr and a crunch, the car glided out of the powerhouse, coming to a stop before the group of officials — E. W. Cottrell, chairman of the Citizens Railway; John Fry, the general superintendent; John Winters, Fry's chief assistant; and Lewis Warfield, vice-president and general manager of the Electrical Works.

Warfield was ready with a quote when an Evening News reporter joined the group:

"Our contract specified that we should have the cars running today," he said, "and here you are."

As the officials boarded the car, the reporter noted that a pretty little girl in a starched white dress and blue-ribboned sailor hat had climbed on ahead of them and taken a seat at the front.

Cottrell, who lived nearby on Jefferson, didn't recognize the child. "Anyway, she is taking a ride on Detroit's first trolley car and she won't be disturbed," he said.

Outside the powerhouse there was a delay while the trolley arm was adjusted again. Then a start was made — but within a few yards the car went off the track.

"We shall not leave the track in this shape," Cottrell told the reporter. "It was not intended for this kind of service, and we have not yet gotten around to changing it."

Workmen pushed the car back on the track. "Steady!" shouted Zimmerman at the controls. No. 295 moved smoothly down the short stretch of track to Jefferson.

There the car stopped and the little girl who had become the first passenger on a Detroit trolley stepped off. She disappeared into another knot of spectators gathered there, her identity still unknown to history.

Slowly, No. 295 was switched to the main track

Open summer trolleys, like this one, let passengers enjoy the
scenery or watch the motorman (right) switch tracks with a
hand bar

out Jefferson. For the first time, Detroiters heard a
sound that was to become celebrated in song and
legend — the clang, clang, clang of the speeding
trolley.

Noting that 400 volts had been made available in
the overhead wire, The News' man wrote:

"Foreman Zimmerman chucked the whole 400 on
after 30 rods had been made, and the first half mile
to Orleans was made in a fraction less than three
minutes.

"Pokey one-horse drivers, who have been accustomed to meandering sleepily across the tracks
under the very noses of streetcar horses, took on
scared, excited looks when the clanging of the gong
announced the car's approach. They scurried
across the tracks in a manner which greatly surprised their nags.

"The occupants of the car caught their breath,
and The News' reporter got in the draft with his
coat unbuttoned and began to sneeze. Crews and
passengers in the downbound cars twisted their
necks and gazed after the car.

"At Joseph Campau the stalwart horses attached
to a sprinkler cart took umbrage at the general
appearance and rapid motion of the trolley and
gave their driver a hard tussle to prevent their running a race with it."

Gilbert Wilks, chief engineer of the Electrical Works, who had designed the dynamos used in the new system, climbed aboard at the carbarns. He was delighted when No. 295 reached the end of the line at Baldwin just 18 minutes after the start.

No. 295 waited several minutes for a connecting horsecar from Grosse Pointe, on which George H. Russel, treasurer of the Citizens Railway, was expected. Russel was not on the car, however, and No. 295 started back.

One mishap marred the return trip. At the Detroit Grand Haven & Milwaukee Railroad viaduct, the cowcatcher struck a big paving stone and splintered.

While it was being removed, Russel caught up with the trolley in a friend's buggy and hopped on. No. 295 reached Woodward at 8:58 and the Third Street Depot 1½ minutes later. In every way, the trip had been a success.

"The car upon which The News rode ran smoothly, and it was noticeable that there was but little of the loud whirring noise which reputedly accompanies operation of the trolley system," the reporter wrote.

"Warfield attributes this to the fact that but one motor of 40 horsepower is used to turn both axles, instead of having a 20-horsepower motor attached to each axle, as is the case with other trolley systems."

Cottrell, too, was pleased with the test. He ordered three more electrified cars to leave St. Antoine at one-hour intervals. Each was piloted by an operator from the Electrical Works and carried several drivers and conductors to learn the ropes.

"If everything runs as smoothly with the four cars today," Cottrell said, "I think the men will be sufficiently well broken-in so that we can start the entire equipment tomorrow. We shall run nine or 10 cars to start with, and more as the service demands."

Everything did run smoothly. After test runs for additional cars Wednesday morning, the trolleys took over the line, reducing the former 50-minute round trip by 10 minutes.

Detroiters climbed aboard in droves. They waved and called to occupants of cars passing on the other track. They thoroughly enjoyed the new marvel of the age. It was a gala day all around, and the clang, clang, clang of the trolleys would remain a part of the city symphony for more than half a century.

The honeymoon between Detroiters and their trolleys, however, did not last long. Soon all the lines were gathered up into a single-traction combine, the Detroit United Railways (DUR), and complaints about inadequate service and monopoly exploitation swelled into a rising tide of dissatisfaction.

In the early years of the 20th century it became a common sight to see hardy passengers, eager to get home through a winter storm and tired of waiting while fully loaded cars passed them by, clinging to the outside of a streetcar for miles.

On Feb. 10, 1910, The News assigned a reporter to study what it was like going home on the Baker line. He boarded a westbound car at Michigan and Griswold at 6:15 p.m.

"On every corner along the route were little groups of work-weary citizens anxious to get home to their meals," he wrote.

"They were too tired and too hungry to care just how they got home as long as they got there as quickly as possible. When the car stopped, they piled on, fighting and twisting to get a foothold."

With the inside of the car full, soon every inch on the front and rear steps were occupied by men clinging to the car. Other would-be passengers, unable to find footing on the step, piled on the fender and rested against the front of the car.

"A winter blast howled down Michigan and, as the car started, it beat into their faces, but they knew that those at home were waiting for them and they were too cold to bother about a little thing like pneumonia," the reporter added.

"They stuck to the fender and cursed the DUR when the motorman pleaded with them to get off."

Such conditions had everybody up in arms, and on Feb. 11 Mayor Philip Breitmeyer and Alderman James Vernor came out in favor of the city's purchasing the car lines.

Some citizens were too irate to wait for that. They took motormen to court under a city ordi-   *63* nance making it a misdemeanor to fail to stop a car with space for more passengers when patrons were waiting at a legal boarding point.

When one defendant, motorman George Brown, denied in court that he ever did such a thing, Judge William F. Connolly adjourned the case and went out in the rush hour to see for himself. What he saw made him so mad he disqualified himself from the case and announced he would be a witness against the motorman.

The DUR era had its lighter side, however. On the "owl cars," as those running after midnight were called, the atmosphere could be distinctly clubby.

"Look over the cargo. Forty passengers aboard, and every one of them asleep," a conductor remarked to a reporter who boarded an owl car running out Woodward.

"We're operating a Pullman service after 12 o'clock. Everybody rolls over against the next fellow and starts snoring, and expects me to know where they get off."

The conductor said he would go through the car when it reached Grand Boulevard and waken anyone he did not recognize. His regular customers were allowed to doze until their stops were reached.

A novelty that winter was a side-seater car installed on the Michigan line. Another newsman compared it to a three-ring circus. The car had just two seats, one running the full length of the car. Its opposite number was bisected by a hard-coal stove. Between the long seats was "an uninterrupted speedway from the motorman's vestibule clear back to the rear railing."

Half a dozen times, the reporter saw unwary passengers caught off balance as the car lurched forward. They "did acrobatics the full length of the car, all the way to the back platform."

Passengers quickly learned to grab a strap as soon as they boarded the new-type car, however. "The side-seat car is the triumph of the straphanger," the report added. "On other cars, the straphanger is an afflicted individual, but on the side-seaters the straphangers are in their glory. They step on the feet of those seated at will."

Another peril for those seated also was noted:

"When the car started quickly the seated passengers, beginning with the people nearest the motorman, rolled into their neighbors.

"The neighbors rolled into their neighbors — and so on down the car like a row of dominoes."

It was perilous to bring a package aboard, too: "There's no chance for the man with baggage on a side-seater. There's nothing to set your suitcase or your egg-basket against. You have to drop them in the middle of the aisle and take your chances of finding them after the car jerks."

Detroiters voted to buy out the DUR and establish their own municipal transit system in 1922, and Detroit's own product — the automobile — finally ended the long reign of the trolley 34 years later. The last street car was replaced by a bus on April 7, 1956.

10. The Clock and the Cannonball

The trains were on time — it was the railroad station that was late. Two years late, in fact.

No one could miss the date, 1891, on the Fort Street side of Detroit's venerable Union Station. It was carved in large figures over what was a main entrance for many years. But the station wasn't finished until 1893.

Some of the city's most solid citizens were among those who pulled the switch that delayed its completion long after the target date was chiseled out by the stonecutters.

Lawsuits wrecked the timetable for the depot's completion and property owners in the vicinity petitioned the City Council to withdraw the building permit. They charged the promoters used high-handed methods in getting rights-of-way across Fourth, Fifth and Sixth streets.

Many viewed the proposed station as a crass encroachment on one of Detroit's finest residential neighborhoods. The corner chosen for it, at Fort and Third, was opposite the highly fashionable Fort Street Presbyterian Church. Across Fort stood the mansion built by Zachariah Chandler — a residence worthy of a Detroiter who rose to the Senate, the Cabinet, and even to the role of president-maker. Three stories high, there were arched windows, a porte-cochere and an elegant conservatory.

Fort Street's tall elms set off other mansions built by such Detroiters as Russell A. Alger, James F.

Joy, Allan Shelden, Henry P. Baldwin and William J. Chittenden. Other community leaders had built a block north, on Lafayette — Walter Buhl, Thomas B. Rayl and Edwin S. Barbour among them.

Not all the residents were opposed to railroads. Joy was the Midwest's most eminent railroad builder, and at 70 he undertook a plan that would give his home city a direct line to St. Louis, and the Sheldens and Buhls were associated with him in the venture. The result was the Wabash Railroad, a major mover — along with the Pere Marquette — in promoting the Union Depot.

On the whole, citizens were reconciled to the fact that the hub of transportation through Detroit centered on Third Street, in the blocks north of the waterfront. They just didn't want it to expand up to Fort. Third sloped down sharply below Fort, and its teaming commercial activities were out of sight of the fine homes above the brow of the hill.

In the '90's, lower Third was the visible center of Detroit's heritage as a frontier outpost at the crossroads of the waterway up the Great Lakes and the east-west land route over it. When the Michigan Central Railroad deposited travelers at its depot, they were only a few steps from the docks of the busy steamship lines.

It was almost a town in itself. Those waiting overnight for morning sailings could find an abundance of hotels — the Wayne Hotel, the Griffin House and the New Western Hotel in a competitive row on Third, and the Tremont House around the corner on Front Street.

Entertainment was available, too. Adjoining the Wayne Hotel was the Wayne Pavilion, pleasant for dining, drinking and dancing. River Street, west of Third, had the adjoining saloons of Michael Quinn, E. A. Voght, and Swan & Co. Commercial enterprises occupied most of Fourth and Fifth below Fort, such as the Cooperative Foundry Co., the Detroit Paper Novelty Co., and the Eagle Iron Works.

Steam was supreme, and in spite of the opposition the railroads won their way to put the Union Depot in the choice spot they wanted. The new terminal cut off Fourth and Fifth altogether below Fort. Sixth tunneled under the maze of tracks and survived.

The Union Depot, Fort and Third, was once a hub of activity with trainloads of people arriving and departing. But it had quiet moments, too, as this old photo shows.

The court of last resort — time itself — ultimately revised the decision. When expressways arrived, the city took back its lost streets — and considerably more — in putting through the Lodge Freeway.

On Jan. 21, 1893, the day the $200,000 depot was opened, the spotlight in Detroit was on Mayor Hazen S. Pingree. "Big boodle!" was the headline on page one of The Detroit News that day. The story related Pingree's sensational charges against the Citizens Street Railway Co. But "Ping," wrapped in a big fur coat, was in a jovial mood that evening when he appeared at Union Station's gala opening.

All Detroit was there, it seemed. The usual downtown Saturday night crowds strolled out Fort to take in the sights of the new depot. The 19th Infantry Band from Fort Wayne, seated in the gallery where the railway offices were holding open house, played stirring airs. The concourse below was handsomely decorated with national flags and potted palms.

"It's a fine depot, and it will help the city commercially," the mayor said.

In the good-natured crush, few heard his remarks. The News reported: "Such a crowd! From about 8 o'clock until 10, men and women, boys and girls, formed a solid mass of humanity in the waiting rooms, in the corridors and on the stairways. It was a sort of go-as-you-please crowd getting in and out. Even the basement and engine room were crowded with sightseers."

A locomotive and two coaches brought a happy party from Saginaw for the festivities. They waved flags from the platforms and windows as their special pulled out, and resounding cheers went up.

The new station resulted in lower Third Street becoming more of a daily hive of activity than ever. The bustle reached its peak on summer weekends, when crowds of hot-weather refugees from such sultry places as Kansas City and St. Louis rode in on the Wabash Cannonball and other fast trains. They breathed deeply of the cooling breezes from the river, and merrily made their way down Third to the docks of the Detroit & Cleveland Navigation Co. There they embarked for Harbor Beach, Alpena or Mackinac Island.

In a few years Third Street had jams of motor car traffic, too. Drivers heading for the East would line up their automobiles at the foot of the street for hours before the sailing times of such leviathans of the lakes as the Eastern States or the City of Detroit III. A person could put his car aboard and enjoy an overnight cruise, then drive off refreshed in the morning at Cleveland or Buffalo.

After being a neighbor of the Union Station for two decades, the Michigan Central Railroad shifted to a new terminal at Roosevelt Park in 1913. Its departure was hastened by a fire which broke out in the old depot the day before Christmas.

It was a sad moment when the roof caved in at the height of the blaze. The depot had been the finest in the city until the Union Station was built, with *69* turrets that made it resemble a medieval castle. The Union Station's interior was modernized in 1948, but its exterior continued to look much the same as when the first train pulled out, with Victorian architecture and gingerbread masonry that made it a memorial to the golden age of railroading.

And the Wabash Cannonball, its most famous train, continued to operate until the government took over American passenger railroading in 1971, long after the Wabash Railroad itself was taken over by the Norfolk & Western.

Legend said that the Cannonball's speed made it a favorite among more proletarian riders than those who occupied its plush seats.

William Kindt, a turn-of-the-century song writer, picked up the story for his ballad, "The Wabash Cannonball," which achieved a popularity surpassed among the epics of railroading only by the immortal "Casey Jones." Time was when every youngster in town knew the lyrics:

"From the great Atlantic Ocean to the wide Pacific shore,
From the sweet flowery mountain to the southbelt by the moor,
She's mighty tall and handsome, she's quite well known by all,
She's the hobo's accommodation on the Wabash Cannonball."

Kindt used poetic license, of course. The Cannonball never traveled beyond the Midwest. But the song did; as recently as 1942, it was on the hit parade in a recording by Roy Acuff that sold more than a million records.

The train carried the fame of Indiana's Wabash River country far and wide, long before Paul Dresser wrote "On the Banks of the Wabash" in 1898.

The Cannonball already possessed a long history when it first steamed into the new Union Station. It began operations in 1884, preceding such famous

name trains as the 20th Century Limited and

Time—a different one on each face—now stands still on Union Depot clock

the Broadway Limited, and it outlived the others by many years. Perhaps that was because it was a down-to-earth train. Never did it offer the secretaries, barbers, manicurists, valets and showerbath attendants encountered on the New York-Chicago specials, but it was fast.

The Cannonball's last departure from the old depot for St. Louis was noted with suitable requiems on April 30, 1971. The next day, the station itself was boarded up. Someone chalked a last entry on the bulletin board for train arrivals: "All trains are down the drain."

High above this epitaph loomed in aloof serenity the station's tower clock that had told generations of travelers how much time they had before their trains left. Day by day since 1893, it clocked the departure of the Cannonball every morning and the arrival of the twin Cannonball from St. Louis in time for dinner every evening. All the trains might be down the drain, but the tower clock kept right on running for weeks.

In two years since Amtrak, the National Railroad Passenger Corp., began operations, time has stood still at the once busy Union Station. No longer used for passenger trains, the only footsteps in its waiting room are those of watchmen.

All too easily, retrospect can over-glamorize the passenger trains of yesteryear. In truth, they were a mixed bag.

Locals were often late, and almost always slow. Cinders got in your eyes from the open windows of the years before air-conditioning. The most mileage-hardened traveling salesmen could find it difficult to get a sound night's sleep in a jostling lower berth, let alone an upper.

Even in the heyday of the railroad era, freight traffic was the bread-and-butter trade. Passenger operations were simply the frosting on the cake.

Today, Detroit's rail network continues to carry as intricate a complex of cargo operations as ever. Compared to this, the two workaday passenger trains still operated by Amtrak to Chicago daily out of Penn Central Station are small time.

But memory still recalls that it was like a birthday and Christmas and the Fourth of July combined for a youngster to be taken to the busy railroad station of old for a journey on the steel ribbons of adventure.

11. Rescue!—of a Skeleton

Nothing was saved but a Bible and a skeleton. That was when fire destroyed Detroit's first high school on Jan. 27, 1893.

The temperature was below freezing and a blizzard had left a blanket of snow on downtown streets. At 3:55 a.m., a roundsman saw flames in the basement of Capitol High School which occupied the onetime State Capitol building in the triangle north of State and Griswold. He hurried to turn in the alarm.

The first engine came from the Clifford Street firehouse, little more than a block away, but it had trouble. The horses were slowed by the heavy snow, and the old structure's interior was blazing by the time firemen poured the first stream of water on it.

More engines clanged up, but the fire continued to spread. Soon the rear annex was burning, too. An early arrival in the growing crowd of spectators was the school's principal, Frederick L. Bliss. He paced the sidewalk, covering his ears with his hands against the cold.

Bliss stopped pacing to stare when a tall, bareheaded man ran into the burning building. The man was one of his 36 teachers, E. Jay Hale, who taught business courses. Hale soon emerged with the Bible from Bliss' office under one arm and the skeleton from the science lab under the other.

"Too hot to get anything else," Hale panted.

The spectators cheered him, then shouted warnings to firemen on the second floor. The upper walls were beginning to crumble and the men hurried out just seconds before one long section gave way.

By now the coats and helmets of the fire fighters on the hose lines were sheathed with ice. Icicles hung from their hair and their mustaches. And ice formed so heavily on the 186 telephone and telegraph wires running on poles down Griswold that many of them pulled loose and drooped in tangled crystal festoons over the sidewalk.

The crowd drew back as two explosions sent blazing debris high in the air. The blasts came when the flames reached a 15-gallon drum of kerosene in a basement storeroom and the chemicals in the science laboratory.

Hale had turned over the Bible to Bliss, but he was still standing in front of the building when the lab went up. He drew appreciative laughter from the fire watchers as he raised the arms of the skeleton in mock horror.

The second blast scattered firebrands across Griswold and Rowland streets — the latter was soon to become part of Shelby — but the snow was deep enough on the roofs to provide some protection. Windows were broken in the Brown Brothers cigar factory, and the damage inside was bad enough to keep the employes out of work for a week.

The absence of John Miller, the school's chief janitor, was noted, and it was feared that he might have been trapped in the building. Miller usually was at work by 3 a.m. to fire the boiler.

A Detroit News reporter went to Miller's home on Mullett Street to check. He found the janitor at home, eating breakfast. Fortunately, that morning he had overslept.

By daylight the fire was burning itself out. The walls left standing were coated with ice. Smoke and vapor poured from the ruined interior. Four firemen were injured, including Lt. Roderick Morrison of Truck Co. No. 1, who stepped on a nail.

By 8 a.m., the 1,100 students began arriving and joined the throngs still at the scene. In the nearby offices of the Board of Education, a discussion began about where to put them all.

Michigan's territorial capitol building in Detroit was taken over by the Board of Education after the seat of government was moved to Lansing in 1848. For many years it housed the city's only high school.

One of the students, David Holmes, reported he had seen a light in the school basement shortly before midnight, and there was speculation that a burglar might have dropped a match to set off the fire. The loss would total $150,000, Supervisor Ernst Nuppenau told the school board, and there was no insurance.

In fact, the Board of Education didn't even own the building. Mayor Hazen S. Pingree, an advocate for removal of the high school elsewhere, reminded reporters of that. Pingree wanted Capitol Square made into a park.

"The loss is not to be too much regarded," he said. "The building has been unfit for school purposes for years."

Only the day before, two sleighloads of city officials led by Pingree went over the structure from top to bottom. They found many health and safety hazards. Certainly the old landmark had seen better days.

Erected in 1818 to serve as governmental headquarters for the Territory of Michigan, it stood vacant after the capital was moved to Lansing in 1847. The school board petitioned the Legislature for its use as a school, but action on the petition was long delayed. In March, 1848, Divie B. Duffield, an influential board member who took a leading role in the struggle to provide free public education, quietly took action.

Somehow, Duffield came into possession of a key to the building, and soon passersby were surprised to see all the windows open. Workmen were busy, and new lumber was arriving. There were rumors that the state militia would be called to eject the brazen invaders, but nothing came of it. Duffield had good friends in Lansing, and the work went on.

The building was transformed into the Capitol Union School and classes were launched for the fall term. In 1863, a high school was started on its second floor with 126 pupils and two teachers, and in 1875 a new front was built on the structure and it became a full high school, with four grades under one roof.

The school board's squatter sovereignty in the onetime Capitol set something of a record; it lasted 45 years, but the fire brought it to an end. Before the embers were out, however, several possibilities for substitute space were being discussed. At a special meeting called that night, the board voted to take over the old Biddle House at Jefferson and Randolph. Once one of the city's leading hostelries, it became a temporary high school for a rental of $750 a month.

An offer of space in the former Temple Beth El, at Washington and Clifford, also was accepted, and a number of classes began meeting there. While the cause of the fire remained a mystery, it did prove to be a blessing in disguise, as Pingree predicted. The site became Capitol Park, a welcome breathing space of downtown greenery.

Capitol High School was Detroit's best known landmark when a fire broke out in the early hours of Jan. 27, 1893. Only the blackened walls were left after firemen put out the blaze.

The school board lost no time in getting a site for a new building. On Nov. 13, 1894, city leaders gathered to watch the first shovelful of earth being taken out of a lot at Cass and Warren. There were protests that putting the high school so far away would be a hardship on many pupils, but the foresighted Duffield declared the city's great residential growth would go in that direction.

Central High School was built on the site. It inherited not only the traditions of Capitol High, but a continuity dating back to Aug. 30, 1858.

On that date, the Board of Education established Detroit's first public secondary school in a two-story frame building, formerly a dwelling house on Miami Avenue—the Broadway of later years. Here 23 boys enrolled in the first session, with Henry Chaney as their teacher-principal.

Before the end of its first year, the high school　　77

outgrew these quarters, and the demand was heard that girls should be allowed to share in the new opportunities of education.

As a result, the school board erected a brick schoolhouse in the rear of the frame building. Beginning in January, 1860, entrance to the high school was by examination, and enrollment for the new term included 30 girls and 67 boys.

That June the first graduating class, of two members, received diplomas.

The decision after the Capitol High fire to build the replacement in a developing residential area had far-reaching results. From it followed Detroit's regional plan for high schools.

Central was soon joined by Western High, facing the tall trees of Clark Park. Western was completed in September, 1898, after classes met for several years in an annex of the nearby Webster School.

Erection of Eastern High, in what was still a heavily-wooded area at East Grand Boulevard and Mack, followed in 1900. Eastern was renamed Dr. Martin Luther King Jr. High School in 1968.

Lewis Cass Technical High School the first high school named for an individual, opened in 1907. Within a few years, with the addition of Northwestern, Northern, Northeastern, Southwestern and Southeastern, the high schools fairly boxed the compass for a swiftly growing Detroit.

After World War I, high schools were named for Gen. John J. Pershing and for Detroit's own Edwin Denby, who resigned as a congressman to enlist as a wartime private and later became Secretary of the Navy.

Later, high schools were named for the aviation pioneer, Wilbur Wright; labor leader Philip Murray; automotive inventor Charles F. Kettering; Thomas M. Cooley, a chief justice of the Michigan Supreme Court; Board of Education leaders Samuel C. Mumford and Mrs. Laura F. Osborn, and two Detroit school superintendents, Charles E. Chadsey and Frank Cody. Redford High retained its regional designation.

The building erected to replace Capitol High still is cherished as Old Main, the heart of Wayne State

University. This transition came about in a sequence of stages.

Detroit Junior College developed in 1917 out of a program of postgraduate courses at Central High. In 1923, a regular four-year curriculum was offered, and the institution became the College of the City of Detroit.

Other institutions of higher learning then under the jurisdiction of the Board of Education were merged to form the Colleges of the City of Detroit in 1933, renamed Wayne University in 1934. In 1956, new status as a state-supported institution resulted in the present title, Wayne State University.

Oldest of the amalgamated schools was the Detroit College of Medicine and Surgery. Originally Detroit Medical College, it was founded in 1868 by five physicians in a frame building at Woodward and Martin Place, with 48 students.

The City Normal School graduated its first class of young women teachers, in taffeta and crinoline, in 1882. Their alma mater successively became the Washington Normal School, the Martindale Normal School, and in 1929, Detroit Teachers College.

Detroit City Law School and Detroit College of Pharmacy rounded out the university.

When the name of Central High School was passed on to a new educational unit, the Bible rescued from the Capitol High fire of 1893 went along. Nor has it been forgotten that the volume was presented in the first place by the same Divine Bethune Duffield who so providentially came up with a key to the old State Capitol at the beginning of the saga.

12. 'I'm the Luckiest Man Alive'

Newspaper Row was the busiest place in town on the morning of Nov. 6, 1895. It was the day after election, and the voters had given Detroit's most spectacular mayor, Hazen S. Pingree, another term.

Newspaper Row centered at Larned and Shelby Streets. The News was on the northwest corner; the Free Press, the northeast, Just off the southeast corner, on Larned, was the Journal.

The tempo heightened just before 9 a.m. as the two afternoon competitors, The News and Journal, readied their first editions. Newsboys lined up to get the initial armsful of papers off the presses.

Moses Jacobs, a paper dealer, had business that morning at Hiller's Bindery, one of a number of enterprises in the publishing field which rented space in the five-story Journal Block. Jacobs lingered to greet some of the five youths and 20 girls employed at the bindery, and it was close to 9 o'clock when he stepped out the rear door of the building. At the same instant Arthur D. Lynch, a stereotyper stooped under a 400-pound steam table in the Journal's composing room. Lynch turned the steam higher for more heat — and the blast of a terrific explosion shattered the building.

The sound was heard throughout the city. Buildings swayed along Newspaper Row, their windows bursting into fragments. Jacobs was blown across an alley, and a fraction of a second later the space across which he had been blown was covered by tons of falling debris.

Jacobs was dazed, cut and bruised, but he picked himself up and could find no broken bones. "I'm the luckiest man alive," he gasped, and for the rest

Spectators watch activity on Larned near Shelby after Nov. 6, 1895, explosion leveled the five-story Detroit Journal Building

of his days he would often repeat the phrase. He knotted a handkerchief around his bleeding head, and hurried to Larned Street. He could hardly believe his eyes.

Where the Journal's entrance had stood were tangled bricks, mortar, timbers and machinery, piled on the foundations and spilled into the street. A wide section of the building, including Hiller's Bindery, had been blown skyward. The pieces had fallen back on the ruins.

As Jacobs reached the street, flames burst out of the rubble. The cries and moans of the injured could be heard. He ran to join passersby already trying to dig into the smoking pile.

The first fire engine clanged up the street. Fire House No. 1 was only a block away, and the blast was its alarm. Soon the firebells were sounding.

Near the top of the debris, an arm and a leg protrudes. Charles Boston, the first rescuer to reach this point, was startled to hear his own name spoken from below as he tugged at a mass of masonry.

"I'm all right, Charley," called the voice. "Don't worry about me."

It was Boston's friend, Arthur D. Lynch. With his feet still pinioned, the stereotyper told his own story of miraculous survival, one that would be paired with that of Jacobs' accounts of the disaster as seeming interventions of providence.

"I was carried down five floors under the steam table," Lynch told his friend. "Bricks fell all around, but I was protected by the table. Steam scalded me from the moment the pipes burst on the top floor, but I never lost consciousness."

While the rescuers worked, several victims managed to push their way unaided from the ruins. A News reporter saw two of them emerge. Soon he was writing his account of it:

"One staggered up, one down Larned Street. Their faces were unrecognizable, owing to the dust and ashes with which they were covered.

"Blood was streaming from their faces and other portions of their bodies, leaving a trail behind.

"One reached the outer door of The News office and was helped within, where he sank helpless on the tiled floor."

Thomas Thompson, engineer of the Journal, was among the occupants who crawled out of the ruins, half his clothes torn off and injured painfully.

"I don't know any more about it than you do," he told questioners. "The boilers were inspected in August."

Ambulances joined the fire engines in the street, and shocked relatives and friends of those who were in the building gathered around them. Mayor Pingree came, his face gray, his triumph at the polls forgotten. He ordered a temporary morgue set up in the nearby Michigan Exchange Building where relatives could try to identify bodies.

In the confused melee, one victim narrowly escaped a further hazard. Fireman Thomas E. Sullivan of Engine Co. 2 needed to rescue him twice. Sullivan stepped back after dragging him from the ruin—then returned indignantly as two

Firemen hosing down tons of smoking debris

undertakers' runners tried to put the poor fellow into a coffin.

"Can't you see he's still alive!" Sullivan shouted. He kicked the coffin lid aside and helped the man into an ambulance.

Like this unfortunate, the Evening Journal itself was prematurely considered about to give up the ghost, long before the explosion that shook Newspaper Row.

The original editor and publisher, Lloyd Brezee, was called "Brezee by name and breezy by nature." It was apparent from the start that his paper would be breezy, too.

Detroit's political pot was at the boil when the Journal's first issue appeared on Sept. 1, 1883. A front-page column offered much speculation over who would succeed Mayor William G. Thompson, who had just announced he would not run for another term.

Another front-page story left no doubt that the Journal realized it faced tough competition. This was a full column aimed at The Evening News, then well into its 11th successful year.

With tongue in cheek, the Journal reported "great consternation" in The News office over the new rival. These were bold words for a paper starting on a shoestring. Silas Farmer, in his "History of Detroit," reported the Journal's starting capital at $3,200.

Before the first paper came out, the Journal chartered the Sappho, one of the ferries steaming between Detroit and Windsor, to give the city's newsboys a free ride. Once aboard, they were plied with ice cream and urged to include the Journal among their wares.

The elegance of Detroit in 1883 came through in a big ad on page one. Roehm & Wright, importers and jewelers in the Opera House block, offered "European Wares." They elaborated:

"Our Mr. Roehm in his recent trip through Europe made such selections of diamonds and other precious stones, marble statuary, bronzes, clocks, art pottery, fine fans and fancy articles generally as will render our stock unusually attractive."

The journal was saved from early extinction by W. H. Brearly, a newspaperman with expansive ideas who bought up its 500 shares of stock. It was Brearly who, in the autumn of 1883, fathered a project which resulted in a contribution to Detroit's growth.

Brearly suggested that the city should have an Art Loan Exhibition. He enlisted an impressive group of Detroiters willing to subscribe $1,000 each for the plan.

Included were James E. Scripps, George H. Scripps, Gen. Russell A. Alger, Christian H. Buhl, Moses W. Field, Dexter M. Ferry, E. S. Heineman, George H. Hammond, James F. Joy, G. V. N. Lothrop, Christopher R. Mabley, James McMillan, Hugh McMillan, Simon J. Murphy, John S. Newberry, Cyrenius A. Newcomb, Thomas W. Palmer, Francis Palms, Philo Parsons, George B. Remick, Allan Shelden, David Whitney Jr. and Richard Storrs Willis.

With Brearly as chairman of the executive committee, a one-story brick structure, 135 by 153 feet, was put up on a tract on the north side of

Larned, between Bates and Randolph, at a cost of $15,000. Here was assembled on loan from the wealth of art in Detroit residences, 950 oil paintings, 250 watercolors, 102 sculptures, 1,000 etchings and engravings — in all, more than 4,800 items.

Brearly even secured an exhibit from the Vatican in Rome. Pope Leo XIII sent a painting of "The Betrothal of St. Catharine" which proved a hit of the exhibition.

Over a 10-week period, 134,050 visitors paid to see the show, and receipts were $45,000 as against expenses of $43,500. Nor did it end there.

In a canvass after the exhibition closed, $40,000 was raised toward a permanent art museum. On May 17, 1884, Brearly announced a gift of $50,000 from James E. Scripps, and on April 16, 1885 the Detroit Museum of Art was incorporated. Today its successor, the Detroit Institute of Arts is recognized as one of America's leading museums.

To return to the aftermath of the Newspaper Row explosion, 35 of those rescued recovered. The death toll was 42. Months of investigation followed, and the conclusion was that low water in a massive boiler caused the tragedy.

Like the city itself after the great fire of 1805, the Journal arose from its ashes, moving into an unoccupied church building on the southwest corner of Fort and Wayne. The Journal built a new front on the structure and continued publication there until it was absorbed by The News in 1922.

13. The Quadricycle and La Petite

It didn't make much of a stir, at the time. On June 4, 1896, there wasn't a line in the paper about the odd happening on Bagley Avenue. That was the day Henry Ford, engineer of the Detroit Edison Illuminating Co. plant, ventured forth for the first time in the contraption he had been putting together for weeks. He called it a quadricycle.

In fact, about the kindest thing said about Ford was that for a fellow who wanted to be an inventor so badly, he certainly had picked the right mate. Ford's wife, Clara, hadn't complained when he spent all this spare time during the spring tinkering in his workshop at the rear of their home, on the north side of Bagley between Grand River and Clifford.

Clara didn't say a word when it turned out that Henry, just like all the absent-minded inventors in the jokes, failed to plan how he was going to get the quadricycle out of the workshop when it was finished. She didn't say a word when he picked up an ax at 2 a.m. and began flailing away at the brick wall of the shop as if he had gone berserk. She didn't say a word when he kept right on with the ax until he had knocked down enough of the wall to wheel the quadricycle into the alley. She didn't say a word when he poured enough gasoline into it to send the whole kit and kaboodle sky-high.

She didn't say a word when he gave the flywheel a spin and the quadricycle started shaking and roaring, and neighbors up and down Bagley threw up windows and peered out trying to find out what in tarnation was going on in the middle of the night. She didn't say a word when Henry climbed into the machine, lit a lamp, and went bouncing over the alley cobblestones, hanging on to the steering tiller, in the dark and drizzle of the street.

Holding an umbrella, Mrs. Ford stood at the back door and waved as Ford drove off, just as it were the most natural thing in the world.

Perhaps she thought about how nice their neighbor, old Felix Julien, had been when Ford started using his half of the brick shed for a workshop. Julien stored wood and coal in his half, but when he saw Ford working so hard on his project he tore out the partition down the middle and moved his fuel into the house to give Ford more room.

Julien would sit there by the hour watching Ford at work. Most of the quadricycle came from bits of scrap metal, machined on the lathe. Ford bored and fitted sections of the exhaust pipe of a steam engine to make the two cylinders. The crankshaft was forged at the Detroit Dry Dock works.

Ford used four 28-inch bicycle wheels and rode on a bicycle saddle mounted above the three-gallon gas tank, that first night. Later on he substituted a buggy seat big enough for two.

Two belts from the engine to the countershaft gave him a choice of speeds — 10 or 20 miles an hour. There weren't any brakes.

Ford wasn't the first experimenter to drive a horseless carriage in Detroit. Charles B. King, a young mechanical engineer in one of the railroad car shops that were Detroit's big business then, was ahead of Ford by three months. King saw a model designed by a German inventor at the Chicago World's Fair in 1893. He built a machine himself, and on March 6, 1896, drove down Jefferson and out Woodward as far as Grand Boulevard.

What set Ford apart was an idea of his own about the strange little machines. Ford was certain they could be more than an expensive toy. They could be more than a passing fad for the rich to play with until they grew tired. His idea was that automobiles could be made fast enough and cheap enough so that almost everybody could afford them.

On that rainy night of June 4, 1896, we know what Henry Ford said when he came back from his first drive in the quadricycle.

87

Henry Ford and his wife, Clara, in the quadricycle Ford built in 1896

"The darn thing ran!" he exclaimed.

Did he tell Clara about his big idea that night, or later? Whenever it was, we can make a likely guess as to what she said about it. It would be the same thing she said every time he came up with something new, even if it seemed as if there were bats in his belfry.

"Yes, Henry," she would say, just as if he were making good sense.

Clara always understood when, perplexed by some mechancial difficulty, Henry would seem to retire into the silences to brood about it. She never appeared to mind if an inspiration awakened him in the middle of the night and he hurried out to the workshop to bang hammers and clang pipes.

The quadricycle really had its biggest day 50 years later. Through the first week in June, 1946, the great men of the motor world gathered in Detroit for the Golden Jubilee of the Automobile. Fourteen pioneers, Ford and King among them, received "Oscars" marking their election to the Automotive Hall of Fame. It was estimated that a million people watched the big parade down Woodward.

On June 4, Mrs. Ford put on a stylish gray bonnet and Ford did a bit of tinkering with the machine that had put Old Dobbin and the shay well on the road to oblivion. They climbed into the shined-up quadricycle in Greenfield Village, just a few steps from where the workshop in which it was built is preserved. In 1946 there were cameramen present to photograph the scene. There was even a reporter close enough to overhear the answer when Ford asked Mrs. Ford if she were having a good time that day.

"Yes, Henry," Clara Ford said.

Besides bringing together the great men of the industry, the Golden Jubilee also brought to light the contributions of some interesting little people — in particular, the story of Olive LaVigne, who always believed she was the first child of the automobile's dawn era to drive a car.

Olive was born a few months after Ford first drove the quadricycle, and she began her own career of automobile driving when she was 7 years old. That was in 1904. One thing is true. The law being what it is today, no youngster is likely to get as early a start at setting automotive firsts as she did.

Of course, she had an advantage over other 7-year-olds of her day. Her father was Joseph P. LaVigne, a pioneer of the motor car. LaVigne was a veteran in the inventing field before King and Ford appeared on the scene — he was credited with being the first thinker to use the shaft drive, and the first to put the engine under a hood. As early as 1890, his achievements were recognized with a gold medal from the Paris Academy of Inventions and Industry. When he died in 1941, at 81, he held 385 U.S. patents.

Next to his small tomboy daughter, LaVigne's special pride in 1904 was a powerful steam car. He drove it all over Detroit, probably scaring a lot of the 12,000 horses that were registered in the community that eventually was to become the Motor City.

The big car had one drawback. It took a long time to get up steam. LaVigne was impatient about delays, so when he drove home for lunch from his workshop it was his habit to leave the car out front with the fire going and plenty of steam in the boiler.

Young Olive wasn't an inventor's daughter for nothing. She had watched her father at the controls and knew how to operate the car. One day when her father parked the steamer and hurried into the house, Olive was hiding behind a hedge. Seconds later, she had the throttle open and was off with a roar. She toured the neighborhood, waving at her friends and shouting, "Look at me, I'm driving!"

Papa LaVigne heard the takeoff and ran to the front porch to yell at Olive, but he wasn't in time to do much else — except sputter. Olive soon drove back with the steamer intact, contrary to all his expectations. Even so, LaVigne was upset, but a spanking meant little to Olive compared with her undying desire to pilot a motor car.

As often as she could, she seized a chance to joy-ride at the helm of the steamer. Papa knew he was beaten. When Christmas came, he gave her a car he had completed for her at the workshop. It was just big enough for one chum to accompany her. At first it had three wheels, but after Olive suffered several spills rounding corners it was converted to a four-wheeler.

The LaVigne home at Commonwealth and Willis was in a sedate neighborhood, and the residents at first looked askance at Olive's "automobubbling," as they called it. Olive never hit anything, but she did shave it a bit close sometimes. At least one hay wagon wound up tangled in the elms that graced the streets, trying to keep out of Olive's way.

She kept on driving and owning cars, among them models long forgotten except by classic car buffs. La Petite, for example. LaVigne built it for display at Detroit's first auto show. His pet name for Olive was "La Petite." Naturally, the car he named after her eventually became one of her vehicles. She went on to drive just about everything dreamed up in the busy automotive whirl, including a 10-ton truck.

Miss LaVigne never drove the 10-tonner up the

Olive LaVigne, who started driving at the age of 7, is at the wheel of LaPetite, a car built by her father, Joseph P. LaVigne

steps of the Wayne County Building, but her father did. LaVigne hadn't forgotten the excitement that gripped the town in 1901 when the steps were successfully negotiated by Joseph H. McDuffee, a young racing car driver, in a two-seat steamer called a Mobile. No one else attempted the feat until LaVigne built his big truck and used the steps to demonstrate that his creation could go anywhere.

When Miss LaVigne coaxed her father into letting her take a turn at the monster's wheel, she had to promise to stay on the regular thoroughfares. In its way, though, her drive was conceded to be something special. No one would have believed a girl could handle more rolling power than the huskiest brewery teamster in town.

By 1946 Miss LaVigne had become director of the children's garden division of the Detroit Department of Parks and Recreation. She was still going strong and estimated she had driven 500,000 miles.

"I never had an accident," she said. "Well, not a real accident. Once or twice other drivers ran right over me."

She retired in 1949, and continued to roll up more mileage around the land until her death in 1955.

14. From Century Run to Nickelodeon

For Detroit as for all America in the summer of 1896, the greatest test of a hero was the grueling century run. Only the hardiest of cyclists could travel 100 miles under their own power, between dawn and dusk.

Teams bent on accomplishing this feat set out each Sunday morning from the clubhouse of the Detroit Wheelmen, on Washington Boulevard near Grand River Avenue. Under the rules, the 100-mile circuit had to be completed in 10 hours. A typical course, through Ypsilanti, Saline, Ann Arbor and back, covered mostly rough clay and sand roads which were truly formidable.

Rival clubs — the Crescent Wheelmen, the Diamond Wheelmen and the Star Bicycle Club — also encouraged their stalwarts to compete in century runs. Cyclists of less heroic mold didn't go so far afield, but they were out every Sunday, too, by the thousands. They hailed the returning "centurions," as those who completed the century runs liked to be called, with colorful parades on Belle Isle, carrying varicolored lanterns.

The bicycle craze also contributed to another boom. Rustic resorts on the outskirts of town made ideal spots for cycling parties to rendezvous, and beer gardens blossomed in a number of shady groves around Detroit. Most were handy to Germantown on the East Side, where the residents were especially partial to wassail in the woods.

Beller's Garden, near the Belle Isle Bridge, enjoyed the best location, with a bathhouse adjoining. As early as 7 o'clock each clear summer evening, Jefferson Avenue was thronged with cyclists heading for the bridge, nearly half of them female. Many stopped at Beller's for refreshment, and two long racks were provided for wheels. Under the elms large tents were decorated with Chinese lanterns and a family of musicians — four girls and their brother — entertained on zithers and mandolins.

Three blocks past Waterworks Park, where the streetcar line ended, was Jefferson Park, the newest and largest beer garden. The management was negotiating to get the streetcar tracks extended. Meanwhile, ambitious programs of entertainment were luring customers. On the first bill were Lew Dockstader, America's favorite minstrel; Alice J. Snow, a whistling prima donna; and the St. Helmos, who offered $5,000 to any other aerial troupe which could duplicate their daring stunts on the high rings.

Exciting fare also was offered at Boulevard Park, operated by the Detroit Railway at Grand River and Fourteenth as an end-of-line attraction. A big fireworks spectacle, Paine's "The Storming of Vicksburg," was presented nightly.

Pfeiffer's Park, at Beaufait and Sylvester, was smaller than the others. Its standing attractions included an electric fountain and classical music by Schremer's Fourth Infantry Band. Business was slow, however. T. L. Diggins, the manager, steeled himself to hazard the park's reputation for quiet gentility with an untried novelty for the Fourth of July. It was called the eidoloscope.

Detroit News=Tribune

ILLUSTRATED

THREE CENTS — DETROIT, MICHIGAN, SUNDAY MORNING, JUNE 25, 1899 — THREE CENTS

A Cycling Misadventure—The front page of the illustrated section of the Sunday News-Tribune for June 25, 1899, depicted the downtown scene when cycling was everybody's sport. Most of the mishaps, like the one shown, were minor. Bagley Fountain, in the background, then at Fort and Woodward, is in the Campus Martius today.

The device linked Thomas A. Edison's kinetoscope, which showed motion pictures in the small peepshows familiar in penny arcades, with a magic lantern to throw the films on a large screen so they could be viewed by a mass audience.

The eidoloscope had been shown at the Detroit Opera House to press representatives and a few cit-

95

izens especially interested in science, without creating much of a stir. But shouldn't moving pictures appeal to patrons so enamored of motion as cyclists? Diggins had a hunch they might. He took space in The Evening News to advertise it:

"Big engagement of the EIDOLOSCOPE! Producing living pictures — sight of a lifetime!"

Diggins was not so indelicate as to mention beer directly in his ad. There was, however, a reassuring line at the bottom: "Gentlemen waiters in attendance."

Business did pick up in a manner highly gratifying to Diggins. No one seems to have suspected, though, that movies would be big long after minstrels, whistling prima donnas and even Paine's fireworks spectacles were only memories.

Wonderland, which developed from a curio and variety show into the Temple Theater, Detroit's premier palace of vaudeville, pioneered the eidoloscope on a commercial basis downtown. Soon Wonderland was showing Biograph newsreels as a regular attraction.

It was a long time, however, before the little flickering pictures would become more important to America than cycling. In the first springtime days of 1897, enthusiasts gathered on Belle Isle in greater numbers than ever. Each Sunday morning singles and tandems streamed across the bridge in an exuberant cavalcade.

The riders found the island at its best. Huge beds of scarlet geraniums set off the green loveliness of the freshly-clipped stretches of greensward. Inviting pathways led many cycling parties into the woods to enjoy the wildflowers.

But most of the younger wheelmen continued on to the head of the island. It had become their favorite picnicking preserve, and that spring they had a new cycling heroine to boast about.

Their choice as the toast of the town was young Mrs. J.F. Priehs. Her husband sold bicycles. As the first Detroit woman to appear in public wearing bloomers, she raised critical eyebrows, but soon her sensible corduroy riding outfit was widely copied. A skirt hid the bloomers from view when she was off the wheel.

Criticism of the costume was largely silenced when Mrs. Priehs became the city's first woman to qualify for the century bar award of the League of American Wheelmen. Ladies of the Unique Cycle Club wangled permission to take part in an official century run, but heavy rains left the country roads in poor condition on the day set for the test.

Mrs. Priehs was the only woman entrant who didn't back out. Courageously, she started out with 15 well-muscled men on a 106-mile course out of Windsor.

"They kept saying, 'She'll turn back,'" Mrs. Priehs told a reporter afterward. "They just dared me to make the run. We were out 11 hours and made stops of two hours, so we covered the course in nine hours.

"There were few hills but we struck 12 miles of bad going. The rains left the stretch soft and muddy. It was terribly cut up. The experience was one of the hardest of my life, but I made up my mind to live through it."

Mrs. Priehs was no Amazon. She was 4 feet 8 inches tall and weighed only 90 pounds. But she completed the prescribed 100 miles under the rigid supervision of league officials who seemed determined not to show her any favoritism.

The reporter wrote of her: "Mrs. Priehs is one of those delicate, diminutive women who look as if they were made to be admired, some dainty piece of bric-a-brac, some pretty Swiss shepherdess."

After the pioneer of bloomers achieved rank as a lady centurion, the critical chorus shifted to a more vulnerable phase of the cycling boom, a craze for "coming out" parties for new bicycles. Engraved invitations were sent out, and when the guests arrived the wheel stood on a pedestal, decorated with flowers.

A master of ceremonies, usually a centurion, conducted a ritual in which the vehicle was abjured to go over bumps without creaking, to climb hills without balking, and to go down them without running away. This was followed by a cyclists' repast, with ices sculptured in the shapes of saddles, handlebars and pedals.

Such frivolities were forgotten, and the cycling boom itself appeared to be running downhill, by the time Detroit achieved a theater devoted exclusively to motion pictures, nearly a decade later.

This was the Casino, at 28 Monroe, across the street from the Temple. It opened March 3, 1906. The impresarios John H. Kunsky, who later changed his name to King, and George W. Trendle, may have had some presentiment that their small nickelodeon would pave the way to greater things. They celebrated with a banquet in the lobby the night before the opening.

Guests included politicians, policemen and newspapermen. The toastmaster was Judge James Phelan, one of the most articulate and convivial Detroiters of the day.

On the evening of March 3 lively three-sheets out front proclaimed the opening attraction, "The Train Wreckers." The manager, Michael W. Schoenherr, resplendent in a brilliant red uniform piped with blue, found a sizable crowd waiting outside at the opening hour. So many were in line, in fact, that all 260 seats were filled for the first performance.

A piano player pounded out the "William Tell Overture." Then the feature picture, replete with bandits and pistols, took over the screen. The pianist made up for the silence of the film with music to fit every turn of the plot. With cheers, jeers, handclaps and whistles, the audience left no doubt that the nickelodeon was a success.

98   The movie was followed on the stage by a bari-

tone, Chuck Reynolds, who sang "In the Baggage Coach Ahead" as appropriate stereopticon slides in color were flashed on the screen. After this, Manager Schoenherr decided the patrons had received their nickels' worth. Besides, more customers were waiting outside.

A slide reading "The Management Appreciates Your Patronage — Please Come Again!" appeared on the screen. The house lights went up. The pianist gave forth a lively exit march, and the box office was ready for another shower of nickels.

15. 'So Fleet the Works of Man'

A new stage hit and a new producer-star were born together at the Detroit Opera House that night. The play was "A Lady of Quality," a dramatization of a novel by Mrs. Frances Hodgson Burnett which was tops on the 1897 best-seller lists. Its producer and star was Julia Arthur.

Miss Arthur needed no introduction to Detroiters. She made her theatrical debut at the age of 13, at the same Opera House. Detroit took her to its heart and gave her acclaim that launched a brilliant career. It was no accident that years later she decided to open "A Lady of Quality," the play she secured for the first presentation of her own company, in the city which had been so generous to her. And on the opening night, Oct. 4, no one was disappointed.

"Purely from the standpoint of history it was a notable performance and Julia Arthur, in the part of Clorinda Wildair, was something to be remembered," said the next day's review in The Evening News.

All week the comedy played to full houses. On Thursday night, the evening most favored by Detroit ladies of quality and their husbands for showgoing, the audience was particularly responsive. After the final curtain call, many lingered under the marquee to talk enthusiastically about "our Julia" while waiting for their carriages.

The Campus Martius in front of the theater was deserted when at 12:50 a.m., two members of Detroit's police force, Patrolman William P. Rutledge and Roundsman John Springer, stopped to pass the time of night at Woodward and Gratiot.

Their words were interrupted by a huge explosion in the Opera House. Rutledge pulled a nearby alarm box, and the two officers ran up the alley in back of the theater.

They saw the janitor, William Moore, and his wife, who occupied living quarters in the building, climbing down the fire escape in their nightclothes.

It was none too soon. Hardly had they reached the ground when there was a series of five more explosions. The back wall of the playhouse collapsed, exposing the interior which was a mass of flames.

Two additional explosions followed. Later, it was theorized that a cigaret dropped by a careless person in the theater started a fire which reached eight chemical tanks used in lighting the stage. Each explosion hurled burning debris further into the recesses of the auditorium and sent showers of sparks into the air.

When the fire trucks arrived moments later, the structure was past saving. The elaborate scenery in which Julia Arthur had invested much of her savings became fuel for the flames.

The firemen turned their efforts to the Leonard Furniture Co., facing Gratiot across the alley from the Opera House. It was supposed to be fireproof, but the fierce heat twisted its steel girders so violently that the walls were thrown in heaps upon the five-story Foster Building next door. Only the misshapen frame was left standing.

Burning missiles went through the roof of the Foster Building, and it too became a mass of flames. On three upper floors, occupied by the Central Storage Co., household effects burned quickly. Down through the block roared the blaze, reaching a grand piano in the display windows of Vaughan and Tanner on the street floor just before the upper walls of the Foster Building slithered down on the adjoining Parisian Laundry.

The game of fiery dominoes continued until most of the buildings in the block east of the Opera House were charred ruins. The damage would be assessed at $680,000.

Photo of the theater, taken before the fire, has Miss Arthur's name on the marquee.

A general alarm brought Detroit's entire fire department into the fight — 22 engines, nine hook-and-ladder wagons, a chemical engine, a water tower and supply wagons. Of the 328 men who battled the fire, four were injured falling from ladders and two were cut by flying glass.

Stephen Townsend, the playwright of "A Lady of Quality," had stayed up late in his room at the Russell House, writing to Mrs. Burnett about the drama's initial success and predicting a splendid future for it.

At the sound of the first explosion, Townsend carried the still unsealed letter with him when he hurriedly left his room. Before he mailed it he added a dismal postscript: "Opera house burned to the ground tonight. Scenery and costumes totally destroyed. Nothing saved."

Flames race through the Detroit Opera House in the sketch on
page one of The Evening News, Oct. 7, 1897. The fire destroyed
the theater on Campus Martius and scenery in the play "A Lady
of Quality," produced by its star, Julia Arthur.

Edwin Arden, Julia Arthur's leading man, was
among those who rushed to the Opera House after
the first explosions. Running into the foyer, he was
blinded and gagged by the thick smoke.

Arden groped his way out again on hands and
knees, suffering an injured hand when a final blast
banged shut a door upon it.

The one death came after the flames were out.
Among the many sightseers who came to view the   *103*

ruins in the morning was 16-year-old Robert Pennington. He was crushed when a wall collapsed.

Miss Arthur slept through the fire in her room at the Cadillac Hotel. Only when she came down to breakfast did she learn what had happened from her manager, Arthur Lewis.

She took it like a lady of quality. "Have you telegraphed for new costumes?" she asked. "The show must go on."

The show did go on, and "A Lady of Quality" became a memorable hit.

Plans were immediately begun for a new opera House on the site of the old, but meanwhile it was necessary to find a temporary replacement. The only auditorium available was the Empire Theater, several blocks down Woodward.

The Empire had certain drawbacks. For one, it was a burlesque house. And it was located in the middle of what was known as "Whisky Row," a block on which 13 saloons kept things humming nightly.

Nevertheless, the aristocratic bookings of the Opera House were moved into the Empire for the remainder of the season. Every night the denizens of "Whisky Row" ogled the splendid show of silks and satins under the marquee of the former shake-and-shimmy emporium as the coachmen-driven carriages of the elite deposited their occupants.

Detroit wanted no tinkering with the classic lines of its beloved Opera House, and a new structure arose with the same trappings of the Second Empire which embellished the city's Temple of Thespis in the gaslight era.

Over the proscenium appeared once more the quotation from a poem by Charles Kingsley that beguiled playgoers in the earlier theater. It seemed more appropriate than ever:

"So fleet the works of man, back to their earth again;

Ancient and holy things fade like a dream."

16. Forward,
the Light Guard

Perhaps no building anywhere ever boasted a better-timed dedication than the Light Guard Armory. On April 25, 1898, in the wake of the mysterious sinking of the battleship Maine in Havana harbor, President William McKinley asked Congress to declare war against Spain. And at 1:10 p.m. the next day, with their band playing "Yankee Doodle," the men of the Detroit Light Guard marched for the first time into their newly completed armory at Larned and Brush.

It was more than a ceremonial occasion. The men wore field uniforms, and they were prepared to proceed to a training camp when the dedication was over.

Flags waved and the gallery was filled with spectators as the troops took their places on the main floor. Gov. Hazen S. Pingree, standing at the lectern, rapped for order to cheers from soldiers and civilian guests before he could make himself heard. A few hours earlier it had been announced that Pingree would take charge in person, as commander-in-chief of Michigan troops, at the Island Lake encampment, near Brighton, where detachments from all over the state were heading.

Emotional oratory was the order of the day, and the event was one which might well have justified it. But Pingree seldom did anything in the way lesser men might do it. As a hush settled over the auditorium, his words were coolly realistic.

"The demand is not so great that you ought to go if you have to leave a mother depending upon you

Leaving For Camp: This photograph taken at Fort and Griswold streets in 1898 shows Michigan National Guardsmen on their way to the Fort Street Union Depot to entrain for Camp Eaton, at Island Lake.

for support," he advised. "Do not think you will be called cowards if you do not go. It isn't fun and you will be subjected to hardships."

The true dedication of the armory and the men of the Light Guard, Pingree continued quietly, would be far from Detroit, in weathered tents on distant fields.

"War means wounds, fever, lost limbs and sudden death," was the blunt warning of the old Civil War soldier who had survived long months at Andersonville, the most wretched of Confederate prison camps.

The sober mien of the listeners disappeared and the stenographer on the platform recorded "great applause and cheers" when Pingree ended on a brisk note:

"We are in communication with Assistant Secretary of the Navy Theodore Roosevelt, and the Naval Reserves will go at six o'clock tomorrow morning."

Another Civil War veteran, white-haired Col. C. M. Lum, presented the regimental colors and reviewed some history. In 1836, the young men of the city organized the Brady Guard, named in honor of Gen. Hugh Brady. In 1850, it became the Grayson Guard, and in 1855 it was transformed into the Detroit Light Guard, with Lum as its captain.

Now, for the young men of 1898, Lum pictured another springtime with war breaking upon the land. That was in 1861, when after congenial years with plenty of time for cotillions as well as for drills, the Light Guard was faced with a moment of truth.

Unlike at least one kid-glove outfit elsewhere which in this exigency voted to disband — thereby giving rise to the jest, "Invincible in peace, invisible in war" — the Light Guard volunteered to a man and was mustered in as Company A of the First Michigan Infantry, Lum recalled.

When he finished, the guardsmen of 1898 marched out. They paraded along streets lined by 100,000 people to the Union Station and their train for Island Lake.

The first musical function in the armory came just four days later. A capacity crowd heard John Philip Sousa and his band present a patriotic spectacle, "Trooping the Colors." The high point came when a dark-haired young woman appeared on the stage wrapped in the flag of Cuba, and the band played Sousa's stirring new march, "The Stars and Stripes Forever."

During the weekend which followed, Detroit could fully sustain Sousa's high pitch of fervor. Word came of Adm. George Dewey's daring invasion of Manila Bay in the Philippine Islands, the stronghold of the Spanish Asiatic fleet, and the annihilation of all 11 Spanish warships without the loss of an American sailor.

For nearly half a century after that April, the Light Guard Armory was the center for all the functions that in a later era would be divided among Convention Hall, the Masonic Temple auditorium, Olympia and Orchestra Hall.

Its rafters were set vibrating by the oratory of presidential candidates, fashionable balls brought the world of society to its floor, and here Detroiters first heard the voices of John McCormack, Alma Gluck and Enrico Caruso.

Tchaikovsky introduced Russian music to Detroit there, Ignace Jan Paderewski played, and Isadora Duncan shocked the straitlaced by dancing on the creaking boards with bare feet.

A young orchestra conductor, Leopold Stokowski, caused something of a furor when he brought the Cincinnati Symphony to the armory. A latecomer slammed an entrance door after the first number began. Stokowski rapped his baton, stopped his players, and started over. Another late arrival stumbled over a wooden chair in a box, and again Stokowski started over. On his last try he waited until the clock in the City Hall tower boomed nine strokes.

Violinist Mischa Elman always remembered his first recital in the Light Guard Armory, too. Someone forgot to notify the bowling league that a concert was scheduled. In the middle of Elman's first number, strikes and spares punctuated his loftiest cadenzas until he raised his fiddle in a despairing gesture and strode off the stage.

Walter Damrosch also made his Detroit debut at the armory, and returned many times. When plans were announced for a new hall of music to house a symphony orchestra of its own for Detroit, Damrosch commented with a smile that no auditorium would ever be built with finer — or more varied — acoustics than the old armory.

Through all its years, however, the baton most attuned to the home of the Light Guard was that of the conductor who presided at the armory's musical beginnings — John Philip Sousa.

Sousa had as warm a spot in his heart for Detroit as the city had for him, and he always brought his magnificent 100-man band back for one or two concert appearances on each of his annual national tours.

The long love affair between the city and the bandmaster reached its culmination in April, 1927. The March King was 72, and Detroit proclaimed "Sousa Week" a gala which turned out to be as sentimental as the maestro's music.

The weeklong celebration came into being after
Sousa dedicated one of his last compositions,

"Pride of the Wolverines," to the city. It was adopted as Detroit's official march.

During "Sousa Week," there was ample opportunity for everyone to hear the band. Sousa directed four recitals daily, and five on Saturday. In between, serenades in his honor were a daily feature for downtown crowds at Grand Circus Park. The Cass Technical High School Band and the All-City Grade School Band took turns demonstrating how well they knew Sousa marches.

But what delighted the bandmaster most during the week was a stint as a journalist. The Detroit News invited Sousa to double as the newspaper's music critic, and he did an outstanding job.

Some days before his arrival, he asked Detroiters to submit their musical questions. A stack of mail greeted him when he sat down at The News music desk.

Sousa tackled the task with enthusiasm. Writing was familiar to him. He was the author of 10 books, including three novels and his autobiography. During the week he wrote a daily column for The News.

One column about the jazz craze, then at its height, occasioned wide repercussions. Sousa gave jazz his approval — but only for dancing.

Naturally the composer of "The Stars and Stripes Forever" placed the standard high for anything in four-four time. He wrote: "A march that is to live must be able to make a man with a wooden leg keep time." He proved his point in Detroit, many times over.

The prime function of the Light Guard Armory remained military. In 1911, the guard and the Detroit Light Infantry were merged in the First Regiment of the Michigan National Guard.

Battle honors of the Light Guard were carried into World War I and World War II by units of the Red Arrow Division, the 32nd. Men of these units often were regaled with the story of how the Light Guard won the nickname "Tigers" in the Civil War fighting. A tiger emblem carved in stone adorned the old armory, and Detroit's big baseball team naturally became the Tigers and wore orange-and-black-striped stockings.

The armory itself was a lusty citadel of sport throughout the years. A few days before Christmas in 1933 some 400 fans were inside awaiting three games of basketball when smoke began to seep through the floor.

The fans didn't take this distraction too seriously, and many grumbled when firemen insisted that they leave. Later they learned the reason; flames in a basement fire were raging perilously close to stores of cartridges and machine gun ammunition.

The armory was saved that time, but it was fated to end in fire. Another blaze broke out in the basement on April 17, 1945. Flames gutted the building, sweeping through to the roof in less than half an hour.

An editorial in The News the next day spoke the building's requiem:

"For old Detroiters the structure was a landmark around which clustered many memories . . . It was the largest and most central of our public meeting places.

"Looking at its shell now, even the latecomer to Detroit may reconstruct in fancy the older, smaller, cozier town which it accommodated and with which it was in harmony."

17. A Miracle for Juliet

She was called Maggie. Her childhood was spent in a rundown cottage near the Detroit River wharves, described as "an old wooden hospice for the river rats."

Here her father, John Finlayson, kept a boarding-house for sailors. Maggie did the chores of a maid in an atmosphere of oaths and rough humor.

For school her mother put her jet black curls into pigtails, but she lacked suitable clothing. The unfeeling youngsters in the schoolyard above Jefferson Avenue snubbed Maggie and the other girls from the waterfront district as the "dirty dozen."

At 10 she was considered old enough to sell newspapers downtown. She developed her lungs crying headlines, and her strength of will defending a choice pitch in front of the post office, on Griswold Street. Her large, lustrous eyes gave her a gamin wistfulness, and customers remembered her.

Maggie was 16 in 1876, and she obtained employment as a maid in one of the Jefferson Avenue homes. One evening she watched a daughter of the family, no older than herself, depart in party finery for a dance, escorted by a beau from the fashionable Piety Hill development above Grand Circus Park.

All the discontent of 16 years welled up in Maggie. Late that night she hurried toward the river, along an almost deserted street. Under the light of a lamppost she passed a youth about her own age, and the expression of despair he saw on her face gave him a shiver.

Margaret Mather Finlayson

Minutes later she stood at the edge of the dock, gathering her courage for the plunge into the river. Just as she was about to leap a strong hand seized her arm and held her back.

It was the young man who had glimpsed her face by lamplight. Something he had seen there impelled him to follow her. Maggie allowed him to take her to her home.

So the story of this city waif did not end that night. Had it done so, Maggie's brief tale would have gone unremembered. As it was . . .

Years afterward the beautiful Margaret Mather, foremost Juliet of her generation on the American stage, recalled her youthful rescuer as "a nice German boy." She was certain she would have drowned herself had he not intervened.

She was certain, too, that only providence could have given him the impulse to hurry after her. "It was a miracle," she said.

112 Miracle or not, it is true that a marked change

Miss Mather in Shakespearean costume

came about in her fortunes almost immediately afterward. A sister who had married well in New York sent for her.

In the metropolis, she was drawn at once to the theatrical district. Her good looks got her bit parts. She adopted her mother's maiden name, Mather, for the stage.

As Margaret Mather she became the ingenue of a small troupe barnstorming through New York State. J. M. Hill, a prominent theatrical manager, caught the performance in Albany, and the ingenue's talents excited his interest. Predicting a splendid career for Miss Mather, he signed her to a five-year contract.

Hill was so certain of his investment that for two years he kept her secluded from the public, on a rigorous schedule of study and training.

"Romeo and Juliet" was chosen for her debut at McVickers' Theater in Chicago on Aug. 1, 1882. The audience found her a Juliet of striking beauty. From her first words, Hill felt rewarded for the long period of tutelage. Her diction was flawless.

The atmosphere in the theater was electric by the time Juliet reached her familiar exit lines at the end of the first act:

"My only love sprung from my only hate!
Too early seen unknown, and known too late!
Prodigious birth of love it is to me,
That I must love a loathed enemy."

Thundering applause swelled into a standing ovation. Margaret Mather was hailed as a new queen of the American stage.

Hill protected her with safeguards suitable to royalty. He kept her early history shrouded in mystery. Miss Mather never was allowed to give interviews.

During her first engagement in Detroit, she occupied the royal suite at the Russell House. It was the suite used by Queen Victoria's oldest son, Edward Albert, Prince of Wales, at the time when Maggie was an infant.

Hill held back her appearance in New York until acclaim elsewhere sufficiently whetted the interest of the metropolis. When she finally graced the boards of the Union Square Theater the critics came prepared to put down this prodigy from the provinces — and remained to toss restraint to the winds in her praise.

It now was official. A new star of first magnitude blazed in the theatrical sky.

While still under Hill's management, she was married to Emil Havekorn, leader of the Union Square Theater orchestra. The affair was a misalliance from the start and soon was terminated by mutual consent. A second marriage to Gustave G. Pabst, scion of the Milwaukee brewery family, also proved unhappy.

Once she gave Pabst a public horsewhipping. He was glad to settle $100,000 on her in return for a divorce.

During an 1886 engagement at the Detroit Opera House, a reporter pierced the cloak of mystery drawn by Hill around her early years. The true identity of Margaret Mather as Maggie Finlayson, the onetime hoyden newsgirl of Griswold Street, was revealed.

This sensation resulted in sellout performances all week, and in greater adulation than ever. From then on, Detroit proudly claimed her as its own.

B.C. Whitney, the city's leading theatrical impresario, took over her management. He soon was even more devoted to her than Hill, and arranged more sumptuous Shakespearean productions. In 1897, an appearance as Imogen in "Cymbeline" in Detroit was chosen as the occasion to announce a contract for her to continue an additional five years under the Whitney banner.

In the spring of 1898, she was on tour in Charleston, W. Va., when the company manager sent word to Whitney that Miss Mather was insisting on continuing her performances in spite of growing illness. Whitney dispatched his chief aide, W.B. Lawrence, with orders to disband the company if necessary to insure a rest for her.

On Thursday, April 7, before Lawrence reached Charleston, the matinee audience saw a somewhat slow-paced performance. The fourth act did not begin until after 5 p.m.

In the somber setting traditionally given to the scene before the cave of Belarius, with Imogen masquerading in male garb, she was alone in the spotlight on an otherwise darkened stage. Well along in one of the longest monologs in her repertoire, Miss Mather reached these lines:

". . . Good faith,
I tremble still with fear: but if there be
Yet left in heaven as small a drop of pity
As a wren's eye, fear'd gods, a part of it!"

The trembling was real, and so was the supplication. She fell unconscious to the stage.

Many in the audience thought it was the powerful end of a powerful scene, and broke into applause. But the curtain, hastily rung down, marked the end of a cometlike career. Margaret Mather died without regaining consciousness.

The theatrical profession took it for granted that the funeral would be in New York, and Whitney authorized Lawrence to initiate arrangements. But in Detroit, John Finlayson, now 75 years old and a widower for three years, spoke against it from his quarters in a Randolph Street roominghouse.

"They can't take her body from me, can they?" he demanded. "I'm her father. I want her buried beside her mother in Elmwood Cemetery." Whitney's comment was: "Miss Mather has been most generous in support of her relatives, who have been the millstone around her neck."

Nevertheless, he bowed to the old man's wishes. The casket arrived at the house on Randolph on April 9.

Next day was Easter Sunday. Long before the hour announced for the service, the chapel at Elmwood was surrounded by a crowd described as "a curious, jostling sea of humanity."

Policemen forced a passage through the throng for the flower-laden casket. Invited guests were pushed into the small chapel through a side door.

In the little group admitted there were only two relatives, the father and a brother. The rest were of the theater.

Outside rose a babble of many voices. Inside a male quartet from "The Geisha," the musical hit

116

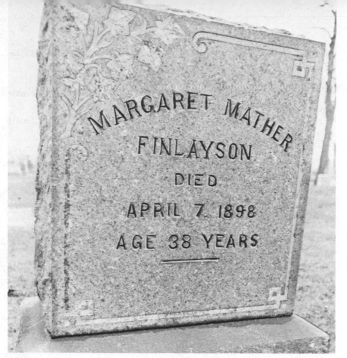

Simple stone marks her grave in Elmwood Cemetery

playing at the Empire Theater, sang "Nearer, My God, to Thee" and "Abide With Me." After his scripture reading, the Rev. C.A. Fulton spoke briefly about Miss Mather.

"I cannot fail to admire the successful struggle through which this life rose to eminence, and I cannot fail to admire her kindliness, generosity and thoughtfulness for others by which it was marked," he said.

Tumult was so great when the chapel doors were opened that a plan to permit the public to pass through the chapel had to be abandoned. With much effort, the officers made a passageway through the throngs for the mourners to pass.

Spectators rushed ahead, and thousands packed the hill slopes until the brief commitment service was ended. Then they stampeded over the grave, clutching at bits of evergreen or rose petals that might be carried away as souvenirs.

Otis Skinner, dean of the actors who served as pallbearers, surveyed the scramble without disap-

117

proval. The turbulent scene was somehow in keeping with Margaret Mather's life, he pointed out.

"She was a chaos of beauty, fancy, ambition, sympathy, generosity, all ill-timed and treading upon the other's heels," he said.

Next day, The Evening News began its account with these words:

"Margaret Mather made her last appearance as Juliet in the death scene of the famous love tragedy yesterday afternoon. Robed in the jeweled gown that she wore so many times in her notable impersonation of Shakespeare's sweet heroine, her body was lowered in Elmwood Cemetery before the eyes of a larger audience than ever greeted her in life."

18. Maude and the Empress Dowager

What girl did not envy Maude Ledyard on her wedding day? She seemed to have everything — wealth, breeding, good looks and charm; the man she was marrying was a diplomat, dashing, handsome and a baron.

No one could foresee that, in only three years, the bridegroom's brutal assassination would hasten the end of the oldest empire on earth, or that Maude would spend the first weeks of her widowhood in terror for her life, sewing the last remnants of velvet and satin from her trousseau into sandbags, besieged by a horde of Chinese fanatics shouting incessantly the one English word they knew—"kill! kill! kill!"

In an era when people talked a great deal about bluebloods, Maude, as she was always called — her real name was Matilda Cass Ledyard — easily qualified. She was the great-granddaughter of Lewis Cass, the first Michigan man to be nominated for the presidency. Perhaps more importantly, in America's Gilded Age when railroad presidents rated at the top of the tree, her father was Henry B. Ledyard of the important Michigan Central.

Finishing at Miss Farnsworth School and later Miss Peebles' School in New York, Maude was noted for her daring horsemanship during summers at home and for her high fashion during winter visits to her grandmother in Paris.

The unexpected death of Maude's mother in 1895

brought her home from France in mourning. After a quiet year at home she was persuaded by her friend Amy McMillan, the daughter of Senator James McMillan, to come to Washington as a house guest. Amy was confident the gay social season in the capital would cheer Maude — and she was right. Excellent help in the process was provided by a highly eligible bachelor, Baron Clemens von Ketteler.

The baron had been in the German diplomatic corps for 16 years, and had come to Washington as first assistant for the consular service after a decade in China. Noted as a good swordsman and a crack pistol shot, he spoke Chinese fluently and was fond of sports, music and opera.

Soon it was apparent that Von Ketteler also was becoming extremely fond of the tall, willowy girl from Detroit, with her light blond hair and her large blue eyes.

The courtship threatened to be longer than either really wanted — Kaiser Wilhelm II did not approve, ordinarily, of foreign matches for his diplomats. But he could be generous at times to bold fellows like Von Ketteler. The permission came through— and a promotion to be minister to Mexico, to boot.

The wedding was set for Feb. 24, 1897. Maude assembled her trousseau from Redfern in New York and Worth in Paris. Von Ketteler arrived in Detroit Feb. 12, with enough baggage to draw stares from the porters at the Hotel Cadillac, where the best suite was reserved. In a round of parties he impressed Detroiters as a man of the world, a sensible fellow, and a man who patiently was much in love with his bride-to-be.

It appeared to be an excellent match. Like Maude, the baron was a blue-eyed blond. He also owned extensive estates in Germany, and there could be no hint of the criticism that was beginning to be prevalent in connection with the marriage of American heiresses to titled foreigners with impaired fortunes.

The wedding was a grand affair. The bride wore white satin, as did her maid-of-honor, Miss McMillan. Von Ketteler was resplendent in a diplomatic blue coat with gilt edging. The 500 guests

Baroness Von Ketteler

found SS. Peter and Paul Catholic Church brightly
decorated for the occasion, too, in green and white,
Mexico's official colors. A reception followed in the
Ledyard mansion, and the nuptials were described
in the press as "the crowning triumph of a brilliant
social season."

Life in Mexico City was exciting enough for the
young baroness, but events on the other side of the
world brought their days there to an end. In totter-
ing China, the old empress dowager, Ts'u-hsi, who
had been regent during the minority of the incom-
petent young emperor, seized back the reins of
power and made him a virtual prisoner. She
seemed determined to turn back the clock against
foreign concessions, and the kaiser felt it was a
good time to return Von Ketteler to Peking as head
of the mission.

121

Off Tientsin there was a reception by the German Asiatic fleet, in battle strength designed to impress the Chinese, with a welcome by the emperor's brother, and much firing of imperial and ambassadorial salutes. It marked entry into a kaleidoscopic world different from anything Maude knew, a world ruled in medieval fashion by the autocratic empress dowager.

Soon she was absorbed by the glitter of the legation quarter, with its array of aristocrats from all over Europe. Maude possessed considerable literary flair, and her friends in Detroit began to receive chatty letters describing the strange Imperial City walled off from old Peking, the ancient craft on the Chinese rivers, the ubiquitous kite flying, the jugglers in the market place, the little black pigs running through the narrow, crooked lanes of the old town.

Then came an invitation to spend an evening with the empress dowager. Accompanied by the ladies of the legation, the baroness was taken into the guarded enclave-within-an-enclave, the Forbidden City inside the Imperial City. The journey was made in the strict fashion prescribed by elaborate court etiquette, in royal chairs carried by court attendants. Maude found the incredible ancient palace gaily illuminated for the occasion.

A priceless touch, she wrote, was the childish curiosity of the rouge-bedizened old empress. Ts'u-hsi walked about on tiptoe, ogling her lady guests, running long bony fingers over their dresses and examining their ornaments with glee. But something in her eyes made Maude shiver.

The cables soon brought grim news from China. They told of the rise of a fanatic native organization opposed to all "foreign devils," whose name translated as the Society of Harmonious Fists. Naturally enough, the West soon nicknamed the sect the Boxers.

By the end of May, 1900, tragedy was in the air. Many missionaries came as refugees to the capital, telling of friends who were murdered in outlying provinces. On their heels came the Boxers themselves, in a regalia of white tunics and red sashes, and it was no longer safe to leave the legation district.

Diplomatic protests to the empress dowager's foreign office were met with polite evasions, but nothing seemed to be done to stem the Boxer influx. The foreign colony felt better when nearly 400 marines, including detachments from eight nations, were hurried in from Tientsin to bolster the legation guards.

In the light of what happened later, it was strange that on June 6, among the many rumors reaching the West about the turbulent situation in Peking, was a report that Baron von Ketteler had been killed. It caused much concern in Detroit, although a four-word cable had just come through to the Ledyards: "All is well. Maude." In Washington, Secretary of State John Hay, a friend of Henry Ledyard, found the report was not believed at the German embassy. But for many long weeks thereafter there would be no direct word from Maude.

In point of fact, Von Ketteler was alive. On June 13, he came upon a yelling Boxer riding in a pony cart and brandishing a sword on Legation Street, the main thoroughfare of the quarter. It was too much for the baron. He seized the Boxer by the collar, pulled him from the cart and pummeled him with his cane.

Later Von Ketteler regretted this lapse from diplomatic niceties. Within a matter of hours enraged bands of Boxers burned the Christian churches in the outer city. On succeeding days fires were set all over the trading quarter. Everything owned by foreigners, or patronized by them, went up in flames. And worse was to come.

Maude wrote in her diary: "On the night of the 16th I was startled by a faint red glow that gradually draped the sky in crimson. The Boxers were burning the north gate, used only by the emperor as his entrance to the Temple of Heaven.

"June 19 is the black-bordered day in my diary. A night of torture. Bloodcurdling yells rising higher and more demoniacal. At dawn we received a message — the Boxers have sworn to kill all foreigners."

On the afternoon of the 19th, each of the 11 legations received an identical message from the Chinese foreign office. China broke relations with them all — and the diplomats were given only until

4 p.m. the next day to get themselves and their staffs out of Peking.

The ambassadors joined in an urgent request for an audience to ask for more time. When there was no reply on the morning of the 20th, Von Ketteler would not give up. Ignoring attempts by his colleagues to dissuade him, he set out for the Forbidden City in a palanquin carried by eight coolies, accompanied by his secretary, Heinrich Cordes.

A hush fell upon the thronged Hata Men Street beyond the legation quarter as the palanquin trundled slowly past the street's great Arch of Honor. A Chinese soldier with a rifle stepped up, and Cordes hoped he would be helpful in getting them through. The secretary had time to note an odd detail, peacock feathers hanging from the fellow's hat. Then the soldier poked the rifle through the palanquin's drapes and shot Von Ketteler through the heart.

Another bullet wounded Cordes as he took flight, but before he collapsed he reached a nearby Methodist compound where an American missionary, the Rev. Frank Gamewell, was rounding up bewildered Chinese orphans for a march to seek safety in the legation quarter. When the diplomats got the news, it was all too clear that the empress dowager had cast her lot with the Boxers.

There was little time for amenities. The stunned baroness was confined with the rest in an area centering on the British compound. It included most of the legations, with a defensible perimeter — of sorts — of about 1½ miles. At 4 p.m. a storm of gunfire came from all sides. The Boxers were joined by more than 20,000 Chinese army regulars, including artillerymen, deployed for a full-scale siege. The defenders could count only 450 men able to handle a gun.

With the other women, Maude worked on the sandbags that were needed everywhere until her fingers were raw, but when every scrap of available material was gone, the full force of the tragedy struck her. The worst terror came at night. The Boxers kept up a calculated bedlam of shots, yells, flaming arrows and blaring trumpets. At the end of the sleepless hours of darkness, in a leaden dawn, Mrs. Gamewell, wife of the missionary, felt an appealing touch on her arm as she stepped near the baroness' window. "I am so alone," Maude told her.

Mrs. Edwin H. Conger, whose husband headed the U.S. legation, tried to rally the young widow from Detroit. Maude pondered in her hearing: "No title, no position, no money can help us here. These things mock us."

An American girl who was visiting with a legation family, Mary Condit Smith — she was called Polly — also tried to be helpful. During a lull she took Maude for a breath of air on the tennis court of Queen Victoria's envoy, Sir Claude MacDonald. A sniper's bullet whizzed past, and Polly hit the turf. Maude remained upright, stony-faced, as more bullets struck trees around her, until a customs volunteer carried her out of range.

But as the casualties mounted and an improvised hospital in the British chancellery filled to overflowing, Maude found work to do that made her forget her own plight. She proved a tower of strength as a nurse and comforter of the wounded.

The story of her efforts became such a legend that more than half a century later, when Hollywood made a film about the affair, the role of a fictional widowed baroness who became the Florence Nightingale of the siege was written into the script.

The siege was relieved by an international column which battled through from Tientsin on Aug. 13. Another old friend of Maude's father, Gen. Adna R. Chaffee, headed the American contingent — the tough 14th Infantry — and Ledyard soon received word that his daughter was safe.

The message reached Detroit in the midst of preparations for another wedding; her brother, Henry, was marrying another Maude — though this one spelled it without the "e" — Maud Hendrie of Hamilton, Ontario. After the ceremony the elder Ledyard arranged a special train to take the couple to Vancouver, where they sailed to meet the baroness in Yokohama and bring her home.

As for the empress dowager, she fled Peking when the international brigade approached. She was forced to pay such heavy indemnities to the Western powers that the dynasty never recovered. *125*

On Dec. 31, in the closing hours of the old century, Su-Hai, the soldier who murdered Von Ketteler, was ceremoniously beheaded in Peking.

One of the penalties imposed by Germany was that China had to erect a three-arched memorial gateway in the principal street of Peking to honor Von Ketteler's memory. It was destroyed by French and Italian soldiers in World War I.

Maude visited Germany in June, 1901. In the company of Baron von Ketteler's mother she dined with Kaiser Wilhelm and the kaiserin. Wilhelm praised her courage and her care of the wounded during the siege, and the kaiserin presented her with the insignia of the Order of Louise. She also toured the Von Ketteler estates near Munster, Westphalia.

Although she outlived her husband by more than 60 years, the baroness never remarried. She had a villa in Italy, near Florence, until World War II brought her back to America. She lived quietly in Bloomfield Hills with her memories, and was devoted to charity. She spent her last years in Falls Village, Conn., where she died Nov. 30, 1960, at 89.

In the Detroit Institute of Arts there hangs a rustic landscape by George Inness, "Apple Orchard," presented in 1923 by the baroness and her brothers in memory of their father. Ledyard built a summer home in Grosse Pointe in Swiss chalet style, and for the baroness the Inness canvas must have evoked memories of happy vacation days there when she was a schoolgirl.

19. Admiral Dewey's Battle Flag

An admiral cruising on the Detroit River! The entire city was excited about the prospect. It wasn't just any old admiral. The city's honored guest in the bracing June days of 1900 was the most celebrated seadog in the world — Adm. George Dewey.

His great victory at Manila Bay gave America its first real naval hero since Farragut uttered his classic remark in the Civil War, "Damn the torpedoes!" Dewey provided an equally trenchant phrase for history: "You may fire when ready, Gridley." The people bought him a fine house in Washington to show their appreciation, and he was being talked about for a presidential nomination.

Then, less than two months after his return from the Philippines, Dewey surprised the whole country. Sixty-two years old and a widower for 26 years, he took a bride. The lady was Mrs. Mildred Hazen, widow of an army general. While cities all over the land were clamoring for an opportunity to lionize the admiral, Detroit was doubly pleased when he accepted an invitation from the City of the Straits and promised to bring the new Mrs. Dewey along.

A tremendous crush of people surrounded the Michigan Central Depot when a special train bearing the Deweys arrived at 2 p.m. on Friday, June 8. Mayor William C. Maybury and a welcoming committee of leading citizens rode in from Wyandotte on the special.

Proudly, the committee members followed the Deweys through the station between two files of soldiers at attention. Dewey was not in uniform, but

Admiral George Dewey

even in a gray cutaway his deeply bronzed face and
thick mustache were unmistakable, and there was
a burst of cheers and applause. Petite Mrs. Dewey,
at the admiral's side, appeared starched and cool
in a white duck dress. Her smiles quickly capti-
vated the crowd.

An elegant carriage drawn by four bay horses
awaited the city's honored guests, and Detroiters
waved from the sidewalks along Jefferson and
Woodward as the Deweys were taken at a brisk trot
to and best parlor suite at the Russell House. The
onlookers also showed great interest in a second
carriage carrying the admiral's Chinese manser-
vant and Mrs. Dewey's Swedish maid.

That evening the dinner for Dewey at the Fellow-
craft Club was stag, and Mrs. Dewey was enter-

tained separately by Detroit ladies at the Detroit Club. Around midnight, as the laudatory speeches droned on and on, the admiral seemed to grow restive.

"You stay up late in Detroit," he remarked to the toastmaster, William Livingstone. He politely excused himself, strolled out of the banquet hall in the middle of a speech, and went back to his hotel. No one seemed to mind. Like a performance of "Hamlet" bereft of the Prince of Denmark but still bowing to the tradition that the show must go on, the dinner and its eulogies rolled on until 2 a.m. As the yawning banqueters made their way homeward, some of them at least must have felt the admiral had shown excellent judgment, as always.

Detroit was crowded for "Dewey Day" on Saturday, with naval and land parades on the program. Railroad excursions brought in thousands of visitors from outstate points, and many spectators already had gathered outside the Russell House when Mayor Maybury arrived at 8:30 a.m. to escort the Deweys to the riverfront for the first event of what was clearly to be a busy day.

Refreshed by a good night's sleep, Dewey seemed eager to get going. He wore a black Prince Albert coat, striped trousers and a high silk hat. Mrs. Dewey was stunning in a soft gray gown with pearl buttons and a hat of white chiffon. Both waved to their well-wishers on the sidewalks on the drive to the foot of Griswold Street.

The ship's band played a medley of national tunes as the party boarded the Steamer Tashmoo promptly at 9 a.m. The Tashmoo, newly launched pride of the river, had completed trial runs only a few days before. The cream of Detroit society and officialdom was assembled on board to greet the Deweys.

After a brief stop in a parlor on the saloon deck, where Mrs. Dewey was given a bouquet of orchids, the guests ascended to the bridge. A bedlam of applause, whistles and bells sounded as the admiral's four-star battle flag was raised above the Tashmoo's pilot house.

Waiting nearby in the river were the USS Michigan, the chief warship available on the Great Lakes, and the revenue cutter Fessenden. Both had

The four-star battle flag of Adm. Dewey, naval hero of the Spanish-American War, flew on the Steamer Tashmoo when Dewey and his bride were guests of Detroit on June 9, 1900.

yards dressed and bunting flying, and the officers and men were drawn up at attention.

As the Tashmoo glided from her dock, the Michigan boomed a 17-gun salute and marines on her deck presented arms. Dewey bowed repeatedly in through their wake, some of Detroit's smartest response to these honors, and the Michigan and the Fessenden fell in behind the Tashmoo. Weaving yachts followed, the Truant in the lead, followed by the Cascade, the Sea Fox, and the Vita.

Next were the ferryboats. Chartered for the occasion by Detroit schoolmarms, the Pleasure's decks were bouquets of pink and white. The Wyandotte, almost awash with sightseers at 50 cents a head,

struggled to keep up.

Across the river, Windsor was ablaze with flags. The Tashmoo swung close to the Canadian shore and her band played "God Save the Queen." At Walkerville, guns fired another salute and a great streamer was unfolded, bearing the inscription: "Canadians' Best Wishes to America's Great Seaman."

Approaching Belle Isle, the Deweys waved to bicyclists on the shore. "It's the finest park I've seen anywhere," the admiral said. Everyone agreed nature had lent the final touches to all the planning of Dewey's hosts; the sky was bright and sunshine glinted on the water, the air was fresh and bracing. The admiral and his lady looked relaxed and happy.

Passing Windmill Pointe, the Tashmoo opened up her engines to show what she could do. All the following craft were outdistanced and gave up the chase. During the Lake St. Clair crossing, the Deweys stood in front of a floral anchor at a reception in the main saloon.

Even by the hearty standards of 1900, the buffet which followed was ample — whole red lobsters, chicken salad, lobster salad, 50-pound roasts of beef, 3,500 sandwiches, ice cream, cake and coffee.

The Deweys ate with Maybury and Livingstone at a table bedecked with flowers and flags in the center of the Tashmoo's dining room.

In a flurry of whirrings and clickings, a cinematographer from the American Mutoscope and Biograph Co. recorded the idyllic scene for the newest medium of history, the newsreel.

The men lit cigars as they lingered to watch the panorama of the St. Clair Flats roll by, with flags and handkerchiefs fluttering along the shore as spectators at cottages and summer hotels sought a glimpse of the honored guests. Livingstone remarked that the area was often called "the Venice of America," and Dewey nodded appreciatively.

"It's enchanting," he agreed. "Perfectly delightful. I should love to summer here. It would be a charming and unique experience."

While this was going on, a sideshow developed in the Tashmoo's parlor. There Ah Wah, the admiral's valet, was holding court for autograph seekers. Grinning at all the attention he was attracting, Ah

The Deweys were so charmed with their cruise on the Detroit River that the admiral signed his name, date and "Detroit" on one of the flag's stars in memory of what he called a never-to-be-forgotten day.

Wah swiftly stroked odd hieroglyphics on every scrap of paper thrust before him by the importunate crowd.

After their repast the Deweys were invited to return to the bridge. They remained there with the captain until the Tashmoo turned back off Star Island. When the wind freshened considerably, Dewey asked that his four-star flag be taken down. It was too old to stand much weather, he explained.

Then, on impulse, Dewey added a neat touch of his own to the bonhomie of the occasion. Borrowing a pen from the captain in the pilot house, he wrote his name on one of the flag's white stars, adding "at Detroit" and the date, June 9, 1900. "In remembrance of a never-to-be-forgotten day," he said gracefully.

The Tashmoo returned at a fast clip, picking up the fleet of yachts again off Grosse Pointe. Once more there were salutes from the Michigan and the Fessenden, from pleasure craft in the river and from the locomotives on shore.

When the steamer docked, Mrs. Dewey returned to the Russell House. Dewey continued out Woodward in the carriage for a chat with Gov. Hazen S. Pingree in the Pingree residence. He was back at the hotel in time to don dress uniform, with gilt epaulettes and cocked hat, for a 3 p.m. reception of the Michigan commandery of the Loyal Legion.

More than 3,000 marched in the parade which followed, with Gen. Henry M. Duffield, Detroit's own Spanish-American War hero, as marshal. After the Deweys, in the lead carriage, and other carriages bearing the local dignitaries, marched the 14th Infantry, sailors and marines from the Michigan, the First Michigan Volunteers, naval militia, 300 Grand Army of the Republic veterans, the Holy Redeemer Grays, the Hibernian Rifles, and Knights of Pythias, the Knights of St. John, letter carriers and a boys' brigade from Windsor.

For Detroit, it was as Dewey so aptly termed it — a never-to-be-forgotten day.

20. It's Better With the Unions

Detroiters did a lot of worrying about the Labor Day parade in 1900 — but everything turned out all right.

The trend that year toward using the holiday largely for recreation was so strong that unions affiliated with the Detroit Trades Council adopted special resolutions. They set fines to be levied against members who failed to show up for the march.

As an incentive, it was announced that 50 pounds of tobacco would be awarded to the union making the best appearance.

The big threat to the success of the parade, however, was the weather. "For the first time on Labor Day within the memory of man," so The Evening News reported, rain was forecast that morning.

It was coming down in buckets, too, at 9 a.m. on Sept. 3, only an hour before the scheduled starting time. Undaunted, the chief marshal, Malcom McLeod, and his aides hurried about on horseback to get everything ready.

They made sure that the seven divisions of marchers assembled in as orderly fashion as possible on the streets around Grand Circus Park. And by 10:30 the heavens smiled on their efforts. The rain let up and 8,000 paraders were ready to go.

Each division had its own band. As the first moved out there were cheers from the spectators — most of whom still kept close to shelter, in case the rain returned.

Behind the first band came 1,000 iron molders,

comprising the largest single group in the procession. They wore blue shirts with white stripes, white caps and white ties. Blue-and-white canes added a jaunty touch.

Best prepared for vagaries in the September weather were the longshoremen. They wore brown sweaters and black caps.

Patternmakers, stove trimmers and blacksmiths also were in the first division. Smaller units followed, including pressmen, stereotypers, bookbinders, bakers, upholsterers and theatrical workers.

The coopers, 120 strong, managed to put in a few licks of union business. They carried transparencies bearing the names of unfriendly barrel makers with whom the public was advised not to trade.

Painters made up the second largest group in the parade, with 600 men looking natty in white duck trousers and caps.

Other well-applauded groups included the carpenters, steam fitters, plasters, streetcar men, cigar makers, boot and shoe workers, broom makers, ship caulkers and curbstone cutters.

The relatively small array of electrical workers drew applause all along the line of march for the most unusual display — two floats, each bearing a miniature telephone pole. The poles were connected with real wires, too. Careful maneuvering was required, especially when floats were rounding a corner.

Detroit had not one, but two parades that day. Members of the National Letter Carriers' Association were in town from across the country.

After watching the weather anxiously, too, that morning, the mailmen were pleased to see clearing skies for their own parade in the afternoon. There were 3,500 men in line, led by a big band of 65 musicians brought to town by the New York delegation.

The growing contingent of Detroiters who plumped for other forms of Labor Day celebration than parading also found plenty of alternatives available in 1900.

On the day before the holiday, the Rapid Railway System, operating interurbans out East Jefferson and Gratiot, suggested taking its comfortable cars "to any of the pleasant summer resorts of Anchor Bay, North Channel or the beautiful River St. *135*

Clair." Electric cars left the City Hall every half hour for Algonac, Marine City, St. Clair and Port Huron.

The Detroit, Belle Isle and Windsor Ferry Co. advertised that its steamers would continue running to Bois Blanc Island until Sept. 9. The name hadn't yet been officially simplified to Bob-Lo.

Perhaps the best bargain on the river was offered by the Steamer Idlewild. For Labor Day only, it was running a cut-rate excursion to Toledo and return for 50 cents.

For those who could extend their holiday jaunts, the Detroit & Cleveland Navigation Co. scheduled special excursions to Mackinac Island at $4, to Saul Ste. Marie for $5, and to Marquette for $6.

Racing fans had their choice of going to the Highland Park Race Track out Woodward, or the Windsor Jockey Club across the river. Each had six races on the holiday card. There were trotting races, too, at the Grosse Pointe grounds.

The Wonderland Theater offered a novelty — Biograph motion pictures of "Col. Theodore Roosevelt and his staff, maneuvers by a German torpedo flotilla, and the Grand Fountain at Longchamps Palace, Marseilles, France."

Other theatrical attractions included Tim Murphy in "A Bachelor's Romance" at the Detroit Opera House; "The Diary Farm" at the Lyceum, boasting a New York run of 108 performances, and "the Convict's Daughter" at the Whitney Opera House. The Whitney ad urged: "See the escape on the hero."

There was even a free concert at Philharmonic Hall by the Egg Baking Powder Quartet and Mandolin Club.

Labor Day parades persisted for generations, but in the end those who preferred to play won out. The last parade on the holiday in Detroit was in 1966. In the meantime, however, the city emerged as the nation's labor capital. The annual marches were hailed as a flexing of muscle in both the real and metaphorical senses.

President Franklin D. Roosevelt and Harry S. Truman established a tradition for Democratic candidates of kicking off the quadrennial presidential campaign in Detroit on Labor Day. The largest

Detroit's Labor Day Parade: The lithographers, with light green umbrellas, were followed by the retail clerks' union, with banners, mottoes and boycott announcements. View from the corner of Woodward and Jefferson avenues.

crowds in downtown history assembled to hear them speak in the old City Hall area, and later it came to bear the name of another candidate who recieved the backing of Detroit labor in his bid for the presidency, as John F. Kennedy Square.

Detroit automobile workers would see one of their number, Walter P. Reuther, rank as America's most progressive labor leader. In retrospect he seems to have been born for the role.

His father, Valentine Reuther, was president of the Ohio Valley Trades and Labor Assembly, and a grandfather was an organizer in the United Brewery Workers. Instead of playing boys' games, Walter and his four brothers were more often found

137

squared off in debates refereed by the father and grandfather.

Although he left high school after two years to serve an apprenticeship as a tool and die maker, Reuther went on with his education in Detroit night classes while employed in the Ford factory. He followed this with three years' study at the College of the City of Detroit, the future Wayne State University.

Students like Reuther both absorbed and added to the institution's heady intellectual ferment derived from its place in the Motor City. So did faculty members like L. E. Dickinson and Frank G. Tompkins, who somehow imbued those in attendance in their courses in poetry and drama, respectivaly, with the understanding that poetry and drama are native not to books and stages but to the abrasions and vicissitudes of urban living.

In their own version of the grand tour, Walter and his brother, Victor, went off on a bicycle tour of Europe. They saw the Nazis ruin labor in Germany, and after a worker's eye-view of the Soviet Union they came home as militant anti-Communists.

The brothers took major roles in the organization of the auto workers in 1935, and Walter went on to the top of the labor movement. A fluent talker and a man of ideas, he was the very antithesis of the old stereotype of the cigar-chomping, hardboiled union boss.

Looking back with the hindsight of seven decades, it is easy to see the two major assets that would make the city the automotive center of the world.

As the crossroads of the water route through the Great Lakes and the overland route transversing it at the Straits, Detroit was destined to become the transportation hub, which produced the dividends of water and rail excursion points close at hand. The other asset centered on workday Detroit — it was the building up of a labor force with the precise mechanical know-how that the Motor Age would require.

On that turn-of-the-century Labor Day, even the shrewdest of prognosticators might have been misled into a prediction that Cleveland would emerge as America's automotive center. Cleveland had the steel mills, the closer proximity to the big Eastern markets. Cleveland had Alexander Winton, the first automotive tycoon, whose product held all the speed championships until a Detroit upstart, Henry Ford, entered the picture.

The extra dollop tipping the scales in favor of Detroit was part of its frontier heritage. That was the presence of a minion ready to take mighty gambles — men like Ransom E. Olds, Charles B. King, and Ford himself. The 20th century was destined to put the world on wheels, and Detroit stood ready to take on the job.

As for labor itself, it took much struggle to achieve the goals envisioned in the 1900 parade. But the time would come when management would join with the rollicking phrase in a favorite song of labor on the march:

"It's better with a union man."

21. Turn of the Century

People will argue about anything. Even over the date when a new century begins.

Like most Americans, Detroiters were eager to celebrate the arrival of the new 20th century on Jan. 1, 1900. But the mathematicians were adamant; it wouldn't really begin for another year.

America wasn't alone in its impatience. In Germany, Kaiser Wilhelm II disregarded the savants. He ordered 1900 greeted with a salute of 33 guns. But it was pointed out that the Kaiser always seemed to be trying to get ahead of everybody else. The rest of the world waited — Detroit included. After that extra year, the city was determined to make its 1901 New Year's celebration the biggest ever. At 9 p.m. on Dec. 31, the streets were almost deserted; the weather was cold and Detroit appeared to be tucked away for the night. But two hours later the thoroughfares were as crowded as at noonday. Streetcars were busy, heading downtown from the residential districts with every seat filled, and as the cars neared the sound of the celebration — horns and pistols, firecrackers and bells — grew louder.

At 11:45 p.m., the darkened City Hall where the car lines converged burst into light. It had been strung with thousands of red and white electric bulbs.

Thousands of fares reflected the glare of the lights. The area around the City Hall and the Campus Martius across Woodward was thronged. Moments after the signal from the hall, lights blazed in stores and offices. Especially brilliant were the two skyscrapers that topped the city's turn-of-the-century skyline, the Hammond and Majestic buildings.

Across Woodward, on the south corner of Cadillac Square, the Russell House, Detroit's leading hotel, was ablaze with light, too. As at countless functions, the 20th Century Ball being held there was approaching its midnight climax.

Most colorful of all the buildings at the center of the city was the Detroit Opera House on the Campus Martius, with its three arches outlined in electric bulbs of every tint of the rainbow.

At 11:55 p.m., a soft red glow appeared around the top of the Majestic Building. The roof of the city's tallest structure was outlined in red bulbs. In the street below, sticks of Greek fire burst into flame in green, red and blue, and firecrackers exploded in a great crescendo. At 11:58, the white ray of a searchlight on the Majestic roof was turned downward, playing on the crowd below. At 11:59, rockets hissed outward and upward from the skyscraper's top, arching far across the sky.

At midnight the clock in the City Hall tower boomed — and pandemonium broke loose. The clock kept booming, but only those in the tower itself could hear any strokes after the first one. In the churches, from Grand Circus Park northward on Woodward, organs pealed forth. Bands played and uniformed processions marched down th vaulted aisles.

In the packed City Hall, Mayor William C. Maybury held court in his office, decorated for the occasion with flags and bunting. The highlight of his reception was the sealing of a copper box in which were placed records of Detroit's state of affairs as the new century began. With the courtliness for which he was noted, the mayor took the box to the city controller's vault, where it was expected to remain undisturbed for 100 years.

What would Detroit be like on that distant day when the box would be opened, Jan. 1, 2001? The mind boggled at the thought. Perhaps it was just as well that the Detroiters of 1901 could only see through a glass darkly as they peered at the future. It might have been too much of a shock for them to   *141*

A float designed like a throne carried a queen and her court in
Detroit's 1901 bicentennial parade.

know that none of the proud edifices at the center
of the city around which the centennial celebration
took place would last out the new century.

By 1973, the Russell House would be only a memory, the Opera House would be long gone and the
City Hall, too. Even the Hammond and Majestic
buildings, proud skyscrapers that seemed built to
stand forever, would be gone with the years.

As for Maybury, he was a forward-looking man,
but the target date he was thinking about was July
24, 1901. On that day, Detroit would observe the
200th anniversary of the community's founding by
Chevalier Antoine de la Mothe Cadillac.

The bicentennial, Maybury felt, should achieve
something of lasting value. Something posterity
would be proud of—like a peristyle court on Belle
Isle to serve as a forum for civic gatherings.

Not too sure of what a peristyle court might be,
the Council empowered Maybury to set up plans,
but not to spend any money. It was all he needed,
and the mayor named a bicentennial committee
with himself as chairman. He asked prominent citizens able to donate funds to serve on it.

The committee engaged the services of a New
York architect, Stanford White. He was considered
142   to be the best in the land—and the most expensive.

White's plan was completed in time to be exhibited at the Detroit Museum of Arts on Washington's birthday. It called for a lofty Doric shaft of white marble, with an assembly area flanked by long colonnades. The estimated cost was $2,000,000.

Flocking to the museum in droves, Detroiters loved the bicentennial plan. Maybury basked in the widespread approval of his dream, and he won reelection handily.

All that was needed was to raise the $2,000,000. The committee obtained some sizable subscriptions, but one of America's periods of economic stringency set in and the sources dried up. So the operation was scaled down to a modest stone chair. This was erected in Cadillac Square, at the place where Detroit's first hall of justice had been erected.

Designed from a drawing in the collection of James E. Scripps, founder of The Detroit News, it reproduced an 18th century "judgment chair" such as found in the early French tribunals.

The civic birthday celebration turned out to be a humdinger, too, although the weather gave Maybury some anxious moments. The program called for an opening 21-gun salute on the river at dawn, fired by a U.S. Revenue Service cutter, the Fessenden. The News of July 24 described what happened:

"Old Nature stole a march on the USRS Fessenden today. For almost three hours before the guns of the government boat thundered out a sunrise salute, the artillery boat thundered out a sunrise coming of Detroit's natal day with a rumble and roar that eclisped all former thunder efforts of the year."

But the skies soon cleared, and early risers were roaming the downtown streets. Many stopped at the City Hall, once more turned out in flags and bunting, to gaze at a large painting of Cadillac's landing. Above was an immense gilded eagle, made of plaster and weighing 1,500 pounds. In his office, before a replica of Cadillac's flag, Maybury accepted congratulations and passed out souvenirs-cigars for the men and matchbooks for the ladies.

Then the mayor went across Woodward to the Russell House to meet the city's special guest, Pierre de Margerie, French charge d'affaires at

William C. Maybury

Washington. Together they led a parade of dignitaries, including mayors of several Midwestern cities, into Cadillac Square for ceremonies dedicating the judgment chair.

After that the officials steamed up the river on the Fessenden. At Peche Island, they met with Dr. Daniel LaForte, a Detroit physician of French descent who had been chosen to enact the role of Cadillac.

While ships along the waterfront sounded loud blasts, church bells rang and factory whistles blew, the Fessenden returned downriver. It had an honor guard of decorated bateaux, rowed by crews wearing knickerbockers of gray ticking that simulated the garb of Cadillac's voyageurs. At the riverfront downtown, Cadillac's landing was reenacted — without strict historical accuracy, but with much enthusiasm.

This stone chair, erected to commemorate Detroit's bicentennial, stood in Cadillac Square until 1941.

LaFerte wore a red satin coat, glittering with gold braid. His waistcoat, knee breeches and stockings were of white satin. A sword dangled form his broad belt and ostrich feathers graced his hat. The Indians waiting at the dock to welcome the voyageurs were Sioux brought from Buffalo, where they had been playing an engagement all summer at the Pan-American Exposition.

Soldiers in French uniforms with puffed sleeves escorted the party to the City Hall, led by an officer who spoke commands in French. Maybury gave Cadillac a key to the city.

At the bicentennial ball that evening, all eyes were on two Detroit belles in Louis XIV dresses from Paris. Isabel Weir played Madame Cadillac and Alice Chapoton was Madame de Tonty, wife of Cadillac's chief lieutenant.

On Thursday, ladies in French gowns also were prominent on floats in a floral street parade that lasted most of the day. Lining the streets were 150,000 cheering spectators. Friday there were both day and evening parades, the latter being a "great allegorical, historical and electrical demonstration" to top off the whole observance. Maybury had persuaded every firm in town to enter a float.

Unfortunately this grand finale was brought to an untimely end by a storm even worse than the one that greeted the birthday dawn. Many of the floats were damaged. The next day, the mayor was besieged by parade fans who wanted the big show repeated on another evening, hopefully a dry one, but Maybury decided against it. Perhaps he felt he had pushed his luck far enough.

Cadillac's chair endured the weather's buffetings for 40 years. In a way it came to fulfill some of the functions of the civic forum Maybury wanted in the first place. Orators soon began to use the chair's pedestal to harangue the passing masses. But by 1941 its red sandstone had deteriorated beyond repair and it was removed.

As for Maybury, Detroit did not forget him. When he died in 1908 funds were quickly raised to erect a statue in his memory. It stands at the north end of Grand Circus Park's west quadrant. The figure seems to be glancing out Woodward, the great avenue of Detroit's growth since 1908.

Maybury is still looking forward.

22. Fate and the Timekeeper

Was Detroit's automobile bubble ready to burst?

Some people thought so on March 9, 1901. In less than an hour that day, a spectacular fire fanned by high winds destroyed the factory of the Olds Motor Works, on Jefferson at Concord.

Completed in 1899, only three years after the original appearance of a horseless carriage on Detroit streets, the building was the first anywhere especially planned for automobile manufacturing. It was a monument to the faith of Ransom E. Olds that motor cars were more than a passing fancy.

Nearly 300 Detroiters worked there. The three-story structure had 150 feet frontage on Jefferson and extended 350 feet toward the Detroit River.

By the time the 20th century arrived, the busy place was one of the recognized sights in town. Many citizens who viewed its marvels were bitten by the insidious "automobubbling" fever, which cartoonists and the jokesters of America's humor weeklies were beginning to identify as a splendid subject for comedy.

On the other hand, older heads often were sadly shaken at the picture of supposedly sane people spending good money for "buzz wagons," or what was worse, dabbling in fly-by-night auto stocks.

The fad couldn't last, they felt sure. Cars propelled by gasoline were just too dangerous. "Explosions looking for a place to happen," some pessimists called them.

And the blaze on March 9 seemed to indicate they were right. The first alarm sounded at 1:36 p.m. Within minutes, a series of blasts were heard inside the plant.

Ransom E. Olds

Then, like the climactic set piece of a Fourth of July fireworks extravaganza, the whole place seemed to be aflame.

Fortunately it was Saturday, and most of the employes left at noon. Four who remained at work in the paint department on the top floor were forced to jump for their lives. They suffered broken ankles and sprained backs.

By 2 p.m. the factory was a mass of wreckage. Firemen quenched flames that spread to the roof of the Detroit United Railways barn on the east, and the wind saved the Detroit Stove Works on the west. But the Peninsular Iron Works at the rear of the Olds lot was badly damaged.

Olds himself took his departure shortly after the noon whistle blew. When he hurried back to the scene he found only smoking, blackened fragments

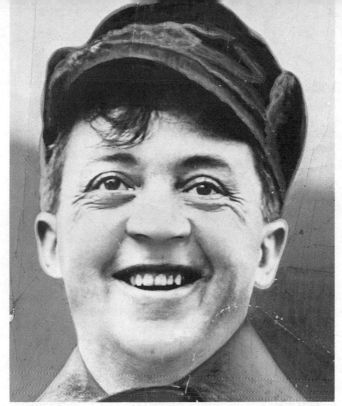

James J. Brady

of the walls still standing. He gathered as many of his workmen as he could find and put them to the task of rescuing the fireproof safe from the ruins.

To reporters, Olds denied that the blasts inside the building were the result of the fire reaching stores of gasoline. Only a small amount of fuel was on hand for test runs, he said. Insurance would cover the loss, he added, and plans would begin at once to get back into production.

In spite of this brave front, Olds was in real trouble. The company was $80,000 in the red, he knew only too well.

The Oldsmobile offered for $1,250 was a good buy, but so far sales were a disappointment. The market seemed to be dominated by expensive cars —Winton, Locomobile, De Dion, Columbia.

Facing this bind, Olds had decided to gamble his

An early Oldsmobile leaves the Olds Motor Works, Detroit's first auto plant

company's chance for survival on one far-out venture, a one-cylinder runabout that would sell for $650. At that bargain price, he hoped a lot of middle-income folks who couldn't afford the big machine would jump at the chance to become automobilists.

The decision was still a closely guarded secret. One prototype runabout was completed. It was stored inside the plant when the fire broke out. So were all the patterns and blueprints.

Months of effort had gone up in smoke, it appeared, and with it the dream that had driven Olds relentlessly all of his adult life. He was just 22 when he built a steam-operated horseless carriage in 1866. He followed that up with a one-cylinder gasoline engine, and in 1892 he organized the Olds Gasoline Engine Works, in Lansing, to manufacture gas engines for farm and machine use. A Detroit copper magnate, S. L. Smith, was his principal backer when he launched into automobile manufacture, and the Olds Motor Works was incorporated for $350,000.

On that fateful day in March, 1901, Olds was deeply shaken by the apparent completeness of the disaster, But just as the safe was being hauled from the debris, he learned that something else had been rescued.

James J. Brady, timekeeper at the factory, 150 pushed through the crowd to his employer's side.

In 1904, William McIntyre, Detroit News city circulation manager, was photographed in a company-owned curved dash Oldsmobile runabout. More than 14,500 of this model were sold between 1900 and 1905. Much of its popularity was attributed to Gus Edwards' lilting tune, "In My Merry Oldsmobile."

"Mr. Olds," he said, "I'm sorry. I didn't have time to bring out the records. But I did drive the runabout to safety."

Olds always remembered that he was so delighted he could have ordered a monument erected to the man on the spot. But at the moment, the timekeeper's action gave him pressing things to do.

Nevertheless, fate might well have smiled at the notion of a monument. In due time, Detroiters would indeed erect one to honor James J. Brady though for reasons which had nothing to do with saving Olds from oblivion.

A quick check by Olds showed no vacant factory building in Detroit large enough for his needs. But immediate space was available in Lansing.

The runabout was driven there and taken apart. New blueprints were made from the pieces.

In the autumn, Olds' test driver, Roy D. Chapin —he would become president of Hudson Motors— drove a curved-dash model to New York. This was a remarkable feat in 1901, and Chapin received much acclaim.

So did the runabout. As sales for it ballooned, Olds took a further gamble. He plowed back every cent into more cars.

The risk was obvious. If demand suddenly dried up as the fickle-minded public turned to some other motoring sensation, the company could still go broke.

But the models continued to sell — 2,400 of them in 1902, and 4,000 the following year. In 1904, sales hit 5,000. By 1905 the saucy runabout was the success story of all motordom. On Tin Pan Alley, Gus Edwards and Vincent Bryan teamed to turn out a classic auto song, "In My Merry Oldsmobile."

Having made a fortune, Olds decided to retire at 41. His former associates, convinced that the runabout was a lucky fluke, went back to turning out higher-priced cars.

The vacuum thus left in the low-priced field soon was filled. Henry Ford moved into it with his Model T, and the results were—to say the least—impressive.

Restless Olds couldn't stay out of the auto game for long. He used his initials to provide the name for a new car, Reo, and it turned out to be a money-maker, too.

Eventually, Olds' fortune exceeded $40 million. He gave most of it to colleges, churches and charitable institutions.

When the motor pioneers held their greatest get-together in Detroit in 1946 at the Automotive Golden Jubilee, Ford and the others conceded to Olds the title of "Father of the Auto." He outlasted the other early giants, lingering on the scene until 1950, when he was 86.

Now, about the timekeeper. The life of James J. Brady deserves a second look. He was born on the site of Tiger Stadium—the front door of the Brady cottage stood about where third base came to be anchored.

It seems hard to believe, but the record is that
152 Jim ran away from home at the age of 6 and managed

to support himself by shining shoes and selling newspapers. He never went long to school, but while working as a telegraph messenger he found time to teach himself bookkeeping.

Brady was as sure as Olds that the motor car boom would continue, and he was one of the organizers of the Thomas-Detroit Co. In 1914 he was appointed collector of internal revenue for the Detroit district.

On Dec. 10, 1914, a cartoon by Burt Thomas on page one of The Detroit News caught Brady's eye. Titled "The Boy He Used To Be," it depicted a business man, laden with Christmas packages, led to the home of a needy family by memories of his own youth as a newsboy.

Brady called his best friend, David A. Brown, who was his competitor selling papers in boyhood, and decided to act. In all, 60 former newsboys answered their call to sell papers again in the cause of Christmas charity.

Their modest goal of $400 was exceeded. The Old Newsboys Goodfellow Fund became a cherished tradition of Detroit, with annual collections over the $100,000 mark, and inspired similar funds elsewhere.

"His Monument—Love" was the headline in The News when Brady died in 1925. Three years later, a bronze statue of Brady, with a tattered child leaning at his side, was unveiled on Belle Isle.

A plaque reproduces the Burt Thomas drawing which inspired Brady, and opposite it is a cartoon by Tom May in the Detroit Free Press, "Forgotten," deepening the grief of a child overlooked on Christmas morning. May's cartoon inspired the Forgotten Club, a forerunner of the Goodfellows.

23. The Race Between Two Centuries

One thing is certain. There never will be another race like it.

Navigation men, to this day, hail the 1901 event as the high point of the whole fabulous era of steam on the Great Lakes.

The Mississippi River had a storied race, too, between the Natchez and the Robert E. Lee. But old-timers on the lakes insist it couldn't compare with the mighty contest between the Tashmoo and the City of Erie — "the race between two centuries."

Built in 1898 for the Cleveland and Buffalo Transit Co. (C&B), the City of Erie established herself as the fastest ship the Great Lakes had seen in the 19th century. No brash challenger ever seriously threatened her reign — none, that is, until the fresh winds of 1900 blew across the lakes.

From the start, the Erie was a well-loved ship. Her specialty was carrying newlyweds bound for Niagara Falls from Cleveland and Erie, Pa., to Buffalo. Her nickname became famous. She was the Honeymoon Special.

But the first lake steamer built in 1900 was something special, too. That was the Tashmoo, the new flagship of Detroit's White Star Line.

Her builders embodied every new trick of construction and design. No expense was spared. They wanted speed and more speed.

Almost immediately, the Tashmoo acquired an affectionate nickname of her own — the White Flyer. She was the most luxurious day-cruise steamer on the lakes. But was she faster than the City of Erie?

The answer to this question was achieved through a chain of circumstances that began with a minor-league contest in September, 1900, between the City of Chicago and the City of Milwaukee. Both boats were owned by the Graham & Morton Co., of Chicago. Their race from the Windy City to St. Joseph, Mich., was just a friendly, intramural affair. The Chicago was the winner by a full minute.

No one would have paid attention to this event outside Chicago and St. Joe except for a bit of braggadocio indulged in by a Chicago newspaper, which acclaimed the local steamboat as "the fastest on the lakes."

This ill-advised boast was the occasion of much merriment elsewhere. In Detroit, one published riposte enumerated nine steamers that could easily leave the Chicago in the lurch: "The North West and the North Land, four Detroit & Cleveland Navigation Co. (D&C) boats, the City of Erie, the City of Buffalo and the Frank E. Kirby."

Omission of the Tashmoo from this list was plainly inadvertent, but A. A. Parker, president of the White Star Line, was miffed. He promptly offered to post $1,000 that his new steamer could beat anything on fresh water.

Just as promptly, T. F. Newman, president of C&B, accepted on behalf of the City of Erie. Each line deposited its $1,000 check with J. W. Westcott, dean of Great Lakes marine reporting, with the understanding that both would be turned over to charity in either Detroit or Cleveland, depending on the winner of the race.

The course, it was arranged, would cover 94 statute miles from Cleveland to Erie.

With the onset of the 1901 navigation season, little else was talked about on the docks. The official purse was only a drop in the bucket. Rivalry between the sportsmen of Detroit and Cleveland was intense, and it was estimated that $100,000 wagered by enthusiasts in the two cities would change hands on the outcome of the race.

On Thursday, May 30, the Tashmoo was put through her paces on a 100-mile trial cruise. Her speed was a closely guarded secret. The crew was *155*

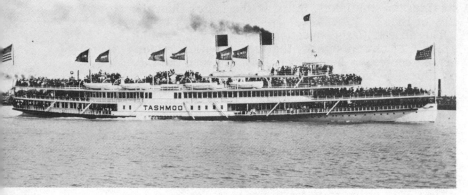

The Tashmoo was nicknamed White Flyer

under orders to make no statements to the press.

The line let it be known, however, that the trials were considered "most satisfactory, even exceeding expectations." The scuttlebutt was that the Erie would have to do better than 22 miles an hour to win.

Especially pleasing was the fact that the Tashmoo's time for the last 50 miles was even faster than for the first 50, indicating her excellent endurance qualities for a long race.

On Saturday, the Tashmoo laid at her dock near the foot of Jos. Campau. Her engineer force was busily engaged, taking a last look at the machinery.

"Fears the Tashmoo" was the headline of a story in The News-Tribune on Sunday. "The City of Erie people are getting scared by the record-breaking trials being made by the Tashmoo," declared the story, "and it was reported yesterday that arrangements have been made to put her in drydock to have her bottom cleaned."

On Sunday afternoon, a large party of Nobles of the Mystic Shrine drew the envy of all Detroit. The nobles and their wives boarded the D&C steamer City of Mackinac for a cruise that would take them to Erie to witness the finish of the race, after a visit to the Pan-American Exposition at Buffalo.

For the cruise, the steamer was temporarily rechristened the City of Moslem and handsomely decorated in the Shrine colors, red and yellow. Toby, Moslem Temple's papier-mache elephant, had a

The City of Erie was known as the Honeymoon Special

prominent spot on the aft promenade.

No bigger than a man's hand, one small cloud sullied Detroit's confident horizon. The course agreed upon followed the Erie's regular route, a clear advantage for the ship representing the 19th century. Nevertheless, the betting was even money.

Enthusiasm reached fever pitch on the morning of Tuesday, June 4. Excursion vessels from Detroit, Buffalo, Toledo and other lake ports carried capacity loads to the starting scene. Steamboat men were there from the Mississippi, and salt-water yachtsmen from the East, too.

More than 20,000 spectators thronged the Cleveland waterfront. It was a perfect day for the race. The sky was clear except for smoke wafted out over the blue water by a gentle breeze.

At 9:18 a.m. a cannon roared and the two greyhounds of the lakes moved out amid cheers. Slim and trim, they looked almost like sister ships.

The Erie gained headway first. She was two full lengths ahead as the rivals cleared the Cleveland breakwater. Once the open lake was reached, however, the Tashmoo showed her class.

Even from shore it was clear that the White Flyer was gaining on the Honeymoon Special. The Detroit boat closed the gap as they passed into a haze three miles east of Cleveland.

One by one, the excursion boats that had steamed to vantage points ahead along the course were overtaken. Eager to give her passengers their money's

157

worth, the little Hawk lurched so close as the Tashmoo passed that a seaman swore at her. The steamer Frank E. Kirby considerately hove to until the racers passed.

The latter vessel had a special reason to be neutral. Kirby himself, the greatest of lake ship designers, created both the City of Erie and the Tashmoo. Whichever won, he could not lose.

As the excursion boats fell astern, Chief Engineer Winfield Dubois stood with one foot on the throttle frame in the Tashmoo's engine room, an unlighted cigar clenched between his teeth and his eyes on the gauges. Dubois held the stroke steady at 40 revolutions a minute. Streams of water were constantly played on the giant pistons, and the blackened stokers worked like demons feeding coal into the flames.

Bit by bit the Tashmoo forged ahead, and at the end of 15 minutes she led by three lengths. Then, changing course, she seemed to yaw about uncertainly, and the Erie quickly came abeam.

Arthur D. Walton, The Detroit News correspondent on the Tashmoo, saw what was wrong. "The wheelsman was not used to steering by compass," he wrote.

The steam steering gear also seemed slow in responding to the helm. Walton noted that the Erie was stripped of every possible extra pound for the race — even her rafts and lifeboats were removed — while the Tashmoo did not take down so much as a pennant.

The shoreline was five miles away now, and no one on the Tashmoo was familiar with it, or with the depth of the water. The Erie was holding her familiar course much better than her rival.

Suddenly the Tashmoo dropped back as her stroke was reduced to 38. In the engine room flustered men were shouting as they worked on a condenser that had become overheated. The Erie shot ahead half a dozen lengths, and now the cluster of boats waiting at the finish line in her namesake city could be seen ahead.

Quickly the Tashmoo's condenser was put back in shape, and her stroke went to 42. Her upper works creaked and the whole ship trembled under the strain. To reduce resistance, cabin doors were

Frank E. Kirby: Designed Erie and Tashmoo

opened and the wind whistled through. A canvas, put up to keep the wash from the lower deck, was ripped off.

There was no bad steering now. The Tashmoo's pilot, accustomed to keeping his course by shore sights, could set the pole on the stake boat and keep it there. The Erie was straining to the utmost, black smoke pouring from her funnel. Still the Tashmoo shortened the gap, and yard by yard she made up the lost precious distance.

But not quite enough. Staggering under the pressure, the Erie passed the stake boat 30 yards ahead.

The old century had won, yet it was a hollow victory. Few doubted now that on the straightaway the Tashmoo was the faster boat. On the spot, the

White Star Line offered to post $10,000 for a return match.

It was in vain. Never again would her owners let the Honeymoon Special be inveigled into a race with the White Flyer.

24. The Shoemaker Who Looked Like a King

King Edward VII did his best for the stricken visitor from Detroit. The king sent his own physicians to the tall-ceilinged suite in London's Grand Hotel where Hazen S. Pingree was fighting for his life in June, 1901.

It was more than a courteous gesture to an honored guest who had served multiple terms as mayor of Detroit and governor of Michigan. The king was genuinely concerned. On a previous visit by Pingree to England, the London press and public had been delighted by the marked resemblance between Pingree and the future monarch, then still the Prince of Wales.

Caricaturists of the metropolis had a field day drawing the distinguished look-alikes. They pictured "Ping" wearing the British crown, and Edward in a hat to match the Detroiter's well-worn campaign fedora.

Michigan's favorite son enjoyed it. He even changed the style of his chin whiskers a bit to further the effort. And there was no doubt that Edward was pleased, too. He admired such forthright American leaders as Pingree.

The new sovereign's easy, democratic ways became the talk of the Continent as the Edwardian era swept away the prim formalities accumulated in six Victorian decades.

For weeks, The Detroit News carried dispatches with Pingree's by-line. They came from exotic places like Lorenzo Marques, Madagascar and Aden. Pingree was a duly accredited correspondent.

He was making a tour around East Africa on the steamer Melbourne, with jaunts inland from ports enroute. In June, 1901, a picture of the Pingree party on camelback in front of the Great Pyramid of Giza appeared on page one. In an accompanying article, Pingree told of a strenuous climb of the pyramid. He explored the interior extensively.

On the same page, another story announced elaborate plans by Detroit Mayor William C. Maybury and the City Council to greet Pingree on his return home, with a public reception at the City Hall.

The first word that all was not well with Pingree came in a cable to The News from his son, Joe, on June 15. Stricken with peritonitis, his father was too ill to leave London and to embark for America, Joe reported.

The next day Pingree was much worse. Mrs. Pingree and their daughter, Hazel, left Detroit to catch a transatlantic liner in New York. Pingree failed to rally, and on June 18 it was over. Word of her husband's death reached Mrs. Pingree in New York in time to turn back before sailing.

In Detroit, the Council quickly adjourned. Newsboys cried the extra with the same magic word that had sold papers for a decade: "Pingree."

In a page one editorial, The News suggested that the citizens' welcoming committee become a committee to build a monument. Carl E. Schmidt, the group's chairman, who was a close friend of Pingree, agreed. Schmidt's first thought was for an equestrian statue, on the Campus Martius or Cadillac Square.

Drawings in the paper that day recalled dramatic highlights of Pingree's career:

One portrayed his beginnings in politics. A successful manufacturer of footwear, Pingree was urged by a committee of leading citizens to run for mayor against the corrupt political machine which dominated City Hall.

His first reply was: "I'm too busy making shoes."

But he did run, and the sketch showed a turning point of the campaign. That came in the Larned Street auditorium, where a mass meeting was packed by cohorts of the opposition. Pingree stood before a hostile mob for 90 minutes, refusing to be

Famous look-alikes Hazen S. Pingree (left) and King Edward VII wearing British crown

shouted down, and the machine's strong-arm tactics roused the city into a turnout at the polls that became a landslide victory for Pingree.

For many readers that day, the most poignant drawing of all was labeled "In Memoriam." It recalled the hard times of the 1890's, when thousands in the city would have gone hungry except for the "Pingree potato patches" that provided food for the needy.

The winter of 1893-94 was difficult. Because of the money panic of 1893, some of Detroit's biggest industries were forced to shut down. The railroad car shops and the stove factories were among them.

It was estimated that 25,000 workers were unemployed, in a city whose population was less than 250,000.

Pingree was the first American mayor to hit upon public works as a means of reducing unemployment. His projects helped, but when the hoped-for revival of business failed to come with the spring of 1894 and the city's poor funds were exhausted, something else was needed.

Pingree noted that, as a result of real estate speculation in the previous boom, plots of land held for a rise in value were standing idle all over town. He made a public appeal to the owners to permit the use of their properties for vegetable gardens.

The response was hearty. Among the first landowners to respond was John B. Corliss, who provided 15 acres along West Grand Boulevard, between 12th and 14th. William Livingstone followed with 40 acres in north Detroit. Frank H. Croul and Bryant Walker also offered large plots.

Applications from the unemployed for garden plots poured in. To raise money to provide seeds and garden tools, Pingree asked for special collections in the churches. He put up his thoroughbred Kentucky saddle horse at auction and turned the proceeds over to the potato-patch fund.

After this start, owners of small parcels and single lots all over town came in by the hundreds. At a cost of a few thousand dollars for seeds and implements, food shortages were reduced to a minimum.

The plan was widely heralded, and other cities took it up. "Potato Patch Pingree" became nationally known as a champion of the needy.

The garden plots were continued through 1895 and 1896, until the effects of the 1893 panic were over. Even then, the plan was not forgotten.

Similar projects were developed in various countries during periods of stress. In Germany, city garden plots were used during World War I to offset food shortages occasioned by the Allied blockade. When the United States entered the war, Detroit revived potato patches, and some patriots went so far as to plow up their front lawns to raise vegetbles.

During his three terms as mayor from 1890 to 1896, Pingree began the fight for municipal ownership of Detroit's street transportation system. He built more than 50 miles of new track to prove that streetcars could be operated for a 3-cent fare, in place of the 5 cents then being charged.

To do battle with Pingree, the traction interests brought to Detroit Tom L. Johnson, who reputedly possessed the most resourceful brain in their industry. Johnson came to admire Pingree so much that when he returned to Cleveland he ran for mayor

While touring the Union of South Africa, Hazen S. Pingree (right) had this photo taken with Eli Sutton, a member of his party, in Port Elizabeth. It was Pingree's last photo before his death.

and campaigned for 3-cent fares in the Pingree style.

"Some day Hazen S. Pingree will be remembered and recognized as one of the foremost leaders in our era of national awakening," was Johnson's assessment of his old foe.

As governor from 1896 to 1900, Pingree locked horns with an even more formidable power than the traction trust. This was the railroad lobby.

When he undertook to push legislation to force the railroads to pay equable taxes, the House of Representatives was with him. The rail lobby, however, maintained a tight grip on the allegiance of 19 of the 32 members of the Senate.

Upon this latter group, Pingree bestowed an ironic designation, "The Immortal 19." The immortals closed ranks against a storm of popular pressure raised against them throughout a special session called in December, 1900, but the measure he sought became law soon afterward.

Pingree's accomplishments in public office were still fresh in the public mind when his death occurred the following June. He was only 59, and the shock was great.

Within minutes after the first edition hit the street, readers were calling The News with offers of donations for a Pingree monument.

It was decided to issue memorial certificates with his picture to contributors. The initial certificate went to a 10-year-old black newsboy, George Throgmartin.

On July 2, a delegation of city officials went to New York to escort Pingree's body to Detroit. The following day a catafalque was placed in the main corridor of the City Hall. The flags and bunting that decorated the building for the Fourth of July were replaced by wreaths on July 5, and a silent crowd began assembling outside for the arrival of the casket.

The long line of those waiting to pay tribute grew until it extended for six blocks. When the cortege arrived it was led by a carriage bearing Mayor Maybury, Pingree's son, Joe, and the ex-governor's brother, Frank. All that day, Detroiters filed past the bier.

At dawn the next day the casket was taken to the spacious Pingree home on Woodward. The service there was simple, with the Rev. Nehemiah Boynton, of the First Congregational Church, offering prayers and the Rev. Reed Stuart, of the First Unitarian, giving the eulogy.

By 2 p.m., 20,000 members of military and civic organizations lined Woodward near the home. The flag-draped casket was placed on a caisson from Fort Wayne, painted deep olive green and drawn by 35 soldiers of the Michigan State Troops.

The cortege moved slowly down Woodward, through crowds of people lining the curbs, and out Jefferson to Elmwood Cemetery.

It was on Memorial Day in 1904 that the Pingree statue was unveiled in Grand Circus Park, to become one of Detroit's most familiar landmarks.

At the end of the parade that day members of the Hazen S. Pingree Command, United Spanish War Veterans, formed a circle around the monument and soldiers of the First U.S. Infantry from Fort Wayne were massed near by on Park Avenue.

Hazel Pingree released an American flag draped around the figure, and Mayor Maybury accepted the statue for the city. Only four years later, after Maybury's death, his statue joined Pingree's in the park. For Detroiters of later generations they stood as bronze sentinels of the past.

25. 'There's a Guy Here with a Buzz Wagon'

No one on board the steamer Sappho seemed to recognize that history was in the making that sunny Sunday morning in 1901 when the ferry eased up to the dock at the foot of Woodward Avenue for another trip across the Detroit River.

The ticket-taker on shore, however, did note a possible problem in one unusual vehicle in line among the buggies and drays waiting for passage to Windsor.

"Hey, captain, there's a guy here with a buzz wagon," he shouted up to the pilot house.

The ferries had begun taking electric automobiles across the river the summer before. They were accustomed to seeing the score of well-to-do Detroiters who owned such machines and who liked to cross the river for Sunday drives. The well-behaved electrics caused no trouble.

But the noisy, dangerous, inflammable gasoline auto, or "buzz wagon," of 1901? That was a horseless carriage of another color. The Sappho's captain saw red, too. When he descended to the dock to express his displeasure, he found that the automobile's chauffeur was well-equipped with documents.

The driver, Theodore E. Barthel, patiently had cut through the difficulties dreamed up by the Detroit, Belle Isle & Windsor Ferry Co., following his application to take a gasoline car across the river. He even posted a bond for the trip through a customs broker.

Barthel was an Oldsmobile employe, and his company wanted him to road test a car in Canada so it could be advertised as an international run. Luck was with him, too. A Detroit congressman, Rep. John B. Corliss, happened to be on the ferry dock at that moment. Corliss interested himself in the problem and assured the master of the Sappho that Barthel's papers were in order.

Bowing to this opinion, the captain ordered the gasoline drained from the Oldsmobile's tank.

"Push him on the boat last and push him off last, so he won't scare the horses," he told his deckhands.

Recalling the story decades later when he was 80, Barthel described the cloud that went up when the Sappho reversed her engines at dockside in Windsor.

"Her stacks emitted a hail of steam, oil spray and soot that made us look as if smallpox had descended on us en masse," he said. "Though I was last off and had to refuel, there was a gang of onlookers watching to see if the car could make the grade up Ouellette Street to Sandwich. There was a great cheer when the car made it."

Barthel had an extra errand in Canada that day. Another Olds employe, Jonathan D. Maxwell, asked him to take along some patent applications to his uncle, Adolph Barthel, a patent attorney.

Maxwell's patents would lead to his becoming the father of the Maxwell car, a sturdy machine that for a time gave strong competition to Henry Ford's Model T in the economy field.

In the strange ways of history, however, the Maxwell would be remembered by posterity chiefly through the japes of the voice of parsimony, Jack Benny.

Maxwells, Fords and every other kind of car followed the trail Barthel blazed. The Sappho and her sisters on the Windsor and Walkerville runs — the Garland, the Excelsior, the Victoria, the Essex and the Ariel — became accustomed to heavy traffic as the automotive era burgeoned. But many amenities continued.

Ferries operated on the river for a century and the Detroit, Belle Isle & Windsor Ferry Co., organized in 1873, made it a big business, but it kept its eye on the family trade. You could ride all day on the boats for a dime, and in warm weather family parties often boarded in mid-morning. Carrying pic-

Theodore E. Barthel and his associate, Arthur Z. Mitchell, in a 1903 Oldsmobile

nic lunches, they would enjoy a day of river breezes at a small cost.

The newest and biggest ferries were assigned to the Belle Isle run in summer, and Detroiters young and old loved them. Every steamer carried a dance band. Ginger ale, at 5 cents a glass, foamed steadily from refreshment stands on each boat.

But trouble began brewing for the ferries early in the summer of 1907. Detroit's aldermen approved a record $85,700 contract to build a new casino on the island, and they argued that as long as the ferry company would benefit by increased patronage from this improvement, it was only fair that it should shoulder some of the cost. To this end, the city's license fee for each boat was raised from $150 to $500.

That seemed steep, but it was only the beginning. The boats long had operated to the island at an adult fare of 10 cents and 5 cents for children. For the 1907 season, it was decreed, the company also should sell adult one-way fares at a straight 5 cents each.

What bothered the steamer line most, however, was an extension of the route included in the new regulations. West side aldermen joined to insert a provision that the ferries, in addition to the traditional stops at the foot of Woodward, Third, and Jos. Campau, also should journey far enough downriver on each trip for a stop at the foot of West Grand Boulevard.

In an appeal on July 3, 1907, the ferry company said the one-way fares were being misused by purchasers who never got off the boat. Now they were riding the entire day for a nickel.

The Council denied the appeal, and when the ferry line delayed extending the runs to West Grand Boulevard on the grounds that suitable docking facilities were not completed, it was brought into court. Judge James Phelan fined the company $300 — and warned that similar fines would be repeated daily for continued violations of the new ordinance.

Walter E. Campbell, president of the ferry line, protested in vain.

"The Council has not stopped to consider what the extension to West Grand Boulevard means to us," he said. "We would have to buy another boat to continue the same frequency of service on the longer run."

The ferry line's old franchise expired at midnight of July 31. On the morning of Aug. 1, it was ready to drop a bombshell of its own.

New signs went up at the Woodward, Third and Jos. Campau docks that morning. They announced the ferries no longer would operate to Belle Isle. Instead, they offered "pleasure cruises on the river" only, for the old 10-cent fare.

Excited scouts who rushed to City Hall with the news reported that most of the Detroiters who came to the docks carrying picnic baskets seemed to accept the change in service.

Great commotion followed among the city fathers. There was much thumbing of law books, much pounding of desks, much running back and forth from the Council chamber to the mayor's office.

In the end the aldermen dumped the crisis in the lap of Mayor William B. Thompson. He invited

Steamer Sappho sketch by Seth Arca Whipple, Great Lakes Marine artist, *from Dossin Great Lakes Museum.*

Campbell to a peace conference, and the two worked out a settlement. Thompson promised there would be no effort to enforce the aldermen's new regulations, and Campbell agreed to send the steamers back to Belle Isle.

Soon things were back to normal. Most of the island visitors went straight from the ferry dock to the elegant new casino. Philip Breitmeyer, city parks commissioner, received many congratulations on the fine addition to the island's attractions, but there was little time for him to rest on his laurels.

Complaints piled up about the antics of some of the more exuberant canoeists who thronged the island with their craft, stacked high with gaudy pillows, the horns of their side-winder gramophones blaring forth song hits like "Belle of the Ball" or "I'm Afraid to Go Home in the Dark"

Many of them ignored the regulation requiring that a light be displayed on their boats after sunset. There were many collisions and upsets on band concert nights, when traffic was heavy on the winding canals. Even worse offenders were the young men who thought it was smart to paddle their canoes three and four abreast down the canals at full speed. You couldn't get past without a splashing.

"Ladies in canoes without escorts are being subjected to insulting remarks by these young fellows who think they are so fetching in their outlandish attire and freak hats," Breitmeyer declared indignantly.

He called for a special patrol of officers in canoes to catch the rowdies. It was a humdinger of a summer on Belle Isle.

Traffic reached its peak for the Windsor ferries in the Prohibition era. The evening lineup of American cars waiting to come home sometimes extended for miles from the ferry dock. Late comers often had to wait three or four hours. The ferry company prospered — but its prosperity attracted competition that eventually proved lethal. Completion of the Ambassador Bridge and the Detroit-Windsor Tunnel marked the beginning of the end.

The Belle Isle run was the first to go. The ease with which automobiles could cross the wide new bridge outmoded the leisurely ferry rides. Crossings to Windsor from the foot of Woodward continued into the late 1930's with two steamers, but the last run came on July 19, 1938.

The steamer Cadillac's decks were jammed with old-timer organizations and city officials that day. Aboard on the last crossing were Mrs. Louis P. Conklin of Detroit, who had made her honeymoon trip on one of the ferries in 1906, and Mrs. L. B. Tilson of Windsor, granddaughter of one of the line's first skippers, Capt. W.R. Clinton, master of the elegant Victoria.

Service to Walkerville, started in 1861 for his personal convenience by distiller Hiram Walker, continued to 1942.

The ships themselves lived on for a time. The Cadillac and the LaSalle served as icebreakers for the Coast Guard for years. The swift Ariel went to the Straits of Mackinac as a ferry, and later served between Port Huron and Sarnia, Ontario. At a winter mooring in Detroit, she was wrecked in a wild February storm.

The Halcyon experienced the most adventurous last days of all. After serving as a Coast Guard tender and then in a search for sunken Great Lakes treasure, she was used in the Arctic trade. She met her end wrecked on the barren coast of Baffin Island near the Arctic Circle in 1963.

26. The House in Baedecker's

Was Detroit slighted by Baedeker's, the granddaddy of all tourist guides? Some indignant citizens thought so in the early years of the 20th century.

Baedeker's was the travelers' bible, and Detroiters who were able to visit Europe naturally kept their volumes in hand when they went browsing in London, Rome or Paris. But when the American edition of the guide came out, what did it have to say about Detroit?

There wasn't a word about Belle Isle, Water Works Park, the Museum of Art, or any of the other attractions Detroiters liked to boast about. Baedeker's listed only one place in town as worthy of the cultured visitor's attention — and that was a private residence, the home of Charles L. Freer at 33 East Ferry.

What made it worse, not all of his fellow citizens could be said to approve of Freer. He was a wealthy, self-indulgent bachelor. He piqued the ladies by an obvious determination to remain a bachelor, too. The story was that in his youth in Kingston, N.Y., where Freer was born in 1856, he fell in love when too poor to marry, and the girl died before his prospects brightened.

Brighten they certainly did, first in railroading and then, in association with a long time friend, Frank J. Hecker, in the manufacture of railroad cars in Detroit. In 1890 Hecker and Freer built unusual neighboring residences which attracted much attention.

Hecker gave Detroit an example of the turreted French chateau. Freer brought in from Philadelphia the exponent of an avant-garde style, Wilson Eyre Jr., to design a huge, rambling, shingled villa.

In 1899 the American Car and Foundry Co. absorbed their plant. Freer and Hecker retired, both multimillionaires. Freer was only 43, and he became a resolute, full-time cosmopolite. Detroit heard of him most often in connection with glamorous goings-on elsewhere— Bohemian parties given in New York by his friend, the architect Stanford White, or in the Latin Quarter of Paris by the painter James Abbott McNeill Whistler.

Charles L. Freer

It was from Whistler that Freer absorbed a love for Oriental art which made his house worthy of Baedeker's. He found a new keynote for his life in the landscapes created by Asian artists under the inspiration of the Zen philosophy of nature contemplation.

Freer began collecting Oriental paintings in America, but he soon became convinced that dealers were unloading fakes on him. He determined to go to the source. He didn't speak Chinese or Japanese, but he trained bright young men to work with him, digging out rare scrolls, porcelains and jade carvings.

His journeys to the remote Chinese interior were sometimes likened, a bit extravagantly, to those of Marco Polo in the days of Kubla Khan. Once in the mountains he complained about the excessive tumult his guards were making to frighten off marauders. When quiet was restored he asked for an explanation; the guards pointed to a row of dead bandits.

On another occasion, while exploring an ancient temple, Freer glanced down at a river rushing torrent-like far below. He felt a tremor underfoot in time to jump back before the embankment plunged into the gorge, but he lost several mules and much of his equipment.

In 1905 he sold his horses and carriages and remodeled the stable behind the Ferry Avenue home into a private museum. He lengthened the structure, fireproofed the roof, and imported rare hardwoods so his rarities would not suffer from poor backgrounds.

The house was decorated with Chinese bronzes, Japanese scrolls and lacquers, Korean metal work. The bronzes ranged from axes, swords and daggers to clapperless bells, mirrors, basins, food vessels, pitchers and wine cups. Freer's collection went back nearly 4,000 years to the Shang Dynasty, and critics hailed it as the finest outside the Orient.

Freer also lovingly amassed works by his friend Whistler. The artist had Detroit connections; he was named for an uncle, the James Abbott who once served as postmaster.

Connoisseurs who passed the entrance tests to see Freer's treasures—and the host was extremely finicky about admitting only the right people—were entranced by a complete wall devoted to Whistler's "Nocturne in White" series. A long gallery was added to the north side of the house to adequately display the Whistleriana.

This gallery, however, was not reached until after suitable preliminaries. The visitor first saw a reception room decorated in silver and blue by Thomas W. Dewing. Simplicity was underlined; the room contained only a table bearing a massive Oriental vase, one chair and one large Dewing mural.

The main hall, done by Dwight M. Tryon, was in tones of ocher, yellow and gold. Four large murals depicted the four seasons. More canvases by Dewing were to be seen in the dining room; only then was the guest ready for the galleries.

Freer always was a stickler for displaying Oriental art in the Oriental manner. After tea blended by the host or vintage champagne was served, a single Chinese ceramic or a priceless Japanese screen

Old Detroit Showpiece—The Charles L. Freer home, formerly at 33 East Ferry, was listed in an old travelers' guide as the only place to see in the city. Freer, a wealthy bachelor, was selective about guests he invited to climb his ornate staircase and to view his art-filled rooms.

would be brought in. The guest was expected to ingest all the nuances of the piece in respectful silence.

Only the visitor who met all of Freer's requirements got to see the piece de resistance. This was the Peacock Room, subject of a celebrated Victorian scandal. Originally it had been created in delicate blue and white for Whistler's patron, Frederick Leyland, a British shipping magnate. Leyland wanted a room that would show off his blue porcelain collection and a painting commissioned from Whistler to go with it, "The Princess of the Land of Porcelain."

Henry Jeckyll, the architect of Leyland's London home, chose gilded walnut shelving and used flowered Spanish leather on the walls which had been brought to England by Catherine of Aragon. But Whistler, who took a dislike to Jeckyll, obtained permission to make some improvements to the room just before Leyland left for a stay on the Continent. He painted golden peacocks over everything — shutters, walls, ceiling, even

Catherine of Aragon's leather. The biggest peacock fluttered its feathers in contempt at a mass of gold coins, clearly a symbol for Jeckyll's—and Whistler's own —patron.

When Jeckyll saw what had happened to his creation he ran from the room screaming. It may sound like fiction, but in sober truth he died shortly afterward in an insane asylum. When Leyland hurried home he was presented by Whistler with a bill for 2,000 guineas. He survived long enough to battle with the artist in the courts, but upon his death Freer slipped into London, purchased the room, and arranged for it to be shipped intact to Detroit.

After this coup, Freer achieved the reputation of being as coolly inconsiderate of everything and everybody as Whistler. He was likely to suddenly withdraw art works from an exhibition if anything displeased him.

When Alumni Memorial Hall of the University of Michigan was completed, Freer agreed to show some Oriental pieces. The building's heating system was working improperly, and the gallery became extremely warm. When an aide reported that several Japanese paintings on wood were in danger of cracking from the heat, Freer seized folding chairs and heaved them upward until the skylight was demolished, to let in cold air.

Freer's one fling at civic betterment came when Detroit planned its 1901 bicentennial. Perhaps because a design by Stanford White was chosen, he backed Mayor William C. Maybury's project for a colonnade on Belle Isle. When sufficient funds were not forthcoming, Freer accused his fellow citizens of withholding donations just to spite him.

Apparently this experience rankled. At any rate, Freer stunned his home city by announcing that he would bequeath his art collection to the Smithsonian Institution for permanent display in Washington.

If Detroit was unhappy about this decision, so was the Smithsonian. Its traditional purview was strictly scientific. The regents took their time about selecting a committee to inspect the collection. A senator headed the committee, and he seemed determined to give Freer a hard time. The prospective donor was grilled as if his princely offer might be an Oriental plot.

Nor did Freer let the committee off easily. Each of the 2,250 art objects was brought out for contemplation one at a time. The senator fumed, but nothing could hurry Freer. The viewing lasted five days.

When the regents continued to drag their feet, long after the committee returned to Washington, Freer enlisted the aid of President Theodore Roosevelt, who brought him face to face with the regents at a White House luncheon. After the President discoursed knowingly and at length about Oriental art, somehow involving it with the peace of the world, the purview of the Smithsonian widened enough to accept Freer's bequest.

Roosevelt also gave imposing letters of introduction to Freer, and the Detroiter happily returned to the Far East for more art. In the quest he penetrated to even remoter regions by sedan chair, as usual nimbly avoiding torrents, brigands, and pursuing hordes of forgery peddlers.

His journeyings were not limited to Asia. In Cairo he picked up a papyrus roll in a bazaar because he was attracted by its beautiful calligraphy. On a trip across the Red Sea, he inspected the purchase and found a place where strips had been cemented together.

Freer concluded it was a fake. He was about to toss it to the waves when something — it seemed almost an inner force too powerful to deny — stayed his hand.

Afterward, Freer had reason to single out that strange moment as the most important in his life. The manuscript is known now as the Codex Washingtonianus. It provided much material new to scholars, and copies were prepared for the papal library and for the British Museum. Along with the Codex Vaticanus in Rome, Freer's find is cherished among the earliest known texts of the New Testament Gospels.

Before his death at 63 in 1919, Freer's collection numbered more than 9,000 items. With what could be taken for exquisite irony, he left to Detroit's museum a few prints by the minor Dutch engraver, Charles van Gravesende.

The rest went to the Smithsonian, along with $1,-000,000 to build a gallery to house the collection. In Freer's old home on Ferry Avenue, the leading art activity became the finger-painting of the Merrill-Palmer School children housed there.

Yet few Americans have such rich memorials as Charles L. Freer. In Japan travelers exclaim over the monument to him in the Koetsu temple in Kyoto. Framed by delicate trees, a rock of great natural beauty bears an inscription attesting to his contribution to the understanding of Japanese art in the Western world. And in Washington, the Italian Renaissance palace of the Freer Gallery of Art has delighted generations of visitors — Peacock Room, Codex Washingtonianus, and all.

27. The Wayward Sister

The sister ships were charmers.

But somehow it seemed that their contrasting dispositions were what made the steamers Eastern States and Western States so different.

Their splendid appearance largely was responsible for making Detroit their home port in the first place. They were built for the Cleveland & Buffalo Transit Co, which planned to operate them between the two Lake Erie cities.

But early in 1902, while they were still on the ways at Wyandotte, the line ran into financial difficulties. It offered to sell them to the Detroit & Buffalo Steamboat Co. (D & B).

Detroit shipping magnates looked over the shiny new ships — and were hooked. They couldn't wait to close the deal.

Detroiters were delighted, too, when the Eastern States was ready to inaugurate the 1902 season.

The Detroit News marine writer pointed out that the liner was "on a much larger scale and the scheme of decorations is more carefully planned and more artistically carried out than anything of the kind heretofore attempted on lake steamers."

Stepping from the gangway to the ship's social hall, designed in Empire style, passengers saw woodwork of select Mexican mahogany, with carvings in gilt and panels of dark green.

This was only the appetizer. Looking forward from the social hall was the grand stairway, also in mahogany:

The Western States—a reputation for the unusual and the unexpected

"The newel posts are encircled by magnificently carved gilt griffins, and the idea is carried out in the griffin wings on the balustrade leading up to the landing."

The landing was faced by an immense mirror covered with an open screen of carved wood. Five-foot candelabra stood on each side, surmounted by scrolls of cupids and flowers. The grand saloon was of dark mahogany and contrasting ivory, in the style of Louis XIV. An adjoining ladies' boudoir utilized lighter tints, with French windows and jardinieres holding lush ferns.

Detroit took the elegant pair of steamers to its heart. Without question, they were the finest the city ever had seen.

The Eastern States—a model passenger ship

Tycoons of the Detroit & Cleveland Navigation Co. (D & C) gave much thought to this competition. They, too, were hooked. They determined to have the alluring States sisters for their own — even if it meant buying out the D & B line.

As it turned out, they did buy out their rivals. It was a move they never regretted. But the Western States gave them some anxious moments.

As the years passed and the city became Detroit the Dynamic, larger steamers were built. In time the twins were the smallest of six side-wheelers the line kept in operation each season. But they remained proud ships.

The Eastern States always was a model of efficiency and propriety. She was everything a good Great Lakes passenger ship was supposed to be. *183*

But it soon became proverbial that anything could happen aboard the Western States. She achieved much notoriety two years after she was launched, when her upper deck was the scene of a crime that could have sent a man to the electric chair for piracy. As it was, Joseph Kirwin, 26-year-old oiler, went to federal prison on Dec. 3, 1904, for life.

Kirwin admitted entering a locked stateroom with a passkey and robbing a woman passenger. He blamed "a strange psychological influence" on the ship for his crime.

It happened in Lake Erie. The ship was off Rondeau Point, Ontario, about 16 miles from the Canadian shore and 29 miles from the American side.

"I went up to the top deck to smoke," Kirwin testified, "and suddenly took a notion to steal something because my wife and child were sick and starving. I had just received a letter from my wife reminding me that the rent was coming due.

"I opened up a stateroom door with a passkey and took some money and jewelry. A purse was lying on the washstand and I grabbed it. Then I snatched the rings off the fingers of the lady in the berth. I was out in two minutes. I had an opportunity to get away, but I stayed on the boat and finished up my work, and I got caught."

Summoned by the captain after the frightened passenger reported the robbery, detectives boarded the Western States when it reached Detroit and made the arrest. It was this timing which saved Kirwin from the electric chair.

If the ship had been headed the other way, to Buffalo, Kirwin would have faced trial in New York, a capital punishment state. Federal authorities demanded the death penalty only in states which used it themselves. So Kirwin received life in Michigan instead of death in New York. It added 39 years to his life. He died in prison in 1943.

A story in lighter vein about the Western States was given wide circulation. It concerned a passage when the ship encountered heavy going in Lake Erie. Big waves caused her to roll considerably.

A woman passenger was sitting alone on the top

deck, forward of the wheelhouse. After a bigger lurch than usual, she turned and shouted at the officer on watch.

"Just why don't you want me to sit here?" she demanded.

"Madam, I have no objection to that whatsoever," returned the puzzled officer. She retorted:

"If you don't object to my being here, why do you keep rocking this end of the boat?"

Pursers on the D & C ships were more apt to receive gifts from passengers than the captains. They were the ones who gave out stateroom keys. When there were more passengers on board than there were berths — which often happened — regular travelers found it useful to be on good terms with the purser.

It was the rule that pets were not allowed in staterooms. They had to travel in the cargo area. Only on the Western States, surely, could a purser have allowed himself to be sweet-talked by a lady passenger into taking her police dog into his quarters.

The lady explained that her pet was too timid to spend the night without human companionship.

At first, the police dog and the purser got along fairly well. Then the host spread a blanket on the floor for his guest's comfort and prepared to retire.

The dog wouldn't have it that way. He leaped on the bed. When the purser tried to reason with him, the dog snarled with such ferocity that the purser fled to the wind-swept deck in his nightshirt.

In the 1930's an innovation on the D & C liners — indoor practice putting greens — proved popular. But wouldn't you know that it would be on the Western States that a passenger broke into print with a complaint about having too much time for golf practice?

Late in the 1935 season, one of the soupiest fogs ever known on the lakes held 20 ships prisoner at the mouth of the Detroit River. They waited there for two days and three nights, their foghorns moaning mournfully. Naturally, the Western States was among them.

A Detroit News reporter went out in a small boat to interview the stranded passengers. His best quote that day came from Maurice Cohen, president of Detroit's Newburgh Steel Co.

The newsman found Cohen on the putting green, swinging dejectedly at his golf ball.

"I'm getting too good," he said. "Five hours of practice today. We all got up at seven this morning, figuring we'd get to Detroit. But here we are — say, where are we?"

Eventually, faster forms of transportation prevailed. The long, happy era of the Great Lakes passenger steamers came to an end.

In 1956 the Eastern States followed other ships of the line to the wreckers. But the genius of the Western States for being different stood her in good stead — for a time.

A Detroit syndicate was formed to buy her and she was renovated for use as a hotel, restaurant and bar. Her 216 staterooms were converted into 108 larger hotel rooms.

She set up shop at Tawas City as Michigan's only floating inn.

Rechristened the Overnighter, she was advertised as the state's largest resort inn, with the exception of the venerable Grand Hotel on Mackinac Island.

Great things were predicted. Instead, troubles multiplied. The bar never opened. Tawas City saloonkeepers blocked issuance of a liquor license for the "flotel." It was a strange twist of fate for a vessel that blithely survived the prohibition experiment without any noticeable diminution of merrymaking.

In 1959 she was sold for scrap. But the Western States achieved a more spectacular end than that.

As a workman was cutting a steel mast with an acetylene torch, part of it toppled into a fuel storage tank. Oil-soaked planks on the first deck burst into flame.

It was a last hurrah for the wayward old Western States. The blaze didn't burn itself out until dusk.

28. T.R. Rides the Tashmoo

It was a day to be remembered. Only once did an excursion boat leave its Detroit dock proudly flying the blue and gold ensign of the President of the United States. Only once did the 21 guns of a presidential salute boom out on the Detroit River.

Sept. 22, 1902, was such a day for proud Detroiters, and especially for the officers and crew of the Steamer Tashmoo, the vessel chosen to take President Theodore Roosevelt for a sightseeing cruise on the river. Roosevelt had been president for barely a year when he visited Detroit to address a national convention of the United Spanish War Veterans, but already he had made the presidency seem as exciting and new as the 20th century itself.

Crowds gathered at the Michigan Central Station at 6 a.m. Sunday, Sept. 21, two hours before the President arrived. When his special train came to a halt he was met by Gen. Russell A. Alger and Mayor William C. Maybury. The crowd cheered as Alger and Maybury led T.R. to a carriage drawn by four bay horses, the Detroit Police Department's finest. The President, a Detroit News reporter noted, displayed "his famous dentative smile."

Through flag-trimmed streets, the carriage circled past the City Hall, hung with bunting and an allegorical picture of Liberty, to the Washington Boulevard entrance of the Cadillac Hotel, adorned with an oil painting of the President framed in flags.

Later Sunday morning T.R. attended services at the Fort Street Presbyterian C h u r c h. Luncheon followed at Gen. Alger's n e a r b y mansion; this was the occasion when the President took the measurements of Alger's stuffed mountain lion, as related in an earlier chapter.

Theodore Roosevelt
Affectionately called T.R.

In the afternoon Mr. Roosevelt took another carriage ride, this time to see the sights of Detroit. More than 200,-000 were in the streets to greet him. Near the Lyceum Theater, where a woman e l b o w e d through the crowd with her little son, dressed in a soldier uniform, the carriage stopped so the lad could present a bouquet of red carnations.

There was even a brief pause—at the President's order — in front of Billy Dobson's saloon on Shelby Street. Dobson had placed out front a huge barrel chair bearing a sign: "Reserved for T.R." Billy stood in the doorway and doffed a silk hat as tall as the President's own. Grinning, Roosevelt doffed his hat to Billy, too.

On Belle Isle, 70,000 gathered to dine with the President at a huge barbecue. He was an hour late but the crowd forgave him when it was explained that he had stopped en route at St. Mary's Hospital to chat with Tom Doherty, a soldier wounded in Cuba.

The next morning Roosevelt had breakfast in the Hotel Cadillac's Flemish dining room with four Detroit veterans of the war with Spain whom he delightedly called "live wires." The four were Truman H. Newberry, Cyrus E. Lothrop, Strathearn Hendrie and Chase S. Osborn. As governor of Michigan in 1912, Osborn became a bulwark of Roosevelt's last political fling. Newberry was destined to receive from T.R. one of the most ticklish assignments ever thrust upon an American by his president.

Never was the Light Guard Armory decorated more elaborately than it was that morning for T.R. and his fellow veterans. Above the stage was a canopy of beech branches and leaves, surmounting a huge flag-draped oil portrait of the President. Beech branches hid the walls of the building. Flags and green sprigs adorned the sides of the galleries. From the center of the ceiling was suspended an American eagle made of evergreens, with tiny electric bulbs fringing the body and wings. On each side of the eagle was an immense cornucopia of wheat.

Gov. Aaron T. Bliss called the meeting to order, and the Metropolitan Band played "America" and "Hail to the Chief." Then T.R. took the lectern. It was Detroit's first opportunity to assess the new President on the platform, and the judgment of a News reporter was:

"He is not a graceful speaker, but he has a manner that is attractive and diction that is vigorous and direct."

Next on the day's program was the ride on the Tashmoo. Sidewalks adjacent to the foot of Griswold Street were roped off, and the precaution proved a wise one — crowds assembled there long before the armory session was over. The President's carriage arrived at 11:45 a.m. with Mr. Roosevelt and Mayor Maybury in the back seat. Facing them was the President's secretary, George B. Cortelyou.

As spectators applauded, the carriage swung around at the forward gangway and a parade of silk hats went on board. The presidential colors were hoisted over the wheelhouse, and moments later T.R. appeared at the window of the Tashmoo's grand parlor, over the gangway, waving to those on the dock.

As the steamer pulled out the President was escorted to the bridge, and the first gun of the presidential salute rang out. The Tashmoo lay offshore until the last gun was fired, then pushed jauntily upstream.

Sunlight speared down through fast-moving   *189*

Theodore Roosevelt (arrow) with city officials on Tashmoo's upper deck Sept. 22, 1902

clouds, and the sirens of vessels on the river, the whistles of factories on shore, and the tolling of church bells echoed across the river. T.R. was a perfect guest, grinning delightedly at everything.

Soon the Tashmoo turned downstream to give the President a look at the lower river. Off Fort Wayne, The News added its own first to the many recorded that day. Having obtained an exclusive statement from T.R., a reporter dispatched it by carrier pigeon to the paper. The statement appeared as a bulletin in the Home Edition:

"We are having a most enjoyable trip.

THEODORE ROOSEVELT."

For newspapermen, too, it was a day to be remembered. Only once did The News scoop the world with a presidential statement delivered from ship to shore by carrier pigeon.

On his part, the President particularly remembered one of the "live wires" with whom he break-fasted in Detroit. In his second term, he summoned Truman Newberry to Washington to fill a post he once occupied himself, that of assistant secretary of the Navy.

It was no sinecure. When T. R. decided to send America's Great White Fleet on a 14-month tour around the world, Navy Secretary Victor H. Metcalf blithely tossed the monumental task of working out the logistics for coaling and supplies to Newberry.

The assistant secretary had something his superior lacked — wartime experience at sea. In the Spanish-American War, Newberry served as a lieutenant on the gunboat Yosemite, in one of the war's picturesque naval exploits; encountering the enemy transport Lopez, the Yosemite set her afire and forced her ashore under the guns of Cuba's Morro Castle. Then it routed three Spanish gunboats which joined the fray.

The cruise of the Great White Fleet afforded a real challenge. Anxiety about the 14,000 men on 16 gleaming white battleships mounted when the fleet left its anchorage in Hampton Roads, off the Virginia coast, on Dec. 16, 1907.

Ostensibly, they only were going to the Pacific, and the President was criticized for ordering even that. Japan, fresh from an astonishingly quick victory at sea over Russia in their 1904 war, seemed to be spoiling for another fight. Wouldn't she regard our fleet movement as provocative?

England, with her superior knowledge of naval affairs, was certain of it. The London Daily News put it this way: "This American fleet could crumple up and disappear before the forces of a nation which never has thought it necessary to declare war before commencing hostilities."

Across the English Channel, the French were even more blunt. A Paris paper asked: "Is the fleet being watched by the Japanese from some dangerous ambush?"

The Panama Canal was not yet completed. Ambush or not, the fleet's long journey around South America was punctuated with headaches for Assistant Secretary Newberry. When he arranged for a coaling call at Rio de Janeiro, police there announced they had wind of a plot to blow up the entire fleet. Off Chile the presence of a Japanese steamer gave rise to more rumors.

Roosevelt, never given to backing down, announced on March 13, 1908, that the fleet would return home by way of the Suez Canal, thus completing a circumnavigation of the globe. Tokyo responded with typical oriental guile. A suave note invited the fleet to visit Japan en route. T.R. was taken aback, but he had to accept or lose face.

Despite everything Newberry could do, progress of the warships up the California coast was agonizingly slow. Metcalf, a Californian himself, kept ruining Newberry's schedule. He was easy prey for members of the Golden State's congressional delegation, and every representative was determined that the fleet must pay a visit to his district, or at least to the nearest port. The only area not lobbying actively seemed to be Death Valley.

At San Francisco, 60 special trains brought visitors to greet the ships. The Fleet Ball at the Fairmount Hotel lasted 48 hours. Rear Admiral Charles Sperry was as much concerned about his banquet-logged personnel as about what the Japanese were doing.

While the ships were taking on supplies Newberry arranged for them at Honolulu, a paragraph in dispatches mentioned a picnic organized by some officers on a pleasant strip of beach, well shaded by palm trees. The littoral's name would become familiar to later generations for another reason. It was Pearl Harbor.

Australia was reached Aug. 20. At Sydney, 250,000 Aussies cheered the fleet at dawn after waiting all night for the landfall. The celebration lasted eight days. Melbourne was even more hospitable, and the sailors had such a good time that 221 failed to get back to the ships at sailing time.

On Oct. 18 the battleships sailed into Yokohama Bay, expecting anything. Admiral Sperry limited shore leave to the men who had not received black marks at previous welcomes. Back home, America held its breath. What did the inscrutable Japanese have concealed up their kimono sleeves?

A 1905 cartoon of Truman H. Newberry, U.S. Navy assistant secretary, and planner of world cruise by America's fleet

It turned out they secretly had taught 10,000 schoolchildren to sing "Hail Columbia" in English as a greeting for the guests. Their elders, 50,000 strong, paraded by torchlight along the shore.

Marquis Taro Katsura, the premier, was host at a formal ball. Fiery Admiral Heihahiro Togo, who annihilated the Russian fleet in 1904, was all smiles at a garden party he gave for Sperry's officers. The captains were lodged in suites at the Imperial Hotel; the admirals were guests in the Mikado's palace. Tokyo, it seemed, was one big love feast.

It remained for a U.S. marine to add the crowning touch. Throughout the city, bamboo arches covered with bunting honored the Americans. On the night of Oct. 23, one of the arches caught fire, and a large crowd saw the flames reach toward a Japanese flag on top.

Then out of the crowd ran the marine. Nimbly he vaulted past the flames and snatched away the flag. The onlookers cheered, raised him on high, and carried him throughout town waving the rescued Rising Sun.

When the vessels sailed Oct. 24, to cries of "Banzai" and "Sayonara," Japanese-American friendship was at a new high. But the long strain proved too much for Secretary Metcalf. He resigned, and it was left for Newberry, promoted to secretary, to superintend the fleet's return home.

Everything went smoothly. On Feb. 23, 1909, the Great White Fleet proudly appeared off Hampton Roads. America heaved a sigh of relief — Secretary Newberry, no doubt, most of all.

Newberry came back to the Navy as a lieutenant commander for active service in World War I. Later he defeated Henry Ford for U.S. senator, in an election that resulted in a long controversy over funds spent in Newberry's behalf. When he died in 1945, at 80, he was the last survivor of the Roosevelt Cabinet.

29. The Man
Who Lived on Speed

"Who do you think you are — Barney Oldfield?"

In the early days of the automobile, that was the standard approach by traffic cops who stopped motorists for speeding. Backseat drivers also favored it, and no one needed to ask who Barney Oldfield was.

Barney was termed "the greatest race driver of all time" and "the most picturesque figure the speed game has produced." When the names of the first 10 immortals elected to Automotive Racing's Hall of Fame were announced in Detroit in 1953, Henry Ford came in second. First place went to Barney Oldfield.

The two men were linked at the beginning of their fame, too. Barney was 24 years old, a professional bicycle rider who had tried motorcycle competition, when in 1902 Henry Ford teamed with Tom Cooper, another bike racer, to build a racing automobile. They called it the 999. It was so fast neither Ford nor Cooper would risk driving the car in a race. Cooper suggested to Ford that the best man to put at the wheel would be his friend Oldfield, who "lived on speed," and Ford agreed.

Oldfield told what happened next in an autobiographical sketch he put together for The Detroit News, a few months before his death in 1946. Cooper's letter reached him in Salt Lake City, where he was racing a bicycle and motorcycle tandem on the board track at the Salt Palace.

"I drew out my savings from the Wells Fargo   *195*

Bank, $650 in gold, and went to Detroit, riding the cushions to save Pullman fare," Oldfield recalled. "Tom Cooper met me at the depot, escorted me to Ford's shop on Bagley, and introduced me to Henry Ford."

Oldfield then was shown the 999—and learned for the first time that he was expected to drive it.

"But I've never driven a car," he protested.

"It's easy," Ford said. "We'll teach you."

On the morning of the race, Ford demonstrated how the controls worked. Years later, Ford described Oldfield's adventure that day:

"He never looked around. He never shut off on the curves, simply let the car go. He was about half a mile ahead of the second car at the end of the race."

Ford's memory was good. His description tallied with the report in The Detroit News-Tribune for Sunday, Oct. 26, 1902:

"Hatless, his long tawny hair flying out behind him with the speed of his mount, Barney Oldfield, the old bicycle star, gave the crowd at the automobile races yesterday one of the greatest exhibitions of reckless, daredevil driving that has been seen on the circuit this year.

"The ex-bike rider was in his glory. He had the speed of the party in the big Challenge Cup race, but he meant to make his win as impressive as possible.

"With never a slowdown he charged the turns, slewing frequently the entire width of his machine and seeming a dozen times on the verge of a capsize.

"The machine never faltered, however. It tore down the straights like a fiend incarnate, spitting fire with explosions that could be heard clear across the track, increasing to deafening force when the machine passed the grandstand."

The race was five miles, around a one-mile circular track in Grosse Pointe. Competition was stiff. The favorite was the world's champion, Alexander Winton of Cleveland, who was driving a car he had built himself, Winton's Bullet.

That morning before the race Winton's Bullet was regarded as the fastest thing on wheels. Other en-

Barney Oldfield in the 999, the first car he ever drove, and Henry Ford who built it in 1902

tries were called the Pup and the Steamboat on Wheels.

Winton dropped out on the last lap. He was a half a mile behind the 999, and his engine was in trouble. At the finish, Oldfield had lapped the Steamboat on Wheels and he was close to a lap ahead of the Pup, which finished second.

It was an impressive debut, but Oldfield did not surpass the record previously established by Winton. On Dec. 1, he rectified this oversight. The last edition of The Detroit News that day reported:

"Barney Oldfield this morning became the champion automobilist of the world, establishing new records for the one and five miles on a circular track. The first mile was the fastest in both runs, as the cold air affected the carburetors. Between the heats big torches were held against the carburetors, but the cold air would chill them in a mile. Oldfield had no trouble controlling the 999 and seemed to enjoy the terrific risks he was taking."

Barney's new record for the mile was 1.2 minutes. It bothered him that he had not broken the one-minute mile, but that was soon remedied. A few days later he covered a measured mile on West Grand Boulevard in 52.8 seconds. It was unofficial but Barney was happy. He broke the minute mile for the record books the following June on the Indianapolis Speedway.

In his own breezy style, Oldfield's autobiographical sketch catches the swift pace of events following his introduction to auto racing in Detroit:

"These two performances of mine brought world fame to the designer and builder of 999, and also fame for me the kid driver. So much fame that Alfred Reeves (an early racing promoter) offered me 25 percent of gross receipts to ride a match race against Charles Wridgeway on New York's Empire City track May 30, 1903, where I defeated Wridgeway, and in an exhibition ride I drove one mile in one minute flat.

"Indianapolis, June 15, 1903, first time an auto beat one minute flat. I drove it in 59 2/5 seconds . . . Columbus, Ohio, July 4, 1903, lowered record to 56 3/5 seconds . . . The last record I made with 999 was on Empire City track, July 15, 1903, when I drove one mile in 55 4/5 seconds.

"Shortly afterward I went to work for the Winton Motor Carriage Co., driving the famous Bullet racing cars, now in Smithsonian. Henry Ford overhauled 999 and matched it against me with Tom Cooper driving.

"The eight-cylinder Bullet was laid up in Cleveland with a broken axle, so I was forced to use the Baby Bullet, 1,800-pound class. I defeated Cooper and did not have to average 60 miles per hour — so what?

"I took the two Bullets to California in November, 1903, stopping en route at Denver and establishing 5, 10 and 15-mile circular dirt track records.

"I quit the Winton Bullet in August, 1903, and went with Peerless Motor Car Co., driving the Peerless Green Dragon, with which I immediately lowered the track record to 53 4/5 seconds.

"In 1904 Alexander Winton resurrected the eight-cylinder Bullet and matched Earl Kiser against me — best two of three heats, 5 and 10 miles. I defeated him easily and in the 10-mile heat I nearly lapped the Bullet."

Oldfield and his rivals drove on flat dirt tracks, and their cars lacked safety devices that later were taken as essential. Brick tracks, banked turns and retaining walls all came later.

Not always did Oldfield leave the track unscathed. His car crashed through innumerable fences, and many times he appeared headed for the morgue. In later years his many body scars led him to call himself "the tattooed wonder."

In 1906, in a race at Hartford, Conn., he was leading the field when a tire blew off. The rear of the car leaped up seven or eight feet. Oldfield was pinned against the wheel as the car bounced down the track like a giant grasshopper. It crashed into a fence and more of Barney's bones were broken.

His most serious accident came on Sept. 9, 1913, at Corona, Calif. The car overturned while rounding a curve and Barney's mechanic, Frank Sandhoffer, was fatally injured. But Oldfield's luck held and he escaped with a few more colorful specimens added to his scar collection.

As a prophet he ran out of the money. He predicted in 1903 that no one would ever drive much faster than 60 miles an hour, "because at that speed the air is sucked right out of your lungs." By 1910, however, a 200-horsepower Blitzen Benz at Daytona Beach, Fla., set a world record of 131.72 m.p.h. The driver was Barney Oldfield.

In later years, Ford liked to say that he made Oldfield and Oldfield made him. When he mentioned this at a reunion of automotive pioneers, Barney's reply was:

"Yes, Henry — but I must have done a hell of a sight better job than you did."

It was seldom remembered that his real name was Berner Eli Oldfield. Nothing much else about his colorful career was forgotten, however, and the anecdotes long outlived Barney himself.

There was the time in a Los Angeles race when his crew wasn't functioning as he liked.

"What the hell's the matter with the pit work?" he demanded of the pit boss on one of his stops.

"They just haven't any espirit de corps," mourned the manager.

"Well, go and get some!" yelled the outraged Barney.

After his first fame as "king of the roaring road," Oldfield visited Omaha on business. An old friend was promoting a bicycle race and told Barney the tickets weren't selling. Would Oldfield compete?

Barney hadn't been on a bike in five years, but he agreed to help out. He found that an innovation had developed among bike riders; each used a gimmick to insure endurance during the race. One tied a lemon around his throat. One covered his chest with onions. Another carried a bag of salt.

Barney liked the idea. He procured a long-necked bottle and had it filled with brandy, then hung it from his neck. Before the start a local sports writer inquired about the contents.

"Vinegar," said Barney.

He won the race, and the Omaha paper headlined the story:

Barney Oldfield

trains on vinegar,

wins bike classic

A year or so later Barney was back in Omaha and went out to watch the races. He found every rider had a bottle dangling from his neck — filled with vinegar.

The best line in his obituary was Henry Ford's remembrance of Barney's remark as Ford cranked old 999 for that classic race:

"Well, this chariot may kill me, but they'll say afterward I was going like hell when she took me over the bank."

30. Cheers for Miss Emily

It took five days to complete Detroit's longest — and most unusual — Memorial Day observance.

That was in 1905, when the body of Stevens T. Mason, Michigan's first state governor, was returned with elaborate honors to the city where he won youthful glory after it had reposed in a New York City cemetery for more than six decades.

The events began on Memorial Day, a Wednesday. Graying Civil War veterans in the uniforms of the Grand Army of the Republic competed for attention in the day's big parade with the men they called "the youngsters" — the veterans of the Spanish-American War.

Even before the marching was over, spectators hurried from vantage points along the parade route to Capitol Park. They were curious about preparations there for the reburial of the "boy governor."

Detroiters were in an expansive mood in 1905. The project to pay belated tribute to Gov. Mason struck the popular fancy. In the White House, America's youngest president, Theodore Roosevelt, provided the youthful, progressive leadership which appealed to to the residents of the City of the Straits.

They felt their community was at the forefront of everything new. It was good to remember with

Emily Mason when she was a belle of old Detroit, *Michigan Pioneer and Historical Museum, Lansing*

pride a Detroit hero who had been the personification of farsighted young vigor in the days when Michigan's history as a state began.

Plans proliferated until it was decided that four days would be needed to do full justice to Mason's memory. On Thursday, the First Michigan Regiment gave a dress rehearsal of the slow march with which it would escort the casket in procession. In Lansing, Gov. Fred M. Warner announced he would attend and bring his full staff.

On Friday, Mayor George P. Codd issued a proclamation about it all and on Saturday crowds watched a vault being lowered into place in Capitol Park. Cradled in stones which had been preserved from the Old Capitol when it was destroyed by fire in 1893, the vault would — hopefully — provide a last resting place for Mason's casket.

The climax came Sunday. Detroit turned out to pay tribute to Mason "with military pomp, eulogistic oratory, and the silent reverence of a vast crowd," as The Detroit News described it.

When the morning train from the east arrived at the Michigan Central Depot on Third Street with the casket, bands played, militia stood at attention — and a slim little lady, 91 years old, with a soft Virginia voice and a pleasant smile, stepped from the train and stole the show.

This was Emily Mason, sister of Gov. Mason. Shaking hands briskly with the governor and the mayor, she was a living link to Michigan's frontier days.

Miss Emily was 16 and her brother was 19 when they accompanied their father, John T. Mason, to Detroit after President Andrew Jackson appointed him secretary of Michigan Territory in 1830. Soon Miss Emily became a reigning belle of old Detroit. The territory was still mostly wilderness and the town scarcely more than a fringe of settlement along the riverfront, but already it had considerable wealth from the fur trade and traditions of social elegance.

Stevens T. Mason

In 1905, a reporter asked Miss Emily about a passage in Gen. Friend Palmer's volume of historical reminiscences, "Early Detroit," which credited Maj. Lewis Cass, son of Gen. Lewis Cass, with being deeply in love with her.

"Lewis never was a beau of mine," she said. "He was a dear friend up to the last hour of his life. From his boyhood we were great sympathizers and lovers of books, and when we met in Paris the old friendship was renewed."

Miss Emily remembered and confirmed another Friend Palmer vignette. It told of the courtly gesture of a Detroit physician, Dr. Rufus Brown, who spread a handkerchief on the mud of Jefferson Avenue for her to walk upon.

Ensconced in a carriage with other Mason relatives, she was escorted by Gov. Warner, Mayor Codd and the First Infantry to the Light Guard Armory. The practiced slow-step was executed to perfection, as the gun carriage carrying the casket rumbled on the cobblestones.

At the armory the casket was mounted on a dais, with the militia as honor guard. The governor and the mayor took Miss Emily to the Russell House for breakfast.

In the afternoon she listened attentively to eulogies of her brother before an audience that crowded the armory to the rafters. The speakers included Gov. Warner and Dr. D. M. Cooper, dean of the city's clergymen.

Dr. Cooper told the story of how, after a few months in Detroit, John T. Mason became interested in a Mexican land deal. He returned to Washington to resign the post in Michigan, and as his successor he recommended his son to President Jackson.

The youth's good looks, suavity and talent for conversation charmed Old Hickory. Even though Stevens was only 19, he was given the appointment.

The news of the president's action traveled to Detroit ahead of young Mason. A deputation of citizens who felt the territory was being slighted by the appointment of a minor to a position of such responsibility waited for his boat, with the announced intention of preventing him from landing.

But the young man handled himself well, disarming the deputation with a good-natured speech. They agreed to "give the boy a trial."

He hardly was settled in the duties of the secretaryship when George B. Porter, who succeeded Gen. Cass as territorial governor, died unexpectedly.

The statue of Stevens T. Mason isn't wearing a tricorn—instead, it's a pigeon looking at Capitol Park in downtown Detroit

Michigan now had an acting governor who was not old enough to vote.

But Mason quickly showed his mettle. When Ohio laid claim to a strip of territory which was also claimed by Michigan, he called out the militia and marched them to the scene.

This maneuver became known to history as the "Toledo War." While a confrontation of the two states' forces did develop, the war fortunately remained bloodless. It was agreed the matter was one suitable for adjudication in the courts.

Michigan felt it had the best legal position, but politically the affair threatened to cost President Jackson votes in populous Ohio. With a glint in his eye, he dubbed Mason "Young Hotspur" — and removed him from office.

Mason's stand as acting governor made him a popular hero in Michigan, however. He was elected territorial governor in 1835, and when Michigan became a state two years later he was swept into office as the first state governor.

He was still a bachelor, and so his devoted sister did the honors at his side at the ball in the governor's mansion that celebrated statehood.

The 1905 audience cheered the recountal of this history, and Miss Emily, on the platform, bowed graciously. But there was more to the Mason story.

Borrowing needed funds for the new state, Mason injudiciously let Michigan in for a high rate of interest. When a period of financial stringency ensued, the new state was in a predicament.

Whig opponents made the most of it. Mason was saved from impeachment only by announcing he would not run for another term.

The remainder of his short life was anti-climax. Shortly after he left Michigan and took up the practice of law in New York City, he contracted pneumonia. He died at 31, in 1842.

In the Light Guard Armory, as the story ended, the band played a hymn, "Come Ye Disconsolate Where'er Ye Languish." Six officers carried out the casket as the line of soldiers outside grounded arms.

Gov. Warner and Mayor Codd, with the governor's staff in full regalia, led the procession from the armory on foot. The First Regiment was followed by the Michigan State Naval Brigade and war veterans. Then came Miss Emily in her flag-draped carriage.

At Capitol Park, the band played "Michigan, My Michigan." Rifles of an honor guard fired a triple salute. As the casket was slowly lowered, a bugler sounded taps.

Miss Emily had brought the boy governor home in style, and Detroit was proud of them.

"I'll come back again," she promised before she left.

And she did. Three years later she returned for another Memorial Day ceremony. This time it was the unveiling of her brother's monument in Capitol Park.

For a while that day a steady rain threatened to make a postponement necessary. But by the time the invited guests filled the stand the downpour was over. The clouds broke and sunshine flooded the park and its flag-draped statue.

Gov. Warner was there, as were President James B. Angell, of the University of Michigan, and generals in dress uniform. But all eyes were on the guest of honor.

Garbed in black and leaning on the arm of Sen. Thomas W. Palmer, Miss Emily mounted the platform steps with a firmness which belied her years. She produced a black-rimmed lorgnette with which to watch the proceedings.

After preliminary speeches, Miss Emily grasped the cord which held the folds of the draped flag and gave it a gentle pull. The flag was soaked with rain and clung to the bronze figure until a soldier moved in to aid in loosening it.

Miss Emily dabbed a handkerchief at her eyes, and exclaimed in gratification at the verisimilitude of her brother's statue.

More speeches followed, but the crowd saved its heartiest applause for the end. That was when the band played "Dixie" in Miss Emily's honor.

Once again she was the toast of the town.

31. Genies of G.M.

Why is having a barber use clippers on your hair like riding in a Cadillac or a Lincoln?

The answer is simple.

The clippers and the automobiles that compete in America's top quality class were the creations of the same man — Henry M. Leland.

Leland stands virtually alone among motor pioneers in that he was too modest ever to name a car after himself. But he ranks among the giants of the automotive dawn age.

He wasn't shy about publicity for his motor cars. Leland contrived a famous stunt that first gave Europe an insight into American mastery of automatic machinery.

The date was 1906. Prejudice against American cars was strong abroad.

It developed from a practice of "dumping" inferior bicycles on the European market. Poorly-made American cars sold abroad added to the bad impression.

Leland found a way to change that.

Three Cadillacs were shipped to England to compete for the Dewar Challenge Cup, the era's outstanding motor trophy. At dockside they were taken apart, while Royal Automobile Club officials watched.

The dismembered parts of the three cars were taken to the Broadlands race track and jumbled in a big heap in an open shed. It rained that night, and the shed's roof leaked. When the hour for Leland's "standardization demonstration" arrived the next morning, the parts were soaking wet.

Nevertheless, three Cadillac mechanics reassembled the cars, using only wrench, hammer, screwdriver and pliers.

Then the cars were put through a 500-mile test. Officials gave perfect scores to all three. America won the Dewar Cup.

Perhaps Leland's greatest accomplishment, however, came in 1910, when he determined to make the motor car practicable for women drivers — and brought to Detroit the philosophic genius who could do it.

It happened after five employes at the Cadillac plant suffered broken arms in one month from what Leland called the "unruly, turbulent, vicious starting crank." Before the month was over, Leland further was shaken by what happened to a close friend, Byron T. Carter, manufacturer of the Carter Car.

Carter stopped on the Belle Isle Bridge to aid a woman driver whose car's engine was stalled. The few women who were brave enough to drive in this period depended upon the gallantry of any handy man to perform the task of cranking the engine, when needed — which was all too often.

Unfortunately, the spark was not retarded. The engine kicked back and the flying crank broke Carter's jaw. Complications arising out of the injury caused his death.

"We had to discover a young and generally unknown genius living in Dayton, Ohio, named Charles F. Kettering," was the way Leland told the story.

Kettering liked to call himself a "monkey wrench scientist." According to his own description, he was a rawboned, 6-foot-3-inch country boy of 29 in 1905, when he married Olive Williams, a music teacher.

He caused adverse talk among neighbors by using his bride's savings to finance a period in which he seemed to spend his time in the haymow of his barn, tinkering on "inventions."

As it turned out, American women soon had occasion to be grateful to Kettering. When his self-

Charles F. Kettering

starter freed motorists from the drudgery of the crank, women drivers blossomed all over the land.

Brought to Detroit, Kettering worked out the device with Cadillac engineers. Leland was delighted.

"It worked," he said, "as smoothly and as positively as the falling of water in a perpendicularly arranged penstock would start a waterwheel."

The new equipment first was installed in cars on Feb. 27,1911. It proved to be the sensation of the industry.

Leland's introduction of standardized components for autos stemmed from his training as a teen-ager in the gun factories of New England. There Eli Whitney, inventor of the cotton gin, introduced interchangeable gun parts.

Henry M. Leland

During the Civil War, Leland helped to make weapons at the Colt revolver plant. He invented the hair clippers while working for a firm in Providence, R.I.

He turned over the manufacturing rights to his employers. Soon the company was making $1,000 a day from his device. Leland was given a raise — of 50 cents a day.

It was his anger at this unfairness that led to his coming to Detroit in 1890. With several partners, he started a machine tool plant, making grinders and cutters. By 1896, he was head of a foundry that machined castings, and his first automotive products were transmission gears for Ransom E. Olds' curved-dash runabout.

Leland's career touched that of Henry Ford after

the organization of the Detroit Automobile Co. in 1899, with Ford as head of its mechanical department. Ford concentrated on racing cars, and the company bought for its production models an engine made by Leland to show what close tolerances could be built into gasoline motors.

In 1902, Leland obtained backing to build his own plant at Cass and Amsterdam. Here he produced a car that embodied his advanced production ideas.

Leland selected the car's name, Cadillac, to honor the founder of Detroit. The emblem seen on the car today was the coat of a r m s of Antoine Laumet de la Mothe Cadillac.

Leland's car was a "one-lunger," but it proved more dependable than most of the multicylindered cars on the market. By 1904, more than 16,000 had been sold.

General Motors took over Cadillac in 1909 for $4.5 million. Leland and his son, Wilfred C., who was the financial genius of his father's enterprises, remained with Cadillac until 1917. In that year they withdrew to form another company of their own.

The name chosen this time, Lincoln Motor Co., reflected a lifelong admiration. The elder Leland cast his first vote for Abraham Lincoln in 1864. Beginning about 1915—well before Henry Ford emerged as a collector of Americana—the Lelands were combing the nation for Lincoln memorabilia.

Among their prizes were the chair used by Lincoln in the White House, and the Cooper Union ambrotype of Lincoln. Of them all, Leland's favorite was the arithmetic book used by 15-year-old Abe Lincoln in 1824, with a quatrain on the flyleaf in his boyish script:

"Abraham Lincoln is my name

And with my pen I wrote the same;

I wrote it in both haste and speed

And left it here for fools to read."

Ford bought the Lincoln firm in 1922 for $8 million. Thereafter, Leland devoted much of his time to civic affairs. He was the founder and first president of the Detroit Citizens League.

Henry M. Leland, an automotive pioneer, is shown at the wheel of an early Cadillac accompanied by his son, Wilfred C. (right), and his grandson, Wilfred Jr. In 1902, Leland built his first plant in Detroit which became the Cadillac Motor Car Co. He remained as its head until 1917 when he and his son resigned to form the Lincoln Motor Co.

To the end of his life at 89 in 1933, he liked to recount a favorite story about a salesman who got the ear of his purchasing agent with an item desired by the company. When the matter was brought to Leland for final decision, he raised an objection. The price was too low, he said.

"You can't afford to sell this for so little," he argued. "You can't possibly make a profit."

"We know that," replied the salesman. "But once you adopt this item, every car manufacturer will want it. That's how highly they regard your judgment."

Leland wrote a figure well above the quoted rate into the contract.

"We'll buy at a fair price or not at all," he said.   *213*

As for Kettering, he remained true to his home-spun traditions even when as an apostle of what he called "intelligent ignorance" he was classed as one of the world's 10 most interesting men.

His story about the bumblebee became a classic:

"The bumblebee is unable to fly, according to the theory of aerodynamics. This is because the size, weight and shape of the bumblebee's body in relation to the total wingspread makes flying impossible.

"But the bumblebee is ignorant of such profundities of science. He goes ahead and flies anyway."

Most of the 176 inventions Kettering patented before retiring at 71 in 1947 were sponsored by GM, whose research operations were concentrated under him in Detroit beginning in 1925. He never permitted "retirement" to stick, continuing to regularly turn out new inventions for the last 11 years of his life.

"Retirement only means I won't have to answer any more mail," he said. "We are still reading the first verse of the first chapter of a book whose pages are infinite."

32. A Short Life
But a Merry One

"It was a short life but a merry one," Detroiters declared in 1919, when the Pontchartrain Hotel was torn down. The most famous hotel in young Detroit's history lasted less than 13 years.

They were very special years. They saw Detroit push to leadership in the exciting automobile "game." The Pontchartrain was the cradle in which the game grew into an industry, with the City of the Straits putting the world on wheels.

Throughout its existence, the Pontchartrain was the meeting place of the men who made motordom hum — geniuses and crackpots, go-getters and salesmen, magnates and financiers.

The building went up in 1907, on the southeast corner of Woodward and Cadillac Square. From the start it was the talk of the town.

For generations, the corner was the city's best hotel site. The National Hotel was built there in 1836, during the land boom which carried Michigan to statehood. After undergoing many changes, it became the Russell House in 1857.

The Russell House flourished for half a century. It was the most cosmopolitan place in Michigan. The Prince of Wales — later King Edward VII — was entertained there. The red carpet also went out for the Grand Duke Alexis of Russia.

Detroiters hated to see the Russell House go, but the eye-filling structure that replaced it soon made them forget. The Pontchartrain was 10 stories high at first, with four more floors added later.

In September, 1907, with the hotel nearing completion, Detroiters flocked to the big Newcomb-Endicott department store to gape at the display of elaborate furnishings being prepared for the Pontchartrain. Satin damask-covered furniture, lace curtains from Ireland, oriental rugs — it was fit for a palace, agreed visitors.

Lew Dockstader, prince of American minstrels, and his troupe of 70 opened at the Lyceum that week. After Dockstader viewed the exhibit he said that he would never stay in another Detroit hotel once the Pontchartrain was finished.

At the grand opening in October, old-timers were pleased with a link to the past. The manager, William J. Chittenden Jr., was the son of the chief clerk at the old Russell House. They presented Chittenden with an oil portrait of Count Pontchartrain, for whom the new hotel was named.

The count was the French minister of marine affairs who sent Antoine de la Mothe Cadillac on a mission up the Great Lakes to found an outpost for France in the western wilderness. The outpost, which would later become Detroit, first was called Fort Pontchartrain.

The count's portrait looked down on a busy setting. Anything could happen there, and doubtless the French minister would have approved when a Frenchman walked in one day, set out equipment in the bar, and demonstrated an invention that he thought the motor men would buy.

They did buy it — with alacrity. The newcomer was Albert Champion, and his invention was the porcelain which solved the auto industry's spark-plug problem.

The hotel bar witnessed many demonstrations. Carburetors, magnetos, tire vulcanizers, brakes, rims, valves — there was something new most every day.

It wasn't a sign that you had imbibed one too many if you saw four or five men trundle a heavy piece of machinery into the bar, put it on a table and start its wheels and cogs in motion. Not in the Pontchartrain.

What may well have been the hotel's finest hours came in July, 1909, when Detroit was the starting

The Dodge Brothers, John F. and Horace E.

point for the Glidden Tour, the most celebrated road circus ever.

Detroiters were delighted when high tribute was paid to their city at the pretour banquet in the Pontchartrain's Flamingo Room. Charles J. Glidden, the millionaire who put up the trophy in the annual automobile reliability test, said that Detroit had outdone all previous host cities.

Streaming past the flag-decorated Pontchartrain the next day came what The Detroit News described as "the longest caravan of chugging automobiles ever gathered together in the history of the great 20th century industry, of which Detroit is the hub."

The cavalcade honored the pick of motordom — *217*

30 cars nominated to participate in the Glidden Tour over a 2,636-mile route, through Chicago and Minneapolis to Denver, and looping back to finish in Kansas City. In between were "some of the world's worst roads."

The competing cars were housed in a circus tent erected in Cadillac Square opposite the Pontchartrain. Throughout a tumultuous weekend, citizens marveled at them and their extra tires, jacks, repair kits and spare parts.

Almost to a man, visitors moved on to the Pontchartrain lobby, to rub elbows with the greats of the automotive world.

Henry Ford was there, so were the Lelands, father and son, and the Dodge Brothers, John F. and Horace E.

The Dodges almost were daily visitors at the Pontchartrain. Often they lingered in the bar with their crony and politicaly ally, Mayor Oscar B. Marx. More than any others, the Dodges epitomized the whirlwind, rough-and-ready, dynamic Pontchartrain era.

They were more than brothers. They were inseparable companions.

On the rare occasion when one of them appeared at the Pontchartrain without the other, he was bound to sprinkle his conversation with a favorite phrase: "My brother and I . . ."

When one bought a new suit, he purchased another for his brother. When they entered the Pontchartrain together, the one who reached the door first held it open for the other. Every day, in many ways, they gave evidence of their brotherly empathy.

Some thought they must be twins, but John was four years older than Horace. Born in Niles, Mich., in the 1860's, they learned the machinist trade in their father's shop. Like the pioneering aeronautical brothers, Wilbur and Orville Wright, they went into the bicycle business together.

The Dodges soon advanced into the infant auto industry, manufacturing transmissions for Ransom E. Olds in their shop at Hastings and Monroe. One day Henry Ford offered a one-tenth interest in the Ford Motor Co. on condition they would equip their plant to make Ford engines.

Old Pontchartrain Hotel, Woodward and Cadillac Square, in the early 1900's

The Dodges were drawn to Ford. They discontinued work for Oldsmobile, already a going concern, to string along with Ford — whose company still was on paper.

They prospered together — tremendously.

But in 1914 the Dodges rebelled against Ford's policy of turning back all profits into vast expansion. They sued to compel Ford to distribute profits as dividends, and won.

The Dodges received $25 million in 1919 when Ford bought out his stockholders that year. They competed with Ford with the Dodge Brothers car, built in their own plant in Hamtramck.

Ironically, the boom brought to Detroit by Ford, the Dodge brothers, and the other automotive pioneers doomed the Pontchartrain. Newer hotels went up, with more rooms in less space. Soon the marvel of 1907 became obsolete. Big as it was, the Pontchartrain had fewer than 400 rooms and only 200 baths.

The big wheels put up the Detroit Athletic Club as their gathering place, too, and deserted the "Pontch."

The end came on a Saturday afternoon, Jan. 31, 1920. A chain went up across the restaurant door. Guests, lingering in the Flamingo Room, were asked to leave.

Lew Dockstader, who had kept his promise of 1907 and never stayed anywhere but the Pontch, was the last guest to pay his bill at the cashier's cage. He put on an impromptu comedy skit about being overcharged while Ann Breck, the cashier, sadly made out the last receipt for him.

Charley Finucan, the house detective, made sure the Palm Room and the lobby were empty. Then he joined Frank Harrinan, the last manager, at the Woodward entrance. They waited until Harry Cramer, assistant manager, brought a key which had been in the hotel's safe since the place opened. The key had never been used, but it fitted the front door.

The Dodge Brothers went to New York that same January for the automobile show. While there Horace was striken with pneumonia.

John dropped everything to remain at Horace's bedside. He stayed there until Horace passed the crisis, then submitted to an examination which showed that he too had contracted pneumonia. He went to bed in the room next to Horace's and died there Jan. 14.

Horace recovered, but life was not the same for him without his brother. He died before the year was out.

The Dodge Brothers car lived on to become part of the automotive empire assembled by Walter P. Chrysler.

33. Curtain Call for the Handcuff King

Was the Garrick Theater ill-starred from the beginning?

Many old-timers of the theatrical world thought so. Some said as much on the night it opened, Sept. 6, 1909.

Detroiters' interest in the playhouse was intrigued by promises of a new era in luxury and comfortable seating. But a few hours before the first-night curtain, the management faced a dire possibility.

Comfortable or not, the seats had not been delivered on schedule. The Garrick might begin its career with standing room only — for the entire audience.

In the best tradition of melodrama, however, vans with the seats arrived in time. The last row was installed moments before the first patrons were admitted. The Garrick opened as "a very comfortable little playhouse, handsomely decorated in green, pale yellow and gold."

Actually, the Garrick wasn't entirely new. If ever a theater found its ghosts ready-made, it was this one.

The building, on Griswold north of Michigan, had housed the Whitney Grand Opera House for 30 years. Melodrama had been its lifeblood — the kind where virtue was sore beset, but always managed to emerge triumphant at the final curtain.

Youthful Detroiters of the 1880's and 1890's paid their dimes to climb to the Whitney's "peanut gallery," just under the roof. Hissing the villain,

Detroiters saw the best plays from Broadway on the boards of the Garrick Theater, but stage folk felt it was haunted by its melodramatic past.

whistling and stomping feet was part of the fun. "Why Girls Leave Home," "Too Proud to Beg," "No Mother to Guide Her," "Waifs of New York" — they all played the Whitney.

By 1909, tastes were changing. New York's canny Shubert brothers, Lee and Jake, rode the tide to build a new theatrical empire, and Detroit profited by their enterprise. The Shuberts remodeled the old Whitney, renamed it the Garrick, and sent it road companies of their New York productions.

For the opening attraction, the Shuberts selected a musical which had done well in Manhattan, "Hamlet of Broadway," billed as a "Shakespearean travesty." The star was Eddie Foy.

It was Foy's prominence on the opening bill that was considered by the superstitious to be a bad omen. Foy was one of America's finest comedians, but his name unforgettably was linked with real-life tragedy. The worst catastrophe in the history of

American drama came Dec. 1, 1903, as Foy clowned through the title role of "Mr. Bluebeard" at Chicago's Iroquois Theater.

When an electrical wire broke and flames engulfed the stage draperies, Foy kept his head. Stepping to the footlights, he calmly told the audience the curtain would be lowered, and they could leave the auditorium at their leisure.

But a woman shrieked — and the panic was on. The toll was 602 lives.

Ill-omened or not, the Garrick celebrated its first anniversary before it suffered a backstage tragedy. In a pre-Broadway engagement of her new vehicle, "Sauce for the Goose," Grace George was well received at a Christmas Day opening in 1910.

The next day the show was praised by The Detroit News drama critic as a sprightly comedy. It was about women's liberation.

The theme was as timely then as it is today. The News had a report from Washington that the Daughters of the American Revolution had been "bitten by the suffragette bug." Pictures of New York debs active in the cause also appeared that day.

Frank Worthing, leading man in "Sauce for the Goose," received special praise in the review. A favorite of fellow actors, he was called the greatest wit of the celebrated New York Lambs Club.

That evening a stagehand saw Worthing stumble in the alley as he approached the theater. He fell at the stage doorway. It was a pulmonary hemorrhage, and before he could be carried to his dressing room he was dead.

The Garrick's strangest performance came in 1926. The house was sold out for the first performance of a two-week engagement of Harry Houdini and his magic shows.

Houdini, whose real name was Ehrich Weiss, was an unbelievable contortionist. It was attested that he could bend over backward and pick up a pin with his eyeball.

As a master of all forms of escape, he achieved world fame. Riveted iron boilers, padded cells, zinc-lined piano boxes, straightjackets, burglar-proof safes, iron cages, U.S. mail pouches — none of these could keep Houdini contained.

On a European tour in 1901, he freed himself from shackles constructed to defy his efforts by workmen at Germany's Krupp plant. In Moscow in 1903, he broke out of the massive van used by the czar's police to transport prisoners condemned to Siberia.

In January, 1906, he escaped from Cell No. 2 in the United States jail in Washington, D.C., the high-security dungeon in which Charles J. Guiteau was confined after he assassinated President James A. Garfield.

Later in 1906, Detroit became the scene of one of Houdini's best publicized — and coldest stunts. At 1 p.m. on Nov. 29, Houdini went to the center span of the Belle Isle Bridge, accompanied by Secretary of Police Charles A. Nichols, patrolmen, a press agent, his valet and newspapermen.

The temperature was in the 30's and snow was falling, but Houdini removed all his clothes except his trousers and suspenders. Regulation police-handcuffs were snapped tightly to his wrists under Nichols' direction. Houdini climbed the bridge railing and looked down at the water 25 feet below.

"It's pretty far," he said. "Come what will!" Then he jumped.

Witnesses could see that Houdini was keeping close to the surface by kicking his feet. Once his head appeared above water and he gulped air before going back under.

In less than a minute he was up again, triumphantly, waving the handcuffs. He swam to a waiting boat and delivered the manacles, still locked, to waiting policemen as he was hauled aboard.

Houdini's magic was so potent that he sometimes seemed able to defy death. But he never could escape from a lifelong obsession about ghosts — real or otherwise.

Phony mediums enraged him, and he went to great lengths to expose them. Yet, he repeatedly sought out the friendship and counsel of Spiritualism's great champion, Sir Arthur Conan Doyle, the creator of Sherlock Holmes. Friends described him as a fatalist who felt the hour of his death to be predetermined.

THE GREAT

HOUDINI

Harry Houdini, master of all forms of escape, played his last performance in great pain at the Garrick Theater.

In the light of where his last performance was to be played, it is worth noting that in all his large collection of theatrical memorabilia, the memento he most cherished was the manuscript diary of the great actor, David Garrick.

After waiting long past curtain time for Houdini to appear, the audience in the Garrick Theater on Sunday night, Oct. 24, 1926, whistled and stomped like the gallery gods of the old Whitney days. The sound reached Houdini, who was stretched out in his dressing room in great pain.

Dr. Leo Dretzka, summoned to the theater by Houdini's manager, diagnosed appendicitis and advised immediate hospitalization. But Houdini was obdurate. The audience must not be disappointed, he said.

At 9:35 p.m., with a temperature of 104, he walked on the stage. Apologizing for the delay, he asked indulgence in advance for any imperfections in the performance.

"We have just made a 1,000-mile journey from Montreal," he said, "and we are tired." He did not mention his illness.

Nor did he spare himself. Nothing in the 2½-hour program was curtailed. It was a never-to-be-forgotten evening.

When a skeptic in the balcony tossed down a pack of cards and demanded that Houdini use them in place of his own, the magician was unruffled. His sleight-of-hand was as mystifying as ever.

Alarm clocks disappeared from his fingertips to reappear at the far side of the stage, ringing at his command. Pretty girls locked inside cabinets showed up at the back of the house, every curl and ringlet in place. At the end, the applause was tumultuous.

But Houdini could take no bows. As the curtain fell, he collapsed.

When an operation was performed at Grace Hospital on Monday, it was discovered that the appendix had ruptured several days before — probably on Friday. On that evening a group of university students gathered in Houdini's dressing room in Montreal to challenge his claim that his abdomen was impervious to any blow. While Houdini's attention was diverted, one of them struck him savagely.

Houdini's secret was to tense the abdominal muscles before being hit, and he was not prepared this time. The pain was greater than he would admit. Only his great willpower carried him through the two remaining performances in Montreal.

With the Garrick engagement terminated, a carload of the show's paraphernalia was shipped from Detroit to New York. By an oversight, however, one item was left behind in the warehouse of the Detroit Transfer Co.

This was a heavy brass coffin, built for Houdini at a cost of $2,500. After a committee of physicians said the air in it would be exhausted by an occupant in eight minutes, Houdini remained in it underwater in the swimming pool of the Stelton Hotel in New York for 1½ hours. He inserted a clause in his will specifying that this coffin be used for his burial.

At 10 p.m. on Saturday, Oct. 31, as make-believe Hallowe'en ghosts cavorted in the Detroit streets, Houdini's brother visited him at the hospital. The brother, also a stage magician, used the name Theodore Hardeen.

"I am weaker," Houdini told him. "I guess I have lost the fight." Soon afterward the Handcuff King was dead.

The Garrick outlived him by only two years. "Ringside" was its last attraction. Then bulldozers delivered the knockout blow.

34. Fountain of Mirth

Was it his last and greatest joke?

That was the burning question all over town when Detroit's most eccentric bachelor, James Scott, died at 79 on March 5, 1910, bequeathing his $500,000 estate to the city to build a fountain on Belle Isle.

No near relatives survived to contest this seemingly generous gesture. But none were needed to stir up a hornet's nest. One string was attached to the bequest: Along with the fountain, the will provided, the city would erect a life-size bronze statue of the donor.

"Only a good man who has wrought things for humanity should be honored in this way," protested Bishop Charles D. Williams. The bishop's lead soon was followed by aldermen, civic leaders and citizens. Everybody in town seemed to be talking about Scott.

He was a loafer and a gambler, it was pointed out. He told off-color stories. And he perpetrated vindictive practical jokes.

The "Hog Block" was one. Falling out with his neighbors, the respected McMillans who operated Detroit's leading grocery store at Fort and Woodward, Scott affixed to his house on the side toward the store, a huge carving of a hog.

"Scott's Folly" was another. When the owner of an adjoining lot refused to sell Scott some land that he wanted to add to his property at Park and Peterboro, Scott spent $20,000 to build a sham house. From the Peterboro side it looked like a mansion, but its elegant facade was attached to a high, windowless wall, whose only purpose was to shut out light from the home of the recalcitrant neighbor.

As the furor about building a monument to such a prankster reached its peak, the size of the statue for Scott became a subject of much drollery.

Dr. F. D. Leete, pastor of Central Methodist Church, thought a statue "about 2½ inches high" might not mar the beauty of the fountain, besides being suitable to the moral stature of the subject. But life size? That was too much. On the other hand, a reader proposed in a letter to The Detroit News that the statue of Scott be 12 feet tall, displaying him "surprised, like Diana, in the bath."

Another letter, signed "Monguagon", suggested roulette wheels and poker chips as appropriate embellishments for the fountain. And Dr. William B. Forbush, of Northwestern Congregational Church, argued that there already were too many fountains on Belle Isle. The city should wait, he said, "until somebody donates funds for removing one."

J. L. Hudson, the merchant prince who headed the Detroit Municipal League, summed up the case against acceptance of the bequest in a few brief but telling words: "Mr. Scott never did anything for Detroit in his lifetime and he never had a thought that was good for the city."

Hudson's summary gave pause to some of the proponents of the fountain. It was true that Scott's career didn't seem to have the historic significance that called for a monument.

His father wisely had invested in Detroit real estate and left him a fortune, and it was said that Jim Scott never was known to do an hour's manual labor in his life.

His days were spent as a leisurely man-about-town, enjoying convivial talk and pleasant companionship. His best reputation seemed to be among waiters, newsboys and other servitors, among whom he was known as a generous man with tips.

Just as it seemed that the tumult about Scott's bequest would end the project, strong voices for acceptance began to be heard. One was that of Alderman David Heineman, who carried weight in the City Council.

Scott Fountain—some Detroiters thought the donor's bequest was a joke, but it provides a spot of bravura beauty for Belle Isle.

Speaking to reporters gathered in the office of Mayor Philip Breitmeyer, Heineman said: "I can look around this office and see pictures of men who played poker with Jim Scott. I say the bequest should be accepted." He also recalled that "Jim always liked Belle Isle and loved to see the children there."

The mayor agreed with Heineman. "I don't believe the city has a right to insult any of her citizens by refusing a gift for such a good cause," he said.

In the end, their view prevailed. It took more than 15 years, but Breitmeyer lived to attend the fountain's dedication in 1925. Cass Gilbert, the New York architect who planned the Detroit Public Library, won a competition for design of the glistening white memorial at the lower end of the city's pleasure island.

Gilbert drew motifs from Detroit's history. A great outer bowl of marble was reached by ascending steps, and three concentric marble rims led up to the main bowl. A central pedestal of carved figures upheld the topmost basin.

A many-jetted circular spray of water rose from the rim, with the main jet in the center towering skyward. Visitors found Neptune depicted on the fountain. There were dolphins, lions and turtles spouting crystal streams of water. And, in a touch that Jim Scott surely would have approved, they found plenty of archaic Greek drinking horns.

Today children love it. . . children of all ages. Scott's bronze figure is seated, seemingly watchful of the fountain's sprays and looking beyond them to the towers of Detroit rising against the sky down-river.

Youngsters delight in sitting in Scott's lap. They crawl over his statue as happily as children crawl over the statue of Hans Christian Andersen in New York's Central Park.

If the fountain was Scott's last joke, time has made the jest a kindly one.

Those who knew the period best remain convinced that the Council unlikely would have approved the Scott bequest had it not been for Heineman's calmy reasoned views.

He was an anomaly in the rough-and-tumble of saloonkeepers. Heineman was respected by the strongest critics of a memorial fountain honoring worldly Jim Scott. He moved in the best social circles, was something of an art and music critic, and even did respectable work in art on his own.

Heineman also could consort with enjoyment with such down-to-earth politicians as Addie Barnett, Tony Weiler and Al Deimel, the periods leading ward bosses.

As president of the Council in 1907, Heineman suprised his colleagues by taking time away from such matters as streetcar franchises and saloon licenses to design the now familiar city flag.

With a certain pride that this scholar was one of them, the aldermen listened patiently to his exposition of the flag's symbolism.

To reflect Detroit's history, he combined quaterings from the flags of three nations, the fleur-de-lis of France which flew over the community in its first decades, the imperial standard of England which ruled Detroit until the American Revolution, and the Stars and Stripes.

Heineman superimposed in the center the official seal of the city, with the Latin motto "Speramus meliora, resurget cineribus" (We hope for better things, we will arise from our ashes).

If this paragon of culture approved a fountain memorializing old Jim Scott, that was good enough for Addie, Tony, Al and the rest.

35. Paul Bunyan's Bow

"Paul Bunyan woke up one morning with a bad toothache. He fastened the tooth to a couple of steel cables around Babe, the Blue Ox, and gave Babe a good whack. Babe was so startled she made a jump that pulled the tooth and sent it sailing through the sky 300 miles south.

"Paul dropped the cables in the Straits of Mackinac, and there they lay until they were dredged up for the Mackinac Bridge. That tooth was full of holes but it still had plenty of vim. It landed upright alongside Grand Circus Park in Detroit, and the next day 100 dentists moved in and set up offices in it.

"They named it the David Whitney Building after Paul's boss, and there it stands today."

This story is not an accepted part of the Paul Bunyan legend. Not yet, anyway. But it would be fitting.

The David Whitney Building is a monument to a Detroit lumber baron whose operations were as gargantuan as anything ever ascribed to the mythical hero of American lumberjacks.

David Whitney was a shrewd operator who bought Michigan and Wisconsin pine lands by the hundreds of thousands of acres. He paid from $3 to

$50 an acre — and the profit when the tall timbers were felled sometimes reached 100 times what it cost.

When he died in 1910, Whitney was reputed to be the wealthiest man in Detroit, with a fortune estimated at $15,000,000.

His first job in his native Massachusetts was operating a paper box factory for a lumber company. When he came to Detroit at 29 in 1859 he started a lumber business with his brother, Charles. He foresaw the great future of lumbering in the Midwest and, when the profitable partnership was dissolved in 1877, he put everything he had into buying pine lands.

Whitney's fortunes expanded in the north woods as swiftly as Paul Bunyan's prowess in the loggers' legends. He soon became a millionaire. His instinct concerning the development of land values in Detroit was keen, too, and it led to his becoming the "Mr. Woodward Avenue" of his day.

Jefferson was Detroit's main business thoroughfare for half a century. Whitney's offices were in the Merrill Block at Woodward and Jefferson, and from there he watched the tides of carriages, drays and vans on both arteries. He was the first to perceive a shift in the tides.

Upper Woodward developed a fine residential area. For years Whitney lived at the corner of Woodward and Sproat. Around him clustered the homes of many leading families of the day — the Pridgeons, the Heavenriches, the Farrands, the Heinemans. Residences also surrounded Grand Circus Park, but Whitney foresaw a change. He bought up such properties and, in 1890, he built the Grand Circus Park Building, five stories high, at Woodward and Park.

The same year he had plans drawn for a more stately mansion at Woodward and Canfield. He built it of jasper from South Dakota, a stone that is one of the hardest of all to cut. It took four years to finish the house.

For years it was one of Detroit's showplaces, with streams of carriages driving up to its porte cochere *233*

David Whitney foresaw the great growth of Detroit northward out
Woodward Avenue.

for receptions, teas and musicales. Summer and
winter, the Whitneys kept the circular conservatory
at the south side of the house blooming with plants
and flowers. The main hall had a huge fireplace,
cheery on the coldest days.

In 1914, Whitney's son, David Charles, ordered
the Grand Circus Park Building razed. On the site
he erected the David Whitney Building, naming it
as a memorial to his father. It was planned as a
center for physicians and dentists, with the corridors arranged around a central court.

The mansion, too, eventually came into medical
service. After the death of Mrs. David Whitney in

234

1917, it was occupied for several years by family retainers. It then became the headquarters of the Wayne County Medical Society, and later was turned over to the Visiting Nurse Association.

But Paul Bunyan outlived his boss. The name of David Whitney does not appear in the Encyclopaedia Britannica, as does that of a Detroit News reporter who grew up in the country dominated by Whitney's logging camps.

That's because the reporter, James MacGillivray, minted gold of his own from the lumberjacks, storing up in his mind their stories. The Britannica's extensive piece about Paul Bunyan lists a feature by MacGillivray which appeared in the newspaper July 24, 1910, called "The Round River Drive," as the first appearance of the legendary figure in print.

Scholars and writers were attracted to the robust humor of the loggers and in a short time the story of Paul Bunyan became a national saga.

MacGillivray was the man to start the ball rolling. His life seemed to parallel the legend. Born in Meaford, Ontario, in 1873, he grew up in Oscoda in Northern Michigan when the area was humming with the lumber boom. Loggers flocked into Oscoda to live it up on Saturday nights, and to tell stories. Young James was a good listener, and the tall tales always grew taller when there was a wide-eyed greenhorn present to marvel over them.

The boy grew up to be a lumber broker for Great Lakes cargo shipments from 1894 to 1900. Then he prospected in the Northwest and Alaska. He managed sawmills in Chance, Idaho, and in Reno, Nevada.

The Paul Bunyan legends moved west with MacGillivray, after Michigan's big trees were depleted and the lumberjacks gone. Along the way, MacGillivray picked up newspaper jobs and discov- *235* ered he had a flair for writing. He worked for the Sacramento Star, the Spokane Review, the Alaska News and the Marquette Mining Journal. After he joined The Detroit News staff in 1907 picturesque feature stories became his forte.

"The Round River Drive" appeared in The Sunday News illustrated section, with a drawing by staff artist Joseph L. Kraemer showing loggers gathered around a campfire as one of their number told a tale of Paul Bunyan. MacGillivray cast his story in the form of a monolog delivered on such an occasion. His narrator told of starting out with another of Paul's men, Dutch Jake, to compete for a prize offered by Paul for cutting the biggest tree:

"Dutch Jake and me had picked out the biggest tree we could find on the forty, and we'd put three days on the cut with our big saw, what was three crosscuts brazed together, making 30 feet of teeth. We was getting along fine on the fourth day when lunchtime comes, and we thought we'd best get tn the sunny side to eat. So we grabs our grub and starts around that tree.

"We hadn't gone far when we heard a noise. Blamed if there wasn't Bill Carter and Sailor Jack sawin' at the same tree. It looked like a fight at first, but we compromised, meetin' each other at the heart on the seventh day. They'd hacked her to fall to the north, and we'd hacked her to fall to the south, and there that blamed tree stood for a month or more, clean sawed through, but not knowin' which way to drop 'til a windstorm came along and throwed her over."

MacGillivray's story was widely read and admired. As other writers worked the vein of golden fun from logging days, many sequels were added to the story about Paul Bunyan scooping out the Great Lakes as a watering through for Babe, the Blue Ox. Babe's footprints around the trough made the area's many little lakes, of course. Puget Sound and even Grand Canyon were soon attributed to Paul's gargantuan activities.

236   Inevitably, promoters of tourist attractions found

The David Whitney Building facing Grand Circus Park has a curious
link to Paul Bunyan, legendary hero of American lumberjacks.

a bonanza in Paul Bunyan. Bangor, Maine, built a 30-foot statue of Paul in 1959 as a centerpiece for the city's 125th anniversary program. Bangor soon became embroiled in a long controversy with Bemidji, Minn., which also built a statue of Paul, over their fancied rival claims. Portland, Ore., built a statue of Paul a bit later — and, naturally, a bit higher.

Brainerd, Minn., entered the lists after obtaining a giant depiction of Paul made for a railroad fair in Chicago. Bayfield, Wis., developed an order of aficionados, "Mystic Knights of the Blue Ox." Babe, the Blue Ox, has her 30-foot statue, too, in a California tourist park on US-101. Paul had to be big in California, and he is depicted on the world's largest wood carving, made from sequoia wood, near the entrance to Sequoia National Park.

MacGillivray left newspaper work in 1911 at the behest of Gov. Chase S. Osborn of Michigan, after a forest fire almost wiped out Oscoda, his boyhood home.

For 17 years he lectured on conservation throughout the state, illustrating his talks with his own motion pictures of birds and animals in the wild.

Osborn appointed him educational director of the Michigan Conservation Department, with the task of campaigning for forest fire prevention.

When he retired he returned to Oscoda with his wife, Amanda, who had been an Oscoda schoolteacher. He died at 79 in 1952 — still marveling at all that had followed after "The Round River Drive."

36. On Moonlight Bay

It was a never-to-be-forgotten time on the river —
June 17, 1911—the day set for the maiden voyage of
the Steamer Put-in-Bay, hailed as the biggest excursion boat yet built for Detroit River service.

Despite an early drizzle, the Ashley & Dustin
Line dock at the foot of First Street was crowded
with spectators as invited guests began to arrive
for the trip. Detroit Mayor William B. Thompson,
headed a large delegation of civic leaders.

From the vessel's bridge, high above the dock,
Capt. A. J. Fox saluted the arriving VIP's. George
Finzel, a longtime favorite band leader among plea-
sure-seekers on the river, rapped his baton and the
ship's orchestra blared forth a gay rendition of "On
Moonlight Bay." Over the years, the tune became
the ship's trademark.

Most of the nearly 1,000 passengers who trooped
aboard paid 75 cents for the round trip, but some
smart travelers made it on soap wrappers. The
Queen Anne Soap Co. advertised in The Detroit
News that customers could exchange 75 queen's
heads cut from the soap wrappers for a ticket.

Before the Put-in-Bay left the dock, excursionists
swarmed over the decks, exploring accommoda-
tions that were unique on a day cruise ship in 1911.
They even went down to the orlop deck. The crew's

239

quarters had been placed forward of the engines to leave room aft for a passenger lounge.

On the main deck, murals in the cabins and dining room were much admired. But the biggest attraction was the ballroom on the promenade deck.

America was dance-mad in 1911. Oldsters shook their heads when young folks jilted the stately waltz, but in 1911 there was something even newer — ragtime. And it wasn't just the teen-agers who seemingly had gone crazy. As the No. 1 hit tune of the year put it, "Everybody's Doin' It Now."

Oliver S. Dustin, general manager of the Ashley & Dustin Line, saw the way the winds of the new decade were blowing. He wanted a dancing ship. He got it, too, in the Put-in-Bay.

The central portion of the promenade deck was devoted to the ballroom. On a ship that measured 240 feet from bow to stern and 60 feet across the beam, that was a lot of dance floor. Dustin also arranged for sliding glass doors around the dance area. It could be shut off from stormy winds without impairing the dancers' view.

Many passengers went no further than the ballroom, but those who climbed higher were well rewarded. The observation deck had a luxurious cabin and private parlors. The hurricane deck offered steamer chairs, and just as on ocean liners passengers could reserve chairs for use throughout the voyage.

As his new command left the dock, Capt. Fox's emotions were mixed. He sounded the five blasts of the Great Lakes salute on the whistle in response to a similar tribute from the Steamer Frank E. Kirby, which the Put in-Bay was replacing on the Lake Erie run.

Fox had commanded the Kirby since it was built, 21 years before, and regret at leaving her mingled with pride in his new ship. The Kirby seemed

From the waltz to ragtime, dancing throngs loved the Steamer Put-in-Bay for gay times on the water. Even her end was a fiery affair.

dwarfed by comparison as the Put-in-Bay pulled away from shore.

At Put-in-Bay, Ohio, the greeting for the town's namesake ship was tumultuous. Most of the island's population came aboard to see the steamer's wonders. They crowded into the ballroom for a ceremony at which the island board of trade presented colors for the vessel.

On the return trip, another innovation kept passengers from being bored. This was a giant searchlight which made objects along the shore stand out "plain as sunlight."

Even so, some of the older heads on board found time for long thought on the voyage home. Their big question was, "Where will it all end?"

Perhaps the story from England in the paper that day had something to do with it. London was ablaze with color for the crowning of King George V, but on the eve of coronation week the limelight had been stolen from the king. It was the ladies who did the pilfering—more than 50,000 of them gathered in London from throughout the world for one of the largest suffrage processions yet seen.

Even in Detroit, you couldn't tell what women would do next. The big local story concerned two prominent society matrons who had become the first of their sex in town to go up in an airplane. Mrs. Fred M. Alger said her ride in an open biplane with Frank Corryn, a young disciple of the Wright brothers, was "one of the most pleasant sensations I ever experienced."

"It was glorious," agreed Mrs. Russell A. Alger Jr. "It felt like flying on the back of a great bird."

As the Put-in-Bay gathered coronation-week plaudits in this brave new world, one grand lady of Detroit noticeably was silent. The flagship of the rival White Star Line, the Tashmoo, had reigned as queen of the river for 10 years, and she was not disposed to lightly give up her crown to the newer and larger steamer.

Their regular runs kept them apart. The Tashmoo headed upstream to the St. Clair Flats and Port Huron, while the Put-in-Bay was going down to Lake Erie. But the craze for dancing soon made moonlight trips popular, and the big excursion boats began sailing nightly on dancing cruises up into Lake St. Clair and back.

Whenever the Put-in-Bay and the Tashmoo found themselves on the river together there would be a competitive sprint. They never had a formal race to a decision, however.

Nor was there ever a really decisive answer to the big question of the Put-in-Bay's maiden voyage, "Where will it all end?"

As far as building bigger and bigger excursion boats, it ended right there. The overnight lines took to supplying space for travelers to carry their cars along to Cleveland and Buffalo, and they developed true freshwater leviathans. But among the day excursion boats, the Put-in-Bay never was surpassed.

Nor was the record set by the bandmaster of the maiden voyage, George Finzel, ever surpassed. He continued as the orchestra leader on the Put-in-Bay throughout the ship's career on the river, and he never missed a sailing.

Never, that is, until Oct. 3, 1953, when he kept a last rendezvous with the Put-in-Bay. This time he had to stay on shore, but he watched with a lump in his throat as the superstructure was set on fire in Lake St. Clair and the once-proud steamer went up in 150-foot flames, in preparation for the steel hull being dismantled for junk.

Finzel provided the requiem for the Put-in-Bay's last trip, too. He didn't have an orchestra handy, but he still could whistle. The tune he whistled, of course, was "On Moonlight Bay."

The task of setting the torch to the old steamer fell to a veteran of the Detroit River, Capt. Frank Becker. As his tug picked up the Put-in-Bay at the foot of Mt. Elliott and brought her to Lake St. Clair, Capt. Becker reviewed many memories.

Still active today on the waterfront, Capt. Becker, 78, well remembers the day's emotional impact:

"My phone rang at 4 a.m. on the day before I was supposed to do the job. It was a woman, not anyone I knew, and she was crying.

"She said, 'Are you really going to burn the Put-in-Bay?'

"I said, 'Yes, but why are you calling me about it at this time in the morning?'

'She said, 'I met both my husbands on that boat.'

"I couldn't get back to sleep, thinking of the many good times I had enjoyed on the Put-in-Bay. I remembered George Finzel playing the piano and all those kids dancing and having a good time.

"I really felt sad about the job I had to do, and soon I was crying too."

37. Cadillaqua!

As civic birthday observances go, Detroit's effort
in 1912, the Cadillaqua festival, had rather unusual
results. That was the year the celebration ended
with Detroit aldermen going to jail.

The city's first taste of historical pageantry in the
1901 bicentennial proved to be so pleasant that
there was much talk of making the city's birthday
on July 24 an annual gala. It took more than a
decade to do it, but the talk culminated in a whop-
per of an idea — Cadillaqua.

Cadillaqua, it was planned, would combine a
demonstration to the world of Detroit's emergence
as America's automobile capital with adequate celebration of its facilities for sports and fetes on the
water.

It was decided to enlarge upon the bicentennial
theme in a suitable pageant of the founding of the
city by Antoine de la Mothe Cadillac and his voyageurs. Subscriptions were solicited to finance the
affair, enthusiasm was widespread, and the committee collected $70,000 to get things going.

The bicentennial, lamentably, was weak on historical accuracy. So in 1912 Clarence M. Burton,
city historian, was put to work to make accurate
sketches of historical events. These would form the
basis of the principal floats.

The first float, "The Dream of Cadillac," would
sound the keynote. Succeeding floats would show
Cadillac's ship, Fr. Marquette preaching to the Indians, the conspiracy of Pontiac and the battle of
Bloody Run.

All went well, and on the eve of the festival Andrew H. Green Jr., general manager for the Solvay Process Co., who served as chairman of the arrangements, received congratulations for his work. Michigan Democrats asked him to run for governor on their ticket. "I'm too busy," Green answered. Green was asked to play Cadillac in the pageant. He tried to turn down this honor, too, but the town insisted.

Monday, July 23, was devoted to "The Vision of the Voyageurs," with fireworks on Belle Isle, but the big guns weren't fired until Detroit's 211th birthday arrived on Tuesday. With Green dressed as Cadillac and 100 Detroiters garbed as his soldiers and voyageurs, the longboats were met at the head of Belle Isle by what was described as "one of the greatest fleets ever assembled on fresh waters."

Landing at the foot of Third Street, "Cadillac" was escorted to Grand Circus Park in a parade of 5,000 automobiles. Only the Motor City could assemble such a number. It was noted that for the first time, competitors who had fought vigorously for the title at last were ready to concede it to Detroit.

As a straw to show which way the wind was blowing, the Cole Motor Co., of Indianapolis, took an ad in The Detroit News to explain that, while it manufactured its cars in the Hoosier State, it had established its "factory branch" salesroom in Detroit.

Paradoxically, the prize for the auto that had come the farthest to participate in the parade went to one made on the city, a Hudson. Seventy-five-year-old Edward Jewett drove the Hudson touring car more than 4,000 miles from Phoenix, and it bore the dust of its 22-day journey.

The sponsors of Cadillaqua were gratified that virtually every car maker of importance in the country sent models for the parade. Because of its name, a local product, the Detroiter, was given the place of honor at the head of the procession. It was followed by a squadron of bicycles of ancient vintage, with elevated seats and hard tires.

For the occasion, the manufacturers of the Detroiter called in their car with motor serial No. 1. It was owned by a local florist, Robert W. Jean, who buried the hood under a blanket of roses. Other his-

"Cadillac's Dream Comes True," a cartoon by Burt Thomas, appeared on page one of The Detroit News when Andrew Green, who portrayed the city's founder in the 1912 Cadillaqua festival, was revealed as the moving spirit behind an investigation of City Hall corruption.

torical vehicles included the first Packard, built in 1899, early Cadillacs and the first Grinnell Electric.

Starting from Woodward and Grand Boulevard, the advance guard reached the reviewing stand at Grand Circus Park at 3 p.m. Along Woodward, the winning car in the Vanderbilt Cup Race, a Lozier, drew applause. The spectators also cheered a Jackson which had a dove of peace on the hood, with streamers from its mouth to the body of the car. A Stevens-Duryea, draped in flags, with the driver dressed as Uncle Sam, got applause, too.

But the parade's big surprise was the prominence of the suffragettes. They shouted their message from cars bearing votes for women signs. Represented were the Equal Suffrage Society, the Highland Park Civic Club, the West Side Equal Franchise Association, and the Political Equality and Civic League.

But the major emotion of the day was enthusiasm, and the Cadillaqua spirit survived fitful showers and a 45-minute delay in starting Wednesday night's industrial parade over the same route. Green, as Cadillac, rode at its head in a white Flanders and received ovations along the line of march. On Thursday he had to issue a firm statement declining to run for mayor.

A naval parade Thursday night was even more eye-filling. It was held in the Cadillaqua Court, 2,-000 feet long and 300 feet wide, built on piles in the river opposite the Belle Isle bathing beach. Lights played on two ornate galleys, with a band of 48 pieces on one and the Mendelssohn Singing Club of 150 voices on the other, as illuminated yachts and excursion boats passed in review.

It ended Friday night — far too soon, the enraptured Detroiters felt — with a Venetian Night gala on Belle Isle. The city's "pillow brigade" of canoeists paraded on island lagoons and canals over a course illuminated by thousands of colored electric lights.

"It was an hour in dreamland for the spectators," The Detroit News reported Saturday. "From the electric tips on their canopies to the silver droppings of their paddles, they presented spectacles of a fairy night."

A less agreeable surprise came when the autos passed down Woodward below the park.

The Detroit United Railways, which had achieved a monopoly of streetcar franchises in the city, promised cooperation. Instead, it stacked its cars along the Woodward tracks to be ready for the rush of fares after the parade was over. The decorated automobiles were forced into a single line to pass between the streetcars and the curb.

Some spectators climbed to the roofs of the cars. Detroit was irked by this example of corporate arrogance, and the movement for municipal ownership of the streetcar lines gained many adherents. *247*

The report, however, was relegated to a back page of Saturday's paper. The front page, and half a dozen inside pages as well, were taken up with the year's big story:

While canoes glided through the glitter on Belle Isle, William J. Burns, the famous detective, and his operatives were busy downtown springing a gigantic trap.

For three months they had been secretly at work, gathering proof of corruption and bribery in Detroit's City Council. In coordinated raids, Council President Thomas Glinnan and 10 councilmen were arrested. They were charged with selling their votes in favor of a petition by the Wabash Railroad to close a public street near the Fort Street Union Station.

The story's punchline, however, was the name of the public-spirited citizen who had spent more than $10,000 of his own money to bring the detectives to town to end civic corruption. It was none other than the man who had been receiving plaudits for his impersonation of Cadillac, Andrew H. Green Jr. More a hero than ever, Green continued to decline suggestions that he run for office. "I'm a business man," he said.

Certainly Hollywood could not have contrived a better surprise ending to Cadillaqua, even though the excitement later fizzled out. Glinnan was the only councilman who went to trial, and after long legal wrangling he was acquitted on grounds that the detectives had set up an entrapment.

Detroit had to postpone for a time the dream of having an annual civic celebration, too. But decades later the neighboring Canadian city of Windsor joined with it in staging an annual Freedom Festival with parades, fireworks in the river and all the trappings that made old-timers remember Cadillaqua so fondly.

38. Preacher Mike

Fire in a church on the day before Christmas!

It seemed such a pity. The fine new building cost the congregation of the North Woodward Methodist Church $100,000. At such a time, who could guess that this seeming disaster would turn out to be a blessing in disguise?

At the parsonage a short distance down the block on Melbourne, the first sign of something amiss early on the morning of Dec. 24, 1913, was an insistent ringing of the doorbell, accompanied by a pounding on the front door.

The new minister, Dr. Merton S. Rice, was awakened from a sound sleep. "As I tumbled out of bed, I thought it must be Santa Claus with an early Christmas present," Dr. Rice recalled later.

His six children trooped downstairs on the heels of their father. They heard the excited words of E.A. Walker, the church janitor:

"Fire! Fire, Dr. Rice! The church is on fire!"

Dr. Rice ran to the alarm box at the Woodward corner. He was a big athletic man, and he ran rapidly. His two oldest boys, Eugene, 17, and Allen, 15, followed him.

Once the fire engines arrived, Eugene and Allen seemed to be everywhere at once. Allen showed firemen where the best corridors were to get through to the blaze in a hurry. Gene led a fire fighter through the maze of smoke into the basement to the main electrical switch.

Spectators milled in the street. The four younger Rice children might have enjoyed their front-window

Called "Preacher Mike," Dr. M. S. Rice refused a bishopric to go on preaching to Detroiters.

seats for all this excitement, if it weren't that their father's church was burning.

All felt homesick for the pleasant place in Duluth they still thought of as home. They had left it only a few weeks before, when Dr. Rice accepted the call to Detroit.

The parsonage on Melbourne was old, and much decorated with Victorian gingerbread. The youngsters didn't like it. Everything needed repairs. Even the porch railing was rotten and sagged crazily.

As flames mounted higher toward the huge glass dome in the center of the auditorium, of which the congregation was proud, the two frightened girls, Shanna and Elaine, covered their heads with pillows.

But the roar and crackling of the flames could not

be shut out. Soon the two rejoined Ruskin and Robert at the windows. As Elaine would write about it, many years later:

"We were all too excited to enjoy anything but the glorious sight of the black smoke that began to rise when the big hoses were spraying water through the popping glass of the dome."

Second and third alarms were sounded. Eight engines fought the blaze. In the end, however, little more than the gutted outside walls were left standing.

That evening, when the church board assembled for an emergency session in the parsonage's front room, there was a new reason for excitement on the part of the children.

The board voted to temporarily hold the congregation's services in the Regent Theater. It was only a few blocks away, on Woodward north of Grand Boulevard, and its seating capacity was the largest of any auditorium in the area.

The Regent! The Rice children, discreetly hidden behind the balustrade on the staircase, pricked up their ears at the name. Ever since the family's arrival in Detroit, they were impressed that the Regent was strictly off limits.

They sometimes were given permission to see a carefully selected motion picture, usually educational, but the Regent's entertainment included something else beside movies — vaudeville. The very word sounded wicked.

On Sunday they found the theater's seats were a great improvement over hard church pews. Otherwise, though, the Regent was a sad disappointment.

The stage was transformed with subdued draperies into a church-like setting. Not even the slightest aura of singers, dancers or acrobats remained as their father's stentorian voice ranged easily to the farthest balcony.

Over the next three decades, more and more Detroiters would hear that voice. A tabernacle temporarily replacing the burned out church proved totally inadequate to accommodate the throngs that wanted to hear Dr. Rice. Maybe, he suggested to the church board, the good Lord had something better in mind when He let the old church burn down. *251*

The board members took the hint. They decided to build the biggest edifice in the city's history. It would seat 4,000 and cost $1,500,000. As a church for all Detroit, it would be called Metropolitan Methodist.

The undertaking was ambitious, but Dr. Rice proved outstanding as a fund-raiser, too. In a single day, his golden voice brought in $446,000 in pledges.

On the Sunday in 1926 when the new building was dedicated, the congregation paraded up Woodward triumphantly singing "Onward Christian Soldiers." Mrs. Sebastian S. Kresge offered a blank check to pay off the remainder of the church's cost that day, but as it turned out, $10,000 was all that was needed to complete the $1,500,000.

Big as the new church might be, it was scarcely big enough. The congregation, which totaled 1,200 when Dr. Rice arrived, grew to 6,700, the largest in Methodism. But Dr. Rice's following cut across sectarian lines. His efforts on behalf of the Old Newsboys Goodfellow Fund in providing Christmas gifts for poor children and his leadership in the interdenominational Lenten services of the Detroit Council of Churches made him known and loved by all Detroit as "Preacher Mike."

Many never realized that his first name was not Michael, but Merton. The nickname went back to a summer when as a youth he worked in a grocery store with his brother, Charles, and the two called each other Pat and Mike. In Detroit an Irish Catholic friend, Edward M. Doyle, who once was Dr. Rice's guest at a Masonic banquet, elaborated this into "Preacher Mike." Doyle, who owned the Majestic Building, long Detroit's tallest skyscraper, said he was impressed by a clergyman who could build a structure more imposing than his without a mortgage.

More than anything else, it was Dr. Rice's mastery of words which caused 25,000 American ministers, polled by the publication, Christian Century, to name him one of the 25 greatest preachers in the country.

He turned down an opportunity to become a bishop because it would take time away from the pulpit. When asked what he did for recreation he answered, "Preaching and then more preaching."

Metropolitan Methodist Church was hailed as the largest in Detroit's history when it was completed in the booming 20's.

Nevertheless, he got back to nature when he could. Perhaps the best remembered of his many books is a small volume of musings about such simple things as rocks and clouds, the wind in the trees, the way of a fish in the water. He called it "My Father's World."

"I go floundering about in a flood of water and am challenged at every step of my way, not by the miraculous, but by my ignorance amid the unknown," he wrote.

When he had a heart attack in 1943 he told his daughter Elaine — she had become Mrs. V. George Chabut — that he couldn't rest until he delivered a sermon that he had prepared for the next Sunday. So he sat up in bed and gave it, with just Mrs. Chabut for an audience. Three days later he was dead.

A few years afterward, when Mrs. Chabut wrote her father's biography, there was only one title she could give it: "Preacher Mike."

39. The Man From Whisky Diggings

Even for a California gold rush town, Whisky Diggings was small — little more than a row of shacks, but it achieved its own niche in history.

And history was important to an infant who was born there Nov. 8, 1853. Clarence Monroe Burton devoted a lifetime to it, doing more to preserve things historical than any other Detroiter. Gold had to be in the background to bring anybody to Whisky Diggings — even to be born — and it was true in his case.

His father, Dr. Charles S. Burton, was 26 when he brought his bride to Michigan from their native Seneca County, New York, and started a practice in Battle Creek. But fever struck the doctor — gold fever. The trek west by covered wagon was a rugged experience for his wife, Annie, a talented writer whose poems appeared in Harper's Monthly and Godey's Ladies Book.

Dr. Burton enjoyed fair success in prospecting for gold. One nugget he found later brought $825 in Philadelphia. More and more, however, he found the gold country needed his skill in medicine. Emergencies called him to one mining camp after another, and so it was that his son was born in Whisky Diggings.

By the time Clarence was two, Dr. Burton was completely disenchanted with the goldfields. He decided to return to Michigan and booked passage for the family on a sailing vessel, the Yankee Blade, leaving for the Isthmus of Nicaragua.

The Yankee Blade never reached the isthmus. Gold hijackers wrecked the ship, and it broke in two on the rocks in a heavy fog along the California coast. Of the 900 passengers, 160 drowned.

With the baby in her arms and the gold nugget sewed in the hem of her skirt, Annie Burton tried to leap from the ship to a lifeboat. She missed, but rescuers hauled her—and Clarence—into the boat. Dr. Burton too, was saved. Eventually the family reached Hastings, Mich., where Dr. Burton built a good practice, founded the weekly Hastings Banner, and never again was tempted to journey afar.

Clarence was married and the father of a child before winning his law degree at the University of Michigan in 1873. He also began to collect historical books and records. Coming to Detroit, he studied land titles with the abstract firm of E. C. Skinner & Co., and by 1883 he became a partner. In 1891 he obtained sole ownership and the firm became the Burton Abstract & Title Co.

By this time, Burton knew the vein of gold he wanted to seek above all else — the gold to be mined from the complexities of human experience. Detroit's history absorbed him. He wrote 27 volumes in this field, notably "A Sketch of the Life of Antoine de la Mothe Cadillac, Founder of Detroit" and "The Building of Detroit," about the city's first decade.

In his search for personal data about the early Detroiters whose names he found on old land titles Burton scanned tombstones in cemeteries and went through newspaper files. It was his dismay at seeing documents tossed into bonfires that led to his becoming a champion paper saver. Once he found old papers piled several feet high on the floor of a warehouse that was about to be demolished. He rescued several wagonloads of them — and found invaluable material in the hoard.

Scouting the French colonial archives in Paris, Burton obtained copies of 12 volumes of Cadillac's papers. He scouted auctions of historical collections for material about Detroit. He made 90 scrapbooks of newspaper clippings and tracked down similar scrapbooks made in the past — amassing more than 2,000 such catchalls. He assembled 1,400 volumes of early American imprints, duplicating the great collection of the American Antiquarian Society at Worcester, Mass.

Clarence M. Burton's passionate interest in Detroit's past never wavered. Today it is perpetuated in the Burton Historical Collection. *Courtesy C. M. Hayes & Co., Detroit.*

In Washington, he achieved a major coup by talking the bureaucrats there out of reports made between 1787 and 1793 by William Henry Harrison, when he was governor of the Northwest Territory of which Michigan was a part. He outbid the government of Canada to acquire the papers of Col. John Askin, commissary of the British army in Detroit who stayed on after the American takeover. Askin's manuscripts cleared up many disputed points about the War of 1812.

Burton added a fireproof extension to his home on Brainard in Detroit to house the collection, which ultimately included 500,000 unpublished documents, as well as 40,000 pamphlets and 30,000 books.

Evolving from newspaperman to historian, George W. Stark became the "father" of the present Detroit Historical Museum.

In March, 1914, his collection was presented to the Detroit Library Commission. The only condition was that "the library be retained as an entity to perpetually bear the name of Burton in some way connected with its use."

Burton and his wife also provided an endowment of $50,000 for the collection, which eventually grew to more than $300,000, providing funds for many acquisitions. The collection was given its own reading room in the Detroit Public Library. It has been said that no researcher working in any field of Americana can consider his work complete without consulting the Burton Collection.

But its use is not confined to scholars. Citizens working up their family genealogy pore over its records. Banks, business firms and advertising agencies make use of the collection. Hollywood has sought its help in documenting historical productions for television. It's a rewarding place to visit just for fun, too.

Burton's service to his city didn't end with the collection. He worked on civic commissions and boards. When he helped to organize the Detroit Historical Society of Dec. 15, 1921, he was chosen as its first president. It was under his leadership that Detroit's first historical museum was established.

Before he died at 79 in 1932, Burton meticulously filled out in longhand a form sent him by The Detroit News to provide accurate biographical information for its files. Under the heading "recreation" he set down one of the most masterly understatements of all times:

"Work hard at old books," he wrote.

After Burton's death, Detroit could find no suitable successor for him as city historiographer. At the time, the man who ultimately would bring Burton's work to completion was concerned with historical matters only insofar as all newspapermen are engaged in the day-by-day reporting that builds in the files into year-by-year chronology.

This was George W. Stark. A native Detroiter and a veteran of The Detroit News staff, he won his journalistic spurs covering the Dayton flood of 1913, served as city editor, and in 1932 was happily filling the post of drama critic.

But in 1938 occurred what Stark described as "probably the most important day in my entire career," though he didn't recognize it as such at the time. He was asked to do a daily column about old times in Detroit.

The column proved of special interest to members of the Detroit Historical Society. Stark accepted an invitation to join. He became a trustee and then president.

The museum launched by Burton was housed in a rented suite in the Barlum Tower. Stark decided a full-scale museum building was needed. He took the lead in raising funds for it, urging city officials — and citizens in general — to a consciousness of the tremendous traditions of the o l d e s t city in the
Midwest.

The task took years. Along the way he wrote several books which elaborated his point — "In Old Detroit" and "City of Destiny." Wayne State University conferred upon him an honorary degree of Doctor of Letters.

When the Detroit Historical Commission was created by the city in 1946 as an aid to the museum project, Stark became its first president. In the following year, the City Council conferred upon him the distinction of which he was proudest — the post of city historiographer, vacant since Burton's death.

At the instance of much "nagging and prodding" on his part — Stark's own phrase — two of Detroit's greatest celebrations materialized, the Golden Jubilee of the Automobile in 1946 and the city's 250th birthday celebration in 1951.

The climax of the 250th birthday festivities came with the dedication of the Detroit Historical Museum as part of the Cultural Center complex where the Burton Collection was ensconced in the Detroit Public Library. Stark presided at the realization of Burton's other cherished dream and accepted for the museum a bust of Antoine de la Mothe Cadillac, a gift of the French Republic.

On the 20th anniversary of the Detroit Historical Commission in January, 1966, Stark and Leonard N. Simons, president of the Simons-Michelson Co., Detroit advertising agency, the two survivors of the original commission, were sworn in again in a recreation of the original ceremony. Simons is now the commission's president.

It was Stark's last public appearance. He died Jan. 29, 1966, a few weeks short of his 82nd birthday — having lived to an even riper age, much to his own surprise, than did the man from Whisky Diggings.

40. Requiem for a Happy Bridge

It was a great day for Detroit automobile owners — and for the city's orphans, too.

But it was the beginning of the end for the old Belle Isle Bridge, so long a bridge to happiness for the town small fry.

Orphans Day was a natural in the summer of 1907. The idea was suggested in letter to The Detroit News from W. A. Pungs, head of the Pungs-Finch Auto & Gas Engine Co. Why not appeal to Detroit motorists to give children in local orphanages a motor holiday?

"I am sure the philanthropic men of the city would be more than willing to volunteer the use of their machines," Pungs wrote.

Mrs. Essie M. Moore, matron of the Home for the Friendless, approved the project. "The children see the automobiles whiz by when they are at play," she said, "and I have seen them look after the machines with the most wistful expression on their faces."

On July 2, the appeal appeared on Page One. The response was immediate. Next day, The News announced that an auto outing for the orphans was assured. Offers of cars began to pour in as soon as the papers reached the city's homes.

Enough motorists c a m e forward to include among the guests not only Mrs. Moore's charges, but also youngsters at the Protestant Orphan Asylum, St. Vincent's Asylum, the United Jewish Charities, the Children's Free Hospital, the House of Good Shepherd and the German Protestant Home.

Wednesday, July 10, was the date set. The only limitation was that a youngster must be old enough to sit up alone. That left 700 orphans eligible for the ride. The weather was sunny and mild, and when 100 crowded automobiles rendezvoused at the Majestic Building they were a sight to behold.

Girls from the Fred Sanders Confectionery passed along the line of waiting cars. They handed a sack of candy and an American flag to each child. Then, with much clanging of gongs and honking of horns, the cavalcade set out.

The children cheered, sang and waved their flags as the cars traveled down Woodward and out Jefferson. The first problem occurred at the Belle Isle Bridge; 100 cars created a traffic jam on the two-lane structure, erected in horse-and-buggy days.

Delay meant nothing to the orphans. Enthusiasm was high at the first stop on the island, the casino, where the drivers treated the children to more refreshments.

Tops in excitement, however, was reached at the island zoo. It came as no surprise that the youngsters' favorite turned out to be the brown bear, a natural-born comedian if ever there was one.

"He looks just like my teddy bear, only bigger," said one 6 year old.

The teddy bear craze was sweeping the country. In 1907, almost every child cherished at least one of the stuffed animals. They were named in honor of President Theodore Roosevelt. Some critics of T.R. said they represented the approximate number of baby bears orphaned on his shooting trips.

For Detroit's human orphans, a more serious traffic tangle was in store when their cavalcade recrossed the Belle Isle Bridge. Then came the day's grand finale, a stop at Electric Park. At this popular amusement center adjoining the bridge approach there were free rides for the youngsters on the carousel, the roller coaster, and other attractions.

As his contribution to the outing, former U.S. Sen. Thomas W. Palmer arranged for ice cream for the 700 children. By this time, most of them looked as fully stuffed at any teddy bear.

Clearly, too, they regarded the day as a complete success. As for the motorists, they congratulated themselves that the affair resulted in a boost for their images. There was no doubt that the image needed it — automobile operators were still a much-criticized minority in 1907.

Much credit for the success of Orphans Day was given to Philip Breitmeyer, commissioner of parks and boulevards. Besides donating his car for the event, he was the host on Belle Isle and worked hard to keep everyone happy.

But the commissioner was appalled when he noted how the 100-car caravan taxed the facilities of the Belle Isle Bridge. He became one of the first Detroiters to envision the traffic jams of the Motor Age.

The upshot of his pondering was a special recommendation in the annual departmental report he prepared that month. It urged upon the City Council the need for a new and bigger bridge.

It took considerable time for Breitmeyer's recommendation to bring results. The panic of late 1907 resulted in a tightening of the city's purse strings. Not until 1913 was a committee appointed to plan a new bridge. This body still was exploring the problem when the need suddenly became urgent.

That was on April 27, 1915. Shortly before 2 p.m. a watchman on the bridge, James Kearney, shouted to his colleague, Isaac Cohen, "Here comes that cart again!"

Cohen didn't have to be told what cart was meant. That morning a heavy steamroller, bound for a construction job on the island, plodded across the bridge with a steel cart in tow, the type used for heating irons in asphalt work. Swaying from side to side, the cart dropped hot coals at several points.

"There was no wind and I swept them up before any damage was done," Kearney remembered later. "We often have fires. I put out as many as six a day."

The last week in April was unseasonably warm and dry, and most of the fires were started by cigaret or cigar butts dropped on the flammable creosote blocks which paved the bridge's roadway.

No one worried about it. The watchmen kept

Detroiters loved the old Belle Isle Bridge, and they rallied by the thousands to watch the fight to save it from fire.

buckets of water at hand. They were accustomed to putting out fires.

As the steamroller passed them with cart in tow on its afternoon trip back to the mainland, the watchmen spotted a small blaze on the draw at the middle of the bridge.

They quickly went to work with their buckets — then gaped with horror as they glanced across the bridge toward the island. Fires were blazing all along the span. They ran and turned in an alarm.

Frank Martin, engineer at the draw, was in charge of swinging this section back to permit ships to pass through the channel. He also saw the danger.

"The fires started in half a dozen places at once," he said. "The bridge seemed to be all on fire from the island side past the American side of the draw.

Racing ahead of the inferno came a touring car attempting to cross. Martin waved the driver, J. H. Burns, to a stop. He used a bucket of water to quench the flames on the car's tonneau top. Burns raced on again, reaching the mainland safely; his was the last car across.

Martin and a fellow engineer, Robert Durie, remained at their post until the heat drove them back. They had to run for it then as flames licked along the heavily creosoted yellow pine stringers and attacked the flooring of the sidewalks.

The crew of the fireboat James R. Elliott, stationed at the nearby Parke, Davis & Co. dock, saw the blaze. The fireboat had steam up and reached the draw in a few minutes. Soon afterward Detroit's other fireboat, the James Battle, made it from a downtown dock.

Both boats played streams of water on the draw. Because of the narrowness of the channel, however, they found it difficult to maneuver.

Thirteen fire companies converged on the bridge approach at East Grand Boulevard and Jefferson, with horse-drawn Hose Wagon 7 in the van. F. C. Drengberg, at the reins, drove out to the draw and turned chemicals on the blaze.

Almost immediately, flames darted up through the bridge floor and imperiled the wagon. Quickly turning his horses, Drengberg dashed the hose wagon back from the draw. It was a narrow escape. Drengberg knew it moments later when half of the draw span gave way.

The noise was terrific. Steel girders, twisting under the intense heat, splashed into the water and sent up clouds of steam.

By now the bridge approach was a maze of fire engines, hose lines, firemen and spectators. Fire fighters ran hoses as far as they could out on the remaining bridge span. They took lines from pumpers out on commandeered launches. They clung to the stone piers below the blazing deck of the bridge.

In the river, a fleet of motorboats lined up, with life preservers handy. They were prepared to rescue any firemen forced to jump from the piers.

The thousands of onlookers jostled for vantage points. Many found perilous positions from which they were ousted by police.

On the nearby dock of the Michigan Bolt and Nut Works, Harry DeVries, a foreman, was pushed into the river by the crowd. In the confusion he almost drowned before anyone heard his cries. A fellow employe threw him a rope.

The firemen fought heroically, but it was a losing battle. Forty minutes after the draw disappeared, a span on the island side crumbled. It sank slowly into the channel and after the vapor cleared not a vestige was left above the surface.

F. A. Wilkinson, superintendent of the Detroit and Walkerville Ferry Co., released the Essex from her regular run for rescue operations between Belle Isle and the foot of Jos. Campau.

A Detroit-Windsor ferry, the Garland, joined in this task — the same Garland whose collision with the yacht Mamie 35 years before drowned 12 altar boys and five adults of Holy Trinity parish.

The Garland still was unlucky. Heavily loaded with autos and passengers from the island, she went aground 600 feet from the bridge.

In the end, eight spans of the bridge sank into the river, and only twisted skeletons of the rest remained. Gaunt girders, with paint scorched off, were twisted into fantastic shapes. At the island end four spans still clung together, but they made a bridge to nowhere.

One incident remained especially vivid to those who noted. At the height of the blaze a young woman attempted to dash out on the burning bridge. Stopped by a policeman, she explained she was the daughter of Col. Herman T. Kallman, the Army Corps of Engineers officer who supervised construction of the structure in 1887.

"I loved the bridge," she said. "I wanted to be the last one to set foot on it."

Younger spectators could understand how Miss Kallman felt, and those who crossed the spans often under their own power, the hikers and the bikers the young in heart of all ages. They loved the happy bridge.

41. The Fabulous Vagabonds

It probably was the most publicized campout of all time. The campers were so famous that the President of the United States leaped at a chance to fill a vacancy on the roster.

And President Warren G. Harding never regretted his acceptance in 1921 of an invitation to be initiated into the Nature Club, which had been formed a few years before by Henry Ford, Thomas A. Edison, Harvey S. Firestone and John Burroughs. Through his remaining short life Harding always spoke of his days with the Nature Club as the happiest of his turbulent presidency.

Ford was the host, and he did everything possible to make Harding comfortable. The President's secretary, George Christian, was permitted to visit camp — on condition that he didn't talk politics.

Nor was presidential protocol allowed to abrogate the camp's foremost unwritten rule. Ford's first consideration in all details was the welfare of Edison, whose inventions combined with Ford's automobiles to transform the horse-and-buggy America of their youth into a superpower at whose helm Harding felt all too inadequate.

The idea for the campouts originated with Edison. Meeting with Ford and Firestone at the Panama-Pacific Exposition of 1915 in San Francisco, where all three received honors, Edison intrigued them with his stories about the great outdoors.

Ford suggested that Burroughs, the best-loved naturalist in America, would be just the right companion to round out a camping foursome. Burroughs was 77 in 1915, 30 years older than Ford and Edison's senior by a decade, but he was still active.

Ford long had found enjoyment in reading and rereading Burroughs' nature books. But in 1913 a magazine article gave him pause; in it Burroughs bewailed the encroachments of the motor car on areas forming the habitat of wild creatures. Ford set about to change Burroughs' views in typically sly fashion.

Burroughs noted the result in his journal a few weeks later:

"I had a surprising letter. Mr. Ford, of automobile fame, is a great admirer of my books — says there are few persons in the world who have given him the pleasure I have.

"He wants to do something for me — he wants to present a Ford automobile, all complete. His sole motive is his admiration for me and my work — there shall be no publicity in connection with it.

"I am embarrassed by his offer. What shall I do? I want the machine, but how can I accept such a gift from a stranger?"

Overcoming his qualms, Burroughs accepted the car. Ford's plan worked perfectly. Burroughs quickly became enchanted with the opportunities the Model T afforded to seek out unspoiled regions, though after driving into a barn on his first attempt at the wheel he decided to let others drive.

On June 7, 1913, Burroughs made his first visit to Fair Lane, the Ford estate in Dearborn. He was delighted with what he found.

An enchantment of bird-song filled the woods of Fair Lane. Ford had imported thousands of birds from throughout the world for his sanctuary. Birdhouses were provided to meet the special needs of every species.

Proudly, Ford s h o w e d Burroughs the food receptacles kept filled all winter, the water basins prevented from freezing by electricity.

On Aug. 29, 1916, the first Nature Club expedition reached Burroughs' farm to pick him up for a rambling trip through New England. He wrote: "They camped in my orchard, an unwanted sight— a campers' extemporized village under my old apple trees—four tents, a large dining tent, and at night electric lights."

Even with such elaborate equipment, Burroughs found the going a bit rugged in the beginning. He complained: "Edison is a dictator. He shuns all the good roads and hunts up rough, hilly, dirt roads."

By the summer of 1918, however, the bonds of friendship were firm. Burrougs wrote warmly of Edison: "He is a great character. We are all devoted to him. Whenever the car stops he gets out, collects a handful of flowers, and brings them to me—half a dozen times each day—and I name them for him. Yesterday he brought me a monarda."

On their first journeys, the four went unrecognized by the few travelers they encountered on the winding byways. Each evening the campsite was selected by Edison, who remained commander-in-chief. Ford always swung an ax to prepare wood for the campfire.

Firestone served as the club's unofficial historian. He set down at length his admiration of the others' ability to rough it. He admitted a preference for hotel beds and barbershop shaves— and his companions often gibed at him as a "dude."

"When Mr. Ford is outdoors he is just like a boy," Firestone observed. "He wants to have running races, climb trees, or do anything a boy might do."

A major source of fun for Ford and Edison was building dams on small streams and examining old mills for a calculation of the power output of each. "They think in terms of power," Firestone wrote.

Shy as the deer he loved, Burroughs was non-plussed when a reporter found the campout in a remote Adirondacks area. The newsman arrived when Ford and Burroughs were reclining against a stump, enjoying the early sunlight of a chilly mountain morning. Guides were taking down the expedition's eight oiled-silk tents under the direction of Sato, Ford's Japanese chef. Edison was seated on a log near the dying campfire, immersed in a scientific periodical—and oblivious to everything else.

That first newspaperman proved to be a portent of what was to come as widespread interest was aroused by the campouts.

America's most illustrious "vagabonds" relax at a 1921 Nature Club campout. Seated, left to right, are Henry Ford, Thomas A. Edison, President Warren G. Harding and Harvey S. Firestone. The President's secretary, George Christian, is at far right; the man standing is not identified.

"Instead of a simple, gypsy-like fortnight on the road, we found ourselves in the midst of motion picture cameramen, reporters and curiosity seekers," Firestone wrote. "We became a kind of traveling circus, and it became tiresome to be utterly without privacy."

When Burroughs died in March, 1921, Ford spoke feelingly of his friend.

"He would have been 84 next Sunday," he said. "But it was a marvel to see the hardihood with which he worked and strove in the pursuit of wildlife information.

"When we went camping he was up at daybreak. Many a time at breakfast, he would tell us of something new he had found on an early morning walk.

"Burroughs had a very strong faith in immortality. We used to speculate on what the afterlife will be like. I'm sure that, wherever Burroughs is now, it's a place where there are birds and wild animals and the other things of nature which he loved so devotedly."

269

When plans for the next campout came up, Ford quickly set straight a newsman who asked if President Harding would take Burroughs' place.

"Oh, no," Ford said. "The President will be another member of the party. Burroughs will be there. We won't see him, of course, but he'll be there — make no mistake about it."

As the reporter gave him an incredulous stare, Ford went on quietly:

"One night, during our trip last year, as we sat around the campfire, we talked about eventualities this year might bring. And we agreed that, if one of us was missing from the circle, he'd come back in spirit even if he couldn't come in body.

"And Burroughs' will be there! Every time we sit at the table, we'll leave a place for him. He'll be right there among us, and I'm sure he'd feel hurt if we didn't take some notice of him."

When President Harding arrived at camp that summer, Ford introduced Edison, whom he had never met. The President offered a cigar, but Edison refused it.

"I don't smoke. I just chew," he said.

Actually, Edison's passion for cigars was well known. "But he had the idea," Firestone explained in setting down the incident, "that he was not going to take a cigar just because the President offered him one. Mr. Edison does not take to everyone at once and does not pretend to."

When the President took a tobacco plug from his pocket, the laugh was on Edison. He grinned and gamely took a big bite.

After his first experience with the Nature Club, Harding joined it whenever he could. On one occasion Luther Burbank, as renowned an expert with plants as Edison was with electricity, also was a guest. This was the trip which gave rise to one of the funniest anecdotes in the club's history.

En route to a new campsite on a day of heavy rain, the Linclon touring car carrying Harding, Ford, Edison, Firestone and Burbank bogged down in deep mud on a back road in West Virginia.

Ford's chauffeur went for help and returned with a farmer driving an ancient Model T. After the Lincoln was yanked from the mire, Ford was the first to shake the farmer's hand.

"I guess you don't know me, but I'm Henry Ford," he said. "I made the car you're driving."

Firestone chimed in: "I'm the man who made those tires of yours."

Then he introduced two of his companions: "Meet the man who invented the electric light — and the President of the United States."

Burbank was the last to shake hands. "I guess you don't know me, either?" he asked.

"No," said the farmer, "but if you're the same kind of a liar as these other darned fools, I wouldn't be surprised if you said you was Santa Claus."

In August, 1923, Ford, Edison and Firestone delayed their vacation to attend Harding's funeral in his home town of Marion, Ohio. Then with their wives they took a Great Lakes cruise on Ford's yacht, the Sialia. The vagabond days on the road were over.

42. Those Wonderful Interurbans

Adventure was tantalizingly close for Detroit youngsters half a century ago. It beckoned on every main thoroughfare — Woodward, Grand River, Gratiot, Fort, Jefferson and Michigan — whenever a big interurban car rolled out of town.

If you were old enough to save a dollar or two from a paper route or mowing lawns, you could afford to go highballing across the countryside on the electric trolleys. After you explored the area reached by cars on the major avenue in your part of town, you graduated to the downtown Interurban Station, at Jefferson and Bates. From there cars fanned out in every direction.

Each day the interurban made 330 runs from the city. A dispatcher called out the names of such destinations as Grass Lake, Sibley, Keego Harbor and Imlay City. You decided where you wanted to go while sitting on one of the long cane benches in the waiting room.

The interurbans were a lot more comfortable than city streetcars. They had green plush seats like railroad coaches. Even better were the black leather seats in the smoking section, next to the motorman's vestibule. This section was strictly a male preserve, with plenty of brass cuspidors. Usually several card games were in progress.

The conductor, dignified and urbane, came to your seat to collect the fare with an air that inspired awe. He rang it up on a register which jingled merrily at the front of the car.

272   You soon learned that express runs were faster

than locals and made fewer stops. Fastest of all were the limiteds, the aristocrats of the electric lines.

They really made time. On some stretches they maintained 60 miles an hour, or more.

Such speeds were possible only on the straight-aways, however. The cars could utilize much shorter curves than railroads. Motormen learned to diminish speed just enough to safely round the curves, then quickly accelerate to full speed.

Once in a while a motorman maintained too much speed. One such time was Saturday, Sept. 3, 1910. There were so many passengers for the 6:25 p.m. Flint limited out of Detroit that it ran in three sections. Two sections waited on a siding at Harris Creek, near Rochester, for the southbound limited.

The third section hit the switch at full throttle. It vaulted from the track, turned over, and landed with trucks in the air and all wheels spinning. Miraculously, only one passenger was killed. But 13 were injured.

Fortunately, the Detroit area never suffered a disaster as serious as the one near Fort Wayne, Ind., later that September, when 39 died in a head-on collision. A local carrying an excursion group from Bluffton, Ind., to the state fair at Fort Wayne was rammed by an empty special car heading south. The motorman of the special, getting a report that the local was 10 minutes late, gambled that he could beat it to the next siding—and lost.

In spite of their hazards, the speeding interur-bans were a spur to the prosperity of rural areas around Detroit. They made it possible to ship perishable produce into the city from considerable distances, and both farmers and city dwellers profited.

Even ice could be transported into Detroit by interurban.

This discovery was exploited by Pittman and Dean, an ice delivery company in the years when a fixture of the summer scene was the ice wagon behind its clopping horse. The wagon had a back step that always invited small boys to hop on and filch cooling chunks of ice.

Once the electric line to Almont and Imlay City was completed, Pittman and Dean's major source

273

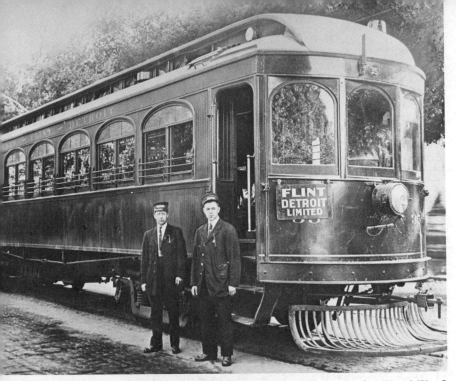

Travel by interurban railways reached its peak after World War I. Limiteds on the run between Detroit and Flint were frequent and well patronized.

of ice for many years was Long Lake, near Oxford. The lake was renowned for the purity of its water.

Businessmen in smaller communities not always were too happy about the interurbans. The cars made it easy for women to board a convenient car, run into the city on a shopping expedition, and be home in time to get dinner.

Every major town boasted about its trolley connections. The colored postcard views that carried such tidings as "Having a fine time, wish you were here" were as popular in Saline and Fenton as in the big cities, and most cards usually showed interurbans trundling down Main Street.

Just as electrification and extension of the old horsecar lines made it possible for Detroiters who worked downtown to make their homes in outlying subdivisions, the interurbans made it possible to expand this trend to bedroom suburbs beyond the city limits. The concept of Detroit as the core city of a three-county metropolitan area had its inception during the interurban days.

It was an era which spanned four decades. In 1893 an electric suburban line was completed from Detroit to Wyandotte. As the tracks were extended, the line became the Detroit, Wyandotte and Trenton, then the Detroit, Monroe & Toledo. Finally, as the Lake Shore Electric Railway, it reached the glory of two-car limiteds speeding all the way to Cleveland.

Another line was built out Michigan Avenue and incorporated in 1897 as the Detroit, Ypsilanti and Ann Arbor Railway. Merged into it was a 7½-mile stub line, from downtown Ypsilanti to the city limits of Ann Arbor, known as the Ypsi-Ann.

After operations were extended to Jackson, the Michigan Avenue route was ambitiously renamed the Detroit, Jackson and Chicago. It never came much closer to Chicago than the Duluth, South Shore and Atlantic steam railroad in the Upper Peninsula came to the eastern seaboard.

The busy interurban year of 1893 also saw the Rapid Railway out Gratiot reach Mt. Clemens. Later it extended to Port Huron. From the start, this service enjoyed prosperity as a speedy means of reaching the St. Clair Flats.

Its success attracted competition. The Shore Line was completed out Jefferson through Grosse Pointe to Mt. Clemens in 1900. After the Shore Line was continued along the St. Clair River to Port Huron, interurban adventurers could enjoy different scenery all day by taking one line to Port Huron and returning on the other. In time, the Shore Line was absorbed by the Rapid Railway.

The Detroit, Lake Orion and Flint line was begun in 1899, and others serving Plymouth and Northville followed. By the turn of the century, Detroit was America's interurban railway capital, with more extensive radial lines than any other city.

All these operations were consolidated with the Detroit United Railways (DUR), an amalgamation of the city traction lines, in 1901. At its peak, this combine served 159 communities within a 75-mile radius of Detroit.

The interurbans reached their peak about the time of World War I. Michigan had 981 miles of track in 1916. The network out of Detroit interlocked with systems in Ohio and Indiana.

It was possible to travel by electric cars from Chicago to New York. Parlor cars and even sleeping cars appeared on popular long-distance runs.

The queen of Detroit's interurbans was the Yolande. This was a deluxe chair car used by DUR bigwigs on inspection jaunts. In 1922 the Yolande was rechristened Ottaway and fitted out as a club car on the Detroit-Pontiac run.

For the benefit of bridge-happy commuters, the forward compartment was equipped with permanent card tables, and there were 13 lounge chairs. A smaller rear compartment with five chairs was reserved for men.

No sex lines were drawn in the card players' section. But the flapper age was in full fling, and the DUR was forced to recognize that women bridge players sometimes smoked.

The management wrestled long with this touchy situation, they came up with a complicated decision. Women players could smoke if the liked, and men players could smoke if the ladies didn't object. If there were objections, the male smokers would have to retire to the little rear compartment.

The DUR maintained its general offices on the upper floors of the Interurban Station. In the 1920's one man was found there who had been a part of Detroit's trolley epic from its beginning.

This was John Cochrane, who as the best horsecar driver for the old Citizens Railway, was assigned to the city's first electrified car on its initial run in 1892. Cochrane's later years came before pension plans were commonplace, but the DUR found a spot for him at the controls of the Interurban Station's elevator.

Another trolley veteran with a talent for survival was Del Smith, who began as a conductor on the Detroit, Jackson and Chicago line in 1907. After the city took over the DUR, Smith became the system's general manager, and later a Detroit councilman.

In Smith's early years as a conductor, Henry Ford was a frequent rider on his car between

Detroit and Dearborn. The sand roads west of Livernois were formidable then, even for the sturdy Model T.

Because of his keen interest in things mechanical, Ford developed an affection for the interurbans. All the while, however, his automobiles were hastening the day when the cross-country electric cars would be preserved only in trolley museums.

Bus competition wiped away the profits. By 1925 only one line in Michigan, the Grand Rapids, Grand Haven & Muskegon, was not in the hands of a receiver. In a last ditch fight, the traction interests lobbied a bill through the legislature to permit them to operate motor routes paralleling their rights of way, but it was vetoed by Gov. Alex J. Groesbeck.

With the exception of segments of Ohio operations which crossed the state line to tap Adrian and Morenci, by 1932 only one stretch of interurban trackage remained in use in Michigan. This was a line from St. Joseph and Benton Harbor to South Bend, Ind.

In 1934 it too gave up the ghost. The haunting wail of the speeding interurbans was heard no more.

One outpost of Detroit's far-flung trolley empire remains, though it seldom is recognized as such. In the palmy days, the DUR built a fortresslike power plant in Farmington, near the junction of the Orchard Lake division with the route on Grand River. Subsequent to the demise of the electric lines, the structure had an honorable second career as a winery.

Today it still stands, a lonely monument to those wonderful interurbans.

43. The Last Alarm

For generations, thundering hooves carried fire fighters and equipment to every Detroit blaze. But the fire horses' biggest audience gathered to watch their response to a make-believe alarm. It was their historic last run.

More than 50,000 people turned out on April 10, 1922, to watch the city's last five fire horses pull their engines down Woodward in a farewell appearance. An army of 500 horses had served the Detroit Fire Department from the arrival of the steam engine to the motor age. The last of them were Pete, Jim, Tom, Babe and Rusty.

The five were ready as always when the fire alarm sounded at the National Bank Building. They didn't know there wasn't a fire. Spectators on Woodward Avenue from Grand Circus Park to Cadillac Square cheered them on.

With Pete, Jim and Tom pulling the fire engine in the lead and Babe and Rusty following with the hose cart, they gave the kind of performance for which fire horses were noted. Nostrils flared, foam flecked the bits, and iron hooves beat sparks from the pavement.

The five veterans were from Engine Co. 37, at Central and Dix. They had responded to the last genuine fire several days before with the dispatch of old pros.

For their last run downtown, there were special trimmings. The fire department band played "Auld Lang Syne." W.M. Sexton, the department's oldest living veteran — he had been a member of Phoenix

278

Co. No. 2 at the dawn of the steam fire engine era — waited at the Soldiers' and Sailors' Monument to reward the horses with affectionate pats and sugar cubes at the end of the run.

Chief Timothy Callahan drove Old Red, one of the oldest equine veterans — brought back from retirement for the occasion — in a shined-up chief's buggy of an earlier era. For the chief himself, the day was more than a poignant moment of history. It was a leave-taking of old companions who had been the mainstay of the department in his youthful years as a fireman.

Callahan deplored any sentimental view of the fire horses. He could remember tough customers among t h e m whose "playfulness" at times amounted almost to viciousness, horses that would strike and bite and kick at their masters, and even chase them into a corner or under a manger and hold them captive until help came.

"But the vicious horse was the exception," Callahan said. "By far the greater number were well-behaved. They were as brave as the firemen themselves, seeming to realize the responsibility that rested upon their broad backs. If a horse can be a hero, they were heroes, too."

Callahan remembered R u f u s W. Gillett, who served on the Fire Commission in the 1880's and was chairman of its committee on horses.

"Gillett loved horses and never was happier than when he added a fine animal to the department's livestock or did something to add to the animals' comfort," he said.

Then there was Commissioner Fred Moran, Gillett's successor as the guardian of the horses.

"If ever there was a genius in his line, Moran was one," Callahan said. "He not only personally bought every horse added to the department, but knew every one of them by sight and by name — and they all knew and liked him.

"He would not t o l e r a t e mistreatment of the horses. If he ever caught a man abusing one, heaven help that fellow!

"On Sundays Moran always went out to the supply stable. He would spend hours at a time ministering to sick horses."

The same type of man was Martin Cooney, boss of the fire horses for their last 27 years in the department. Cooney died in the month following the horses' last run. There were some who said he died of loneliness, because "he loved horses even more than he did men."

Like Moran before him, Cooney knew instinctively when a horse had what it took to be a good member of the fire department. Decades after his death, his daughter, Mrs. Agnes Paul, recalled: "When dad would walk into any of the stations, the horses knew him instantly. They would whinny and crane their necks. He broke them in with gentleness and patience, and they never forgot him."

It was said that Cooney never took a furlough, because of his devotion to his horses. He always hurried to a winter fire; there the horses would be standing, their sleek coats steaming after their run.

Their friend would see that they were blanketed. When they were back in the barns, he made sure that they were rubbed down and made warm and comfortable.

The average working life of a fire department horse was only four or five years. Pounding city pavements at high speed was hard on them. Cooney would see to it that they were sold to farmers on their retirement, and that they went to areas where there were no hard roads to irritate their weakened feet.

On that April day in 1922 it was difficult to realize that the equine age in the department was little more than 60 years. Prior to the arrival of the steam fire engine, things were colorful — but primitive.

After the great fire of 1805, each male citizen was required to have two buckets and a neck yoke for carrying them to fires. Then came the swashbuckling decades of the volunteer fire companies, loosely-knit clubs whose members enjoyed prestige, organized clambakes, and loved dress uniforms and silver trophies.

The city provided their hand-operated pumping engines, but the firemen bought everything else. Their lack of discipline was notorious, and feuds between rival companies often were bitter.

On Oct. 3, 1860, the city bought its first steam
pumper from the Amoskeag Co., of Manchester,

N.H., for $3,150. It was named Lafayette No. 1, and was housed at Larned and Wayne.

The city fathers recognized that skilled attendants would be needed to operate the machine. They hired Detroit's first professional fire fighters — an eningeer, two drivers, a foreman and five hosemen. John McDuff, one of the original hosemen on that first engine, became fire marshal in 1890 and served until 1916. He died in 1921 as the fire-horse era was drawing to a close.

The fire horses had their greatest test on New Year's Day in 1886. Detroiters said the town would never have another New Year's Day like it. Fortunately, they were right.

Headlines in a Detroit News extra at noon, Jan. 1, 1886, told the story:

GREAT FIRE
The Biggest Blaze in Detroit's History

Nearly $2,000,000 in Property Destroyed

After celebrating New Year's Eve, most holiday merrymakers were enjoying a late sleep. If any of the few pedestrians strolling on Brush Street at 9 a.m. looked up at the building of D.M. Ferry & Co., it must have been with a touch of civic pride. Built in 1881, it was the largest commercial block in town.

At 9:10 a.m., a jet of black smoke curled from a broken window in the handsome building, from which millions of garden s e e d s were shipped throughout the country.

Jets of smoke from the Ferry building grew larger. A passerby noticed and hurried across the street to tell officers at the police station.

The first alarm brought four fire companies. Two more followed on a second alarm turned in by the first official on the scene, Police Commissioner Jerome Croul. The streets were nearly deserted, but the clanging firebells quickly changed that. Police lines were drawn to handle the crowd.

Dense smoke inside the building prevented firemen from entering. They broke windows and shot streams of water inside. The openings also let in a brisk wind. Suddenly, the building's dark interior was wild with flames.

281

Detroit's last fire horses are off on their final run, April 10, 1922. Clomping out of Engine Co. No. 37 are Pete, Jim and Tom, pulling the steam pumper, and Babe and Rusty on the hose cart. There was no fire; the alarm was ceremonial, and spectators lined the curbs to cheer the horses' farewell appearance.

Windows in the southeast corner were blown out by the heat. The roof curled back in the flames like the top of a burning box.

One fire engine working on Brush was threatened by the conflagration. As burning boards fell on it, Fire Chief James Battle sent men to try and save it. Streams of water were directed on the men to protect them from burns as they rushed the horses to safety and dragged away the engine.

Enclosed in a solid sheet of flames, the building's south wall collapsed at 10:15 a.m. Heat drove firemen from their positions on Brush. They took their hoses across the street.

At 10:25 a.m. the wind shifted and flames began to sweep toward the north end of the building. Employes saved records on the second floor by throwing them out windows. The last employes got out only moments before flames reached the north windows.

282

Charles O. White, manager of White's Theater on Randolph, across from the Ferry Building, could see that his problems were just beginning. The theater was in danger.

White called members of the "Pavements of Paris" company from their hotel to rescue their costumes and scenery.

The theater's auditorium filled with smoke. A ladder was raised from a fire truck brought to the front of the building as a blaze broke out on the roof. Capt. Richard Filban quickly climbed it.

As he neared the top, a cornice of the building collapsed above him. He was thrown to the ground under a shower of bricks.

Digging frantically, rescuers removed the rubble, but Filban was dead when they reached him.

By 11:30 a.m. only the skeleton of the theater was left.

Flames spread across Monroe to the Bellevue Hotel and the Hilsendegen Block. Dozens of streams of water fought the new threat.

By the time the blaze in the Ferry building had burned out, lesser fires across the street were under control. Detroiters began to realize how closely the city had escaped a holocaust such as that which destroyed the heart of Chicago 15 years before.

But the first concern of the firemen after the flames were out was for their horses.

It seemed as if the fire horse as an institution was destined to go on forever. No one considered it a threat when the first automobile in the department, a Carter two-seater, was assigned to the notification branch in August, 1906. The firemen thought it was a joke. They called it the Hustle Buggy.

In March, 1907, another Carter two-seater runabout was obtained for the superintendent of apparatus. An Olds four-cylinder car was purchased for the chief. The first motor fire engine in the world, a Packard, arrived Nov. 30, 1908.

A storm of objections to the replacement of horses by motor vehicles followed. The early autos frequently were cantankerous about starting; and breakdowns on the road were frequent. The fire horses, it was argued, were noted for readiness and reliability.

But all too soon came the time when the last fire horses were retired to a real equine Elysium in River Rouge Park.

In 1934, only four of them were left, Walter F. Israel, the fire chief at that time, talked about the department's horse days as fondly as his predecessors.

"I was a driver at Ladder No. 3 when the horses were retired," he remembered. "Some of them were so nervous they couldn't sleep, and of course they didn't last long.

"But I knew one that could sleep any time. He'd come in from a run, lie down with his head flat on the floor, and soon he'd be snoring like a man. But when the alarm sounded, he was raring to go.

"One horse liked tobacco. I carried some in my hip pocket for him and he'd pester me until I'd give him some.

"One time he nosed my pocket when I was busy. He touched it again. When I didn't pay attention to him, he took a bite at the spot where he knew the tobacco was. He bit the entire pocket out of my pants!"

44. An Affinity for Laughter

For more than a decade after Henry Ford unloosed his Model T upon the world in 1908, visitors to Detroit expected to hear Ford jokes. They seldom were disappointed.

Teen-age boys who took summer jobs on the big white busses of the Dietsche Sightseeing Co. found a bit of comic relief in the spiel they were required to memorize about points of interest in the city:

"They say that next year Mr. Ford is going to paint his cars yellow and sell them in bunches, like bananas."

Barkers repeated this one through megaphones as the buses approached the Ford plant in Highland Park, then waited for the laughs that always followed. As Ford jokes went, it may not have been the best — but it wasn't the worst, either.

There were all kinds of them. For a generation of Americans, jokes about the Model T occupied as firm a place in folklore as the vehicle itself did on the highways and byways.

Witticisms about the car were an integral part of vaudeville humor. Fittingly, the Temple Theater Building at the Campus Martius and Monroe, seat of Detroit's major vaudeville theater, was surmounted during the T-joke years by the city's first animated electric sign, a touring car with whirling wheels in lights that displayed the slogan: "Watch the Fords Go By."

Even on railroad coaches, train butchers offered 10-cent booklets of Ford jokes along with peanuts and candy bars. Apparently they were unaware

When Henry and Edsel Ford conducted Charlie Chaplin on a tour of
the noisy Ford plant in Highland Park, communication had to be in
Chaplin's idiom—pantomime.

that they were advertising a competition which
might prove fatal.

Many jokes revolved around the assumption that
tin was the major element in the Model T's
construction. In one variation, a farmer stripped
the tin roof from his barn and puckishly sent it to
the Ford factory. In due course he received a letter
of acknowledgement.

"Your car must have been in an exceptionally
bad wreck," it said, "and we shall not be able to
complete repairs for several weeks."

The stories knocked or boosted the Model T
impartially. One owner expressed disappointment
at not getting the Ford dealership in his home
town, claiming it went instead to the 5-and-10-cent
store. Another directed in his will that his touring
car should be buried with him. "I never was in a

hole yet it couldn't get me out of," he explained.

Ford riddles were popular, too. "Why is a Ford like a bathtub? Because you hate to be seen in one."

If the driver of a more expensive car told that one to a Ford owner, the latter could come back with: "Why is a Ford car like a motion to adjourn? Because it's always in order."

Spin-offs from the basic Ford jokes were endless. There were postcards illustrative of such jingles as: "While the big car sticks around the beanery, the Ford goes up and views the scenery." There were songs like "The Packard and the Ford," "In the Back Seat of the Henry Ford," and "The Little Old Ford Rambled Right Along." There was verse, like the many quatrains of "Omar the Ford":

"Come, fill the tank and fix the broken spring,

Your worn-out clutch into the garbage fling;

This car of thine hast but a little way to roll

And then you'll ask what trade-in price 'twill

bring."

Until Jan. 5, 1914, Henry Ford was not particularly well-known outside Detroit. But his announcement that day of a profit-sharing plan whereby he would pay his 13,000 employes a minimum of $5 a day created a worldwide sensation.

Up to then, $1 to $1.50 a day was considered an excellent wage. Ford was hailed as everything from a philanthropist to a crackpot Socialist. Stories about Ford, the man, soon became as widely circulated as those about his ubiquitous product.

Some had to do with his penchant for stopping on the road to aid any Ford driver having trouble with his machine. An early specimen managed to keep the original flavor of the Model T jokes:

It seems a farmer's roadster conked out on a country road .A lanky stranger drove up in another Model T and offered to help. The Samaritan did a bit of tinkering and succeeded in starting the engine, whereupon the farmer offered him a quarter.

"I don't need it," said the stranger. "I make these cars. I'm Henry Ford."

The farmer sniffed, suspecting a leg pull. "If you had all Ford's money," he said, "you wouldn't be driving a tin Lizzie."

Less than a month after the $5-a-day pronouncement sent out global shock waves, a half-pint English stage comic accepted an offer of $150 a week to make films with Mack Sennett and his Keystone Cops. Within three years this recruit, Charles Chaplin, signed his first million-dollar movie contract.

Chaplin did not miss the Model T's affinity for laughter. In a 1919 effort, "A Day's Pleasure," he departed from his usual role as the little tramp to portray a family man, expertly piloting wife and children through traffic tangles at the wheel of a Ford on a holiday outing. The comedy's high point was reached when the car got stuck in hot tar on the roadway.

When Ford and Chaplin met, they were numbered among the world's best known men.

By one of those coincidences dear to the hearts of movie directors but uncommon in real life, Chaplin arrived in Detroit on the same train as another figure of much renown.

The date was Oct. 23, 1923. On that autumn morning, Secretary of Commerce Herbert Hoover was on the way to becoming the successor of President Calvin Coolidge in the White House.

Hoover came to Detroit to preside over the first convention of the American Child Health Association. Through the Pullman window he could make out a large crowd at the Michigan Central Station. Movie cameras were poised; reporters, on hand.

But no one was waiting for the future president. Bag in hand, Hoover eased his way through the excited throng filling the concourse. He found a cab at the depot's side entrance and went to his hotel.

Meanwhile, amid shouts of "Hello Charlie!" and a fanfare of applause, cordon of police made a path through the crush for Chaplin and his party to an open car decorated for a tumultuous ride

downtown.

Chaplin decided to come to Detroit only a few hours before. After he completed "A Woman of Paris," the serious film by which he hoped to add recognition as a dramatic director to his laurels as a comedian, his friend John H. Kunsky, owner of Detroit's biggest chain of movie houses, invited him to the city on a hunch.

Kunsky knew that Chaplin threw everything he had into the making of a picture. He always needed to unwind afterward. Kunsky got the city to add an official invitation to his own, and the Chamber of Commerce arranged a dinner in Chaplin's honor. But Chaplin was noncommittal until another telegram arrived from Detroit.

"The schoolchildren of Detroit want to see you," it said.

That got to him. His response was prompt: "I'll be with you tomorrow morning."

Chaplin may have recalled his first appearance here 11 years before, unknown and unacclaimed. In 1912, he was a minor comic in an English music hall act at the Broadway Strand Theater. The act was called "The Wow-Wow" — but it was far from a wow.

In 1923, Detroit gave him a very different reception. Chaplin was warmly applauded en route to the Statler Hotel. After breakfast he was greeted by acting mayor John C. Lodge and members of the City Council.

Things didn't get out of hand, however, until a motor caravan took him through Highland Park for a meeting with Henry Ford and his son, Edsel. Highland Park High School students lined the corner of Glendale and Second. As the cavalcade approached, they poured into the street in such numbers that Chaplin's car was halted in spite of its police escort.

Not until the comedian stood up in the car, delivered an impromptu speech and threw kisses was he allowed to proceed.

Chaplin entered Henry Ford's office rather diffidently. He apologized for taking up Ford's time.

"Not a bit of it," returned Ford. "Im tickled to pieces to think you came all the way out here to see us."

Photographers took pictures. Then Henry Ford   *289*

caught Charlie by one arm and Edsel took the other. They led him toward the plant.

The three maintained an animated conversation as they walked into the factory, cupping hands to hear until the noise made it impossible. Thereafter, the meeting of minds as they strolled through the Ford domain continued of necessity in the Chaplin idiom — pantomime.

The party lingered longest at the assembly lines. Chaplin was fascinated. He made good use of his impressions later in "Modern Times," hailed by critics for its feat of somehow weaving into a slapstick background all the pathos of the little man caught up in the age of behemoth machines.

After leaving the plant, Chaplin began a tour of Detroit s c h o o l s — and enjoyed, as he said afterward, one of the greatest emotional treats of his life.

At the first school, he asked to be allowed to enter a classroom unannounced. When he did there was a moment of unbelieving silence. Suddenly there was a shout of recognition, and then bedlam.

They crowded around. Charlie talked to them. When he left the room tears spilled out of his eyes.

In other schools, the youngsters were brought from classrooms into auditoriums where they could see and hear Charlie in large groups. It was the same thing all over again.

Cheers, deafening cheers. And Charlie standing there, eyes sparkling, looking as if he had never heard anything like it before.

In one school he lost his derby. In another, someone made off with his handkerchief. Buttons disappeared. Charlie was p u s h e d, hugged and mauled. He loved it.

As he left a school he would say, "Where's the next one?" He kept it up until late in the afternoon.

"The look in those children's eyes!" he exclaimed on the way back to the hotel. "It was one of the finest times I ever had. The confidence and love they showed for me What better praise than to be regarded by the children as their clown?"

In his suite, Charlie still seemed like a boy at a picnic. He signed autographs for chambermaids. He danced around the room.

Chaplin never forgot that day. After "A Woman

of Paris," he returned to comedy. His next production, "The Gold Rush," in nine reels, was among the most ambitious of his career — and in the judgment of many critics, the most successful.

When it was completed, he sat back in the projector room of his Beverly Hills home for its first screening with a gleam in his eye.

"I hope it will please my little pals in Detroit," he said.

45. Light's Golden Jubilee

Never before had the city seen so great a gathering of celebrated persons, but the rain that October day gave them all a common touch.

For example, who would have expected the President of the United States to decline a limousine in favor of being drawn in an antique carriage by horses struggling through a quagmire of mud?

Also, it was something to see starched dignitaries from Tokyo and Budapest getting drenched apparently without a qualm. And there were captains of industry, statesmen, scientists and financiers getting wet, too, and taking it with good humor.

The place was Henry Ford's Greenfield Village in Dearborn, and the time was Oct. 21, 1929 — the Golden Jubilee of Light. Damp or not, the visitors seemed to enjoy the jubilee as much as Thomas Alva Edison liked prowling once more in the laboratory where he had seen the first electric light glow incandescent 50 years before.

Ford staged for his longtime friend that day perhaps the greatest "This Is Your Life" program ever devised, and America's premier wizard was delighted with his host's painstaking magic.

There was a lull in the rain at Detroit's Michigan Central Station, when guests arrived from the East and were transferred to a special train of antique coaches, drawn by a wood-burning locomotive named Sam Hill.

Aboard the special, Edison received an authentically stocked news butcher's bag like the one he had toted as a youth on trains between Port Huron and Detroit. With glee the 82-year-old inventor hawked fruit down the aisle. President Herbert Hoover gave him a dime for a peach.

Everyone knew the story of young Tom Edison setting fire to a baggage car where he experimented with chemicals, getting his ears boxed by an irate conductor and being expelled from the train at a station called Smith's Creek near Port Huron. So in 1929 it was a poignant moment when Edison stepped down from the special at the same Smith's Creek Station, moved brick by brick and rebuilt at Greenfield Village.

Historic though its components might be, the village itself was fresh off the Ford assembly line. In addition to the carriages lined up for a tour, automobiles were available. But when President Hoover gamely chose a carriage, most of the distinguished guests ignored the rain and followed his example.

Edison beamed with delight when he saw the Sarah Jordan boardinghouse, brought intact from Menlo Park, N.J., where it had adjoined his laboratory and housed his assistants. Here it was — flower garden and all — transplanted with care.

Francis Jehl waited at the laboratory nearby. As a youth of 20, he assisted in the 1879 experiments. In 1929, he was the only member of the original group besides Edison to survive.

The rainy day camaraderie continued into the evening. There was an aura of glory in the assemblage brought together to do Edison homage in Greenfield Village's replica of Independence Hall at Philadelphia.

Madame Marie Curie, the co-discoverer of radium, chatted with Jane Addams of Chicago's Hull House, as well as Dr. Charles Abbott, head of the Smithsonian Institution, and Judge Ben B. Lindsey. Orville Wright, survivor of the pair of brothers who put man into the sky, joked with Henry Ford, who put the common man on wheels, and with Harvey Firestone, who made the ride comfortable on rubber tires.

One of the informal witticisms of the evening has been preserved. It rippled across the tables, from Otto H. Kahn to Julius Rosenwald and George Eastman, from Charles M. Schwab and Adolph S. 293

President Herbert Hoover and Henry Ford joined to honor Thomas A. Edison for the Golden Jubilee of Light celebration at Greenfield Village in 1929, fifty years after Edison first produced electric light.

Ochs to Walter P. Chrysler, Henry Morgenthau, James W. Gerard and Daniel Willard. They were saying that you could round up a quorum of directors at the banquet for any billion-dollar corporation you could name — and considering the precarious state of the stock market, it was a good thing too.

The President spoke with a touch of whimsy that night that wasn't much remembered in the grim days following October 1929. He surmised, he said, that Edison's aim in inventing the electric light was "to relieve the human race from the curse of always cleaning oil lamps, scrubbing up candle drips and everlastingly carrying one or the other of them about."

Electric lights were dimmed all over the country while Hoover was speaking. In the banquet hall, they were replaced by candles and flickering oil *294* lamps.

There was a restfulness in the soft nostalgic lighting, even to the most habitually frenetic of the tycoons. For the octogenarian guest of honor, it provided a welcome and needed respite. The day had been long — for him most of all.

No one, certainly not the President, minded if Edison's eyes closed and his head drooped a bit. No one begrudged him a few moments of relaxation. And if he dreamed momentarily, it would have been of a day long before, a day brought back so vividly by the byplay on the ancient railroad car, the new butcher's bag . . .

Detroit was tense on the morning of April 6, 1862. It didn't take the vendor on the 10 o'clock train from Port Huron long to find out why.

From the depot, 15-year-old Tom Edison hurried to the city's newspaper offices on Woodbridge. He found crowds gathered in front of the bulletin boards.

Dispatches posted on them told of a big battle in progress near Pittsburg Landing, Tenn., around a crossroads church called Shiloh. Gen. U.S. Grant's army was under heavy attack by Confederate troops. Already there were 60,000 dead and wounded on both sides — with the outcome still in doubt.

Young Edison hurried back to the depot. After a bit of sharp bargaining — Tom promised to keep the telegraph operator supplied with Harper's Weekly for three months — the telegrapher agreed to send a flash on the battle to all stations en route to Port Huron.

Before train-time, Tom also fast-talked himself into 1,000 copies of the late edition on credit. Ordinarily he carried 100 papers north.

The first stop was Utica. The usual delivery there was two papers. When Tom saw a crowd waiting on the platform, he knew his hunch was a good one.

"The moment I arrived there was a rush for me," was the way he remembered it. "Then I realized the telegraph was a great invention. I sold 35 papers."

At Mt. Clemens the throng was so great that Tom wished he had brought even more papers. He doubled the price, from 5 to 10 cents a copy. They still sold like hotcakes. At Port Huron the crowd was even bigger — and Tom quickly decided to raise the ante again.

"Twenty-five cents a copy, gentlemen!" he shouted as the wheels groaned to a halt. "I haven't enough to go around."

No one argued. The last papers disappeared in a hurry. For the first time in his life, Tom Edison felt rich.

Even in 1862, he was no stranger to Detroit. He acquired the privilege of selling newspapers on the train between his hometown of Port Huron and the metropolis of Michigan at the age of 12. He put his daily layovers in the exciting city to good use.

Often he made a beeline for the Detroit Young Men's Society clubrooms on Woodbridge, at the rear of the Biddle House. By paying an annual fee of $2, Tom became eligible to use the society's library, the largest in town.

Naturally, he gravitated to the science shelves. He wasted no time deciding which book to read. He simply began at one end of a shelf and methodically devoured the volumes piecemeal, one by one.

Another profitable investment that he made in Detroit was the purchase of a hotel's small press which was used for printing daily bills of fare. A supply of type came with it. The press was installed in a baggage compartment turned over to him as storage space for his stock of goods.

Here was printed, as the train bumped along, a little sheet he called the Weekly Herald. Tom was the publisher, editor, compositor and pressman. He sold the paper for 3 cents a copy, or 8 cents a month delivered to any station on the line. Circulation soon built up to more than 400 copies.

It was through the Herald that Edison first experienced fame. Travelers carried copies to England, and the London Times recorded the appearance of this brash product of Yankee inventiveness — the first newspaper to be published on a moving train.

In Detroit, young Edison also met George Pullman, who operated a small shop. He was working on a plan for a railroad car equipped with sleeping berths. Edison was full of questions about it — and about everything else in Pullman's shop. Pullman gave him a supply of apparatus for the chemicals with which he was experimenting in his baggage-car compartment.

The thought of those chemicals always would bring back a painful memory, of how a stick of phosphorus, jarred from a shelf, started a fire in the car. The mounting flames flickered, flickered . . .

A nudge from Henry Ford brought Edison back to 1929 and the candlelight in the banquet hall. The President had finished. It was time for Edison's own part in the Golden Jubilee of Light, the reenactment of an historic moment.

Accompanied by President and Mrs. Hoover, Ford and Mrs. Ford, Edison returned to the laboratory shortly before 8:15 p.m. Jehl poured mercury into the reservoir of a mercury pump and the pump drew the air from the bulb with the charred thread. Edison turned on the current and, once again, light came forth in the laboratory and across the land.

Back in the banquet hall, in the full glare of his own creation, the old man stood up to speak, his snow-white hair a bit disheveled, his hands and his voice a bit shaky. He said:

"I would be embarrassed at the honors that are being heaped upon me this unforgettable night were it not for the fact that, in honoring me, you are also honoring that vast army of thinkers and workers of the past and those without whom my work would have gone for nothing. If I have helped spur men to greater effort, if our work has widened the horizon of thousands of men and given a measure of happiness in the world, I am content,"

His last words were for Henry Ford:

"I can only say that in the fullest meaning of the term he is my friend. Good night."

46. Battle of the Garden Court

It doesn't look like a one-time battleground.

Nowadays smokers, people who want to sit together and chat, and visitors merely resting their feet find the Garden Court at the Detroit Institute of Arts a pleasant place. Students linger there with their books. Some of the loungers study the murals on the walls by Diego Rivera, but most hardly give the frescoes a second glance.

It wasn't always so peaceful. When the murals were new, they were the center of a raging controversy.

The kindest disposition of them proposed by those who thought they were an outrage was that they be whitewashed over. This was the suggestion of the Rev. Ralph Higgins, senior curate of St. Paul's Cathedral. City Councilman William P. Bradley didn't think whitewashing was enough. Whitewash, he said, could be removed. Bradley demanded that the murals be erased completely from the museum walls; he branded them "a travesty on the spirit of Detroit."

The tumult was not foreseen by Dr. W. R. Valentiner, the institute's dignified director. He had long wanted to do something about the Garden Court's huge bare plaster walls. A Burne Jones tapestry and a large painting by Augustus John hung there temporarily, but the effect left something to be desired.

Murals seemed to be called for. Valentiner recommended Diego Rivera, regarded as the world's foremost mural painter, for the job. The arts commission members were impressed by a showing of his drawings and watercolors. The Mexican artist was invited to come to Detroit.

Edsel Ford, one of the museum's greatest bene-factors, agreed to underwrite the project's cost. It was announced to the public by Valentiner on June 10, 1931.

Three tons of lime arrived at the museum the following December, along with Albert Barrows, one of Rivera's assistants. The muralist himself arrived the following April, accompanied by his wife and two more assistants — Clifford Wight, a sculptor from California; and Lord Hastings, of the British peerage.

Plump and affable, Rivera weighed 316 pounds when he reached Detroit. He went on a diet and lost 108 of them in the 11 months he worked in the Garden Court.

It was clear that being an assistant to Rivera was no job for a dilettante. Rivera devoted several weeks to studying Detroit auto plants for inspiration, but once the work itself was under way Wight began operations at 3 a.m. to have wet plaster freshly applied to the museum walls by the time Rivera came to work at 10 o'clock.

Rivera drove himself, too. The section of wall prepared by Wight had to be entirely covered before the plaster dried. Sometimes Rivera put in as many as 20 hours at a stretch on his scaffolding, high above the floor of the Garden Court.

Members of the institute staff were amazed at his endurance. Through the long days of midsummer, when the temperature under the court's glass roof reached 120 degrees, he worked steadily.

He found his theme prowling odd corners of the city, visiting the neighborhoods of workmen's homes near the factories and the areas where ethnic groups centered their activities. He saw Detroit, he said, as an expression of the steel that goes into automobiles and skyscrapers alike. On the walls of the Garden Court he represented the four elements most important in the making of steel by four major female figures.

"The yellow race represents the sand, because it is most numerous," he said. "And the red race, the first in this country, is like the iron ore, the first thing necessary for the steel.

"The black race is like coal, because it has a great native esthetic sense, a real flame of feeling and beauty in its ancient sculpture, its native rhythm and music. So its esthetic sense is like the fire, and its labor furnishes the hardness which the carbon in the coal gives to steel.

"The white race is like the lime, not only because it is white, but because lime is the organizing agent in the making of steel. It binds together the other elements and so you see the white race as the great organizer of the world."

Even while Rivera put finishing touches on the smaller panels, the gates in the court were unlocked for visitors on St. Patrick's Day, 1933. The critical donnybrook began in a matter of hours.

An indignation meeting was called. One of the most vocal critics, Dr. George H. Derry, president of Marygrove College, summed up the objections this way:

"Senor Rivera has perpetrated a heartless hoax on his capitalist employer, Edsel Ford. Rivera was engaged to interpret Detroit; he has foisted on Mr. Ford and the museum a Communist manifesto. The key panel that first strikes the eye, when you enter the room, betrays the Communist motif that animates and alone explains the whole ensemble. Will the women of Detroit feel flattered when they realize that they are embodied in the female with the hard, masculine, unsexed face, ecstatically staring for hope and help across the panel to the langurous and grossly sensual Asiatic sister on the right?"

The arts commission met in a state of siege. Letters of protest were piled high in the board room. But the members also found a growing reaction to the criticism. Telegrams and letters were presented from university professors, museum directors and art critics throughout the country — expressing regret that the murals were put under attack.

In the end, the commission accepted the murals and thanked Edsel Ford for his gift.

Rivera moved on to New York to complete another commission. An even greater storm followed there. The new commission was from John

Controversy was vigorous when Diego Rivera decorated the walls of the Garden Court at the Detroit Institute of Arts with frescoes; some scented Communist propaganda in Rivera's work. But the murals soon became an accepted part of Detroit's cultural wealth.

D. Rockefeller Jr., for the walls of Rockefeller Center. Rivera's design included a Communist demonstration in Wall Street, where banners were depicted bearing such legends as "Down With Imperialistic Wars!" "Workers Unite" and "Free Money."

Rockefeller stood the gaff for a time, but when Rivera added a portrait of Nicolai Lenin he threw in the sponge and ordered the painting destroyed.

Rivera pocketed his fee and bided his time. He was given an opportunity to retaliate when the Palace of Fine Arts in Mexico City asked him to recreate the murals there from his original sketches. He put portraits of the Rockefeller family next to Lenin.

In later years, Detroit would name a freeway after Edsel Ford. Yet the Garden Court murals might well be the memorial that the quiet, self-effacing son of Henry Ford would himself consider most fitting. It was ironic that the heir apparent to one of the world's great fortunes should appear in the controversy as the sponsor of the Communist Rivera — but Edsel Ford's lifetime was full of ironies.

It was said that he grew up under the shadow of his father. Nevertheless, he became president of the Ford Motor Co. in 1919 at 25, and it was no mere titular responsibility. From the first day he visited the company offices as a boy, his father saw to it that he was trained to fill the role.

Greenfield Village bears witness to the omnivorous enthusiasm of the elder Ford as a collector of Americana, but he was not greatly attracted to the fine arts. Edsel Ford, on the other hand, played an important role in Detroit's cultural development.

His appointment to the Arts Commission in 1925, extended by Mayor John C. Lodge for seven years, proved a happy choice. He became president of the commission in 1930 and steered the Institute of Arts through the difficult depression years.

Throughout those years, Ford and Valentiner worked in close partnership.

Dr. Valentiner became director of the old museum on East Jefferson in 1924. His monumental task was to make the collection worthy of the $7,000,000 new building. Formerly associated with the Hague museum of Holland and the Kaiser Friedrich Museum in Berlin as well as the Metropolitan Museum of Art in New York, he ranked as a world authority on Italian sculpture, the art of the Middle Ages, oriental art and other fields.

Edsel Ford purchased and donated treasures selected by Valentiner specifically to round out the collection. It might be a Persian silk animal rug of the 16th century, a marble Madonna and Child by the 14th century Italian sculptor Nino Pisano, or a rare sixth century Chinese gilt bronze Matreya, a "Buddha of the Future."

Together, they built for Detroit's future artistic heritage. Their collaboration put the institute well on the way to becoming one of America's great museums.

47. Latter Days of a Side-Wheeler

It was remarkable that old rivermen should be so persistent in predicting the Tashmoo was bound to come to a bad end.

Never did an excursion steamer have more glory in her early years. But the Tashmoo was a side-wheeler that bore an Indian name. The old timers never stopped shaking their heads over this unfortunate combination.

Still, she was a proud and luxurious ship. For decades she was the best - loved vessel on the Detroit River. Her fame was so great that most Detroiters came to think Tashmoo Park was named after the boat, instead of vice versa.

Tashmoo Park was the pleasure spot set in the pleasant greenery of the St. Clair Flats where the steamer Tashmoo stopped several times daily on trips between Detroit and Port Huron. When the park opened in 1897 it was regarded as the crowning touch that gave Detroit as fine a summer playground as any city on the lakes could boast.

Besides its stately groves of old trees with plenty of picnic tables, a baseball diamond, swings and rides, the park had a casino and a dancing pavilion so big everybody goggled. It had real Indians too. They paddled over from the Canadian reservation on nearby Walpole Island and sold moccasins and beadwork to fun seekers from Detroit.

Developed by the Star-Cole Line, the park was delightful for one-day family excurisons on the steamer Darius Cole or the big new Greyhound. At 50 cents a round trip, it was a real bargain.

A reporter for The Detroit News-Tribune took the trip and was enthusiastic about what he found:

"One's first trip to the Flats is a red-letter day in life's calendar. This western Venice seems to be a spot where tired feet and dusty pavements are no more, but where the people float through liquid streets."

Since establishment of the Lake St. Clair Fishing and Shooting Club in 1872 — later to become the Old Club — private clubs, cottages and hotels proliferated at the Flats. Tashmoo Park broadened the resort's popularity base to include virtually all Detroiters.

The hotels ran a wide gamut. At Joe Bedore's, six-bottle men always could be sure of lusty companions. At the other end of the scale , the Island House offered rustic charm to many families from the South who came year after year to escape the heat back home. The dignified Muir House, operated by Mrs. C. M. Muir, was advertised as "the only temperance house at the Flats."

In 1897, the newest and most pretentious hostelry was Riverside Hotel, a mile beyond Star Island. It attracted admiration for its fine expanse of lawn between the main building and the dock. Under rainbow-hued parasols, women guests paraded on the lawn and verandas to watch the passing show of Great Lakes vessels threading the channel hardly a fair-sized croquet stroke away.

Ore and grain freighters were numerous, but the big attractions were the cruise ships for the Upper Lakes. Waving passengers thronged their decks. The Detroit & Cleveland Navigation Co.'s new steamer, the City of Mackinac, took cruisers to Mackinac Island from Detroit at $12.50 for the round trip, meals and berth included. The Detroit, Windsor & Soo Line offered a seven-day trip to Georgian Bay and Lake Superior for $17. The aristocrat of cruise ships, the Canadian Pacific's Alberta, charged $20 for a journey to Fort William, Ontario.

The most welcome sight of all for ship-watchers at the Flats, however, was the Tashmoo. The schedule she maintained through the resort area seemed incredible. In less than an hour, the Tashmoo made 10 stops.

What words can recapture the excitement of a Tashmoo landing? The seemingly reckless

Breaking loose from winter moorings and blown up the Detroit River in a December gale, the Steamer Tashmoo was battered against the Belle Isle Bridge—but survived for many seasons of pleasure cruises.

approach to the dock; the spouting foam of the reversed paddlewheels bringing her to a sudden halt; the shouted greetings across the narrowing span between ship and shore; the clanging bells. Swiftly followed the accurately tossed hawser loops dropping on the piles, the gangplank lowered and the passengers hurrying off while the never-stilled engines throbbed impatiently.

Within seconds the rising gangplank nipped at the heels of any dawdling passenger. Retracted hawsers whistled through the air; bells clanged again; more spouts of foam. Then the fluttering handkerchiefs of farewell dwindled behind. Only the Tashmoo could do it with such flair.

She had her trial run in 1900. Adm. G e o r g e   *305*

Dewey and his bride were among her first passengers. Her epic race with the City of Erie and President Theodore Roosevelt's ride on her soon after he became President added to her eclat.

But on Dec. 8, 1927, the doubts the old rivermen expressed for so long about the steamer came to the fore. That was the day the Tashmoo, in the worst storm on the river in years, disappeared without a soul on board.

A 60-mile-an-hour gale was blowing, driving snow before it. During the night the temperature dropped 40 degrees, to 8 above. In the predawn blizzard The Detroit News dispatched a reporter and photographer to assess storm damage along the waterfront. At the office of the White Star Line, successors to Star-Cole, at the foot of Griswold, the team for the paper found the big story in the person of a white-faced watchman, Robert McCrumb.

McCrumb waved at the dock where for many weeks the Tashmoo was moored at winter anchorage, made secure by 14 heavy steel cables.

"She's gone," he said. "Gone right up the river."

McCrumb remained at his post while the storm mounted. "Then the cables started snapping," he said. "They went one after the other, like they were grocery string."

McCrumb heard a crash, muffled by the wind, moments after the Tashmoo broke loose. On this tip the newsmen pushed their way a block east, to the Woodward Avenue dock of the Detroit and Windsor Ferry Co.

What the Tashmoo hit, they learned, was the ferry Promise. Anton Mensen, her engineer, and three crewmen leaped to the dock after the impact. They were getting up steam for the ferry's first morning run across the river.

The Promise was badly damaged. Her own cables snapped and she blew upshore, but the Tashmoo veered off after the crash, out into the river.

"Just like she was starting on her regular summer run up to Port Huron," a crewman volunteered.

Taking off in their vintage Model T roadster, equipped with isinglass side-curtains, the searchers made their next inquiry at the foot of Randolph, home base for the fireboat James Battle. Had anyone seen the Tashmoo heading upstream?

"No, and we haven't seen the Flying Dutchman, either," answered a skeptical fireman. When further explanation convinced him that he was not being ribbed, he offered a suggestion: "There's only one thing can stop that fool boat," he said. "The Belle Isle Bridge."

Visibility was near zero when the Model T reached the bridge, but long before the searchers sighted the Tashmoo they could hear the anguished banging of the ship against the concrete abutment. And then, there she was — listing tipsily to port, her sides gashed, but still seemingly determined to batter her way up to Lake St. Clair.

Two tugs arrived, and after a struggle to get lines aboard, they pulled the Tashmoo away from the bridge. In tandem formation, they tried to tow her to the Detroit Shipbuilding Co. dock at the foot of Orleans, where she was built.

Still she wasn't subdued. Abeam of the Walkerville ferry dock at the foot of Jos. Campau, the Tashmoo snapped the hawser and once again plunged upstream toward the bridge.

She was only 10 yards from it when the tugs got lines on her once more. This time she followed them to harbor.

Repaired and refurbished, the Tashmoo lived on for nine more years until the sad night of June 18, 1936.

She was chartered for a moonlight r i d e that evening by the Pals Club, a Hamtramck social group. A crowd of 1,400 gathered at the foot of Griswold. River traffic delayed the Tashmoo's return from her day trip, one of the cut-rate Friday excursions to Port Huron sponsored by the News. She left the dock at 9:20 p.m., 20 minutes after her longtime rival in the m o o n l i g h t trade, the Columbia, was speeding downriver.

The Tashmoo made up most of the deficit. She reached Sugar Island, near Grosse Ile, at 10:35 p.m., and started on the cruise homeward at 11:20. As she came out of Sugar Island Channel a shock was felt throughout the ship.

Passengers were told that there was engine trouble. Jean Calloway's orchestra played on, and the dancing never was more lively. But in the engine room it was different. The Tashmoo had struck a submerged rock. The wound was mortal.

As water poured in through a hole in the hull faster than the pumps could handle it, the engine room crew stoked the boiler fire in a swirling, waist-deep flood. Capt. Donald MacAlpine called for full speed ahead.

Ten minutes after the shock, the Tashmoo docked at the Brunner-Mond Co. coal wharf above Amherstburg on the Canadian side. Only after passengers and crew were safely ashore did the grand old steamer sink to the bottom in 18 feet of water. The Tashmoo's days of glory were over.

48. Olympian of the Freeway

No candidate for President ever had better staff work than John F. Kennedy, but he made one of his rare campaign mistakes in Detroit. Whirlwinding into town in 1960, he told his audience how much he enjoyed the fast ride into town "on your John Cabot Lodge Freeway."

Perhaps it was too much to expect a Massachusetts senator not to link Lodge with Cabot. But Detroit didn't name its first freeway for the Brahmin John Cabot Lodge. It was named for John Christian Lodge.

Even though a generation has matured since Lodge's death, it should never be forgotten why his name went on a Detroit freeway before those of the automotive giants, Ford, Chrysler and Fisher.

Anyone who has been trapped in a rush-hour jam on Detroit's busiest freeway might like to remember the man for whom it was named never owned an automobile and never learned to drive.

At the wheel of city government in Detroit's greatest period of growth, however, he had no rival. Lodge's lifetime covered nearly nine decades. They blanketed most of the century in which the city was transformed from a community of 40,000 to its peak population, close to two million. For more than half of that century he was a potent figure in local government.

He was a boy of 9 when, skittering around the edge of the throng assembled for the dedication of Detroit's new City Hall in 1871, he listened with interest to the orations of some of the most brassy-lunged spellbinders of the day. His own chance to

John C. Lodge never owned an automobile or learned to drive one, but his name was given to Detroit's first freeway. In a long career at City Hall he was a bulwark against civic corruption.

make a beginning in the great American game of politics came just four years later.

One autumn day in 1875 his father, Dr. Edwin A. Lodge, a physician and druggist who kept a vigilant eye on civic affairs, told him: "John, I want you to go out and do some political work."

The job consisted of distributing in the neighborhood a few cards for reform candidates and reporting back on how well the names Dr. Lodge favored were received. John took on the task with alacrity. His estimate of the neighborhood's political temper turned out to be accurate.

In his 20's Lodge became a Detroit newspaper reporter and soon specialized in politics. He proved an astute critic of the corruption that accrued from the city's ward system, which made it easy for saloonkeeper precinct-bosses and their henchmen to become entrenched in City Hall.

Out of his articles grew a better understanding on the part of the citizenry of what was going on. In 1889, when a group of leading citizens sought a reform candidate for mayor to battle the bosses, they asked Lodge's advice. He steered them to Hazen S. Pingree, who never had run for anything, with the result that proved so fortunate for Detroit and Michigan. The friendship between Pingree and Lodge remained steadfast until Pingree's death.

Lodge left journalism to become chief clerk of Wayne County's Board of Auditors in 1896. He served as secretary to Mayor George P. Codd in 1905, then became an alderman.

It was high time. Pingree was gone; the automobile brought Detroit its great boom — and while the city enjoyed its pleasant prosperity the ward heelers became guests at the public trough in greater numbers than ever. After the indictment of 11 aldermen for accepting bribes in the Cadillaqua crackdown of 1912, Lodge and other crusaders belabored the shocked city to adopt a new charter abolishing the ward system.

Lodge made speeches day and night — "whenever I could get four people together to listen," he said. The new charter won, and the nine-man Detroit City Council, its membership chosen by citywide vote, superseded the aldermen. From the beginning Lodge was the Council's strong man.

In the first election under the charter, Lodge topped the Council candidates to become Council president. He received this same honor at many later biennial elections. He filled in often as acting mayor, serving the equivalent of two full terms in the city's highest office in this way.

After World War I, when national prohibition brought new problems to the Detroit River area so convenient to Canada and rum-running gave rise to the gangster mob era, many of the old ward politicians came back out of limbo to join with those who wanted a wide-open city.

Once again, in 1927, a group of leading citizens concerned about the state of the city sought out the man they wanted to run as a law-and-order candidate for mayor.

This time it was Lodge they waited on. Lodge was 65, an age when many men think about retirement. No matter. He ran, but on the strangest platform ever seen: He would make no promises and he wouldn't make a speech or lift a finger to win the office. He won, anyway.

During his term, Lodge's grandnephew, Charles A. Lindbergh, made his epochal flight alone across the Atlantic. When Lindy visited his native city not long afterward, he took the mayor for his first plane ride. Lodge enjoyed the experience, but said it violated one of his cardinal rules — "keep both feet on the ground."

In his lifetime Lodge lost only one campaign. That was when he ran for reelection as mayor in 1929. The issue raised against him was that he was "too old."

Lodge returned to the role that he liked best, that of grand old man of the Council and the watchdog of Detroit's probity. So he is best remembered — the piercing gray eyes, his hair grown white, his wits remaining as sharp as his salty tongue. Married to the city, he remained a bachelor. There was room in his life for no other wife.

The voters wanted no divorce, either. It was Lodge's own decision to retire from the Council in 1947. He was 85. Before his death two years later, he set down his memoirs in a book aptly called "I Remember Detroit." No one had better memories, and no writer about Detroit took a more important part in carrying it through the adventurous decades of the city's greatest century run.

No one would have scoffed more sardonically about a marble monument for the man than Lodge himself, either. But a freeway as a memorial — a freeway for Detroiters on the go, those restless citizens who think nothing of running up a century run in miles between breakfast and lunchtime?

John Christian Lodge must like that.

49. Signpost from the Sea

"My Christmas present from Detroit."

That was what Charles B. King called his favorite piece of driftwood. He found it on the beach, washed up by the tide, shortly before Christmas, 1944. After it was cleaned and polished, he hung it in a place of honor on the wall of the library at Dolfincour, his estate on Long Island Sound.

In the style favored for road markers in the early days of motoring, the board was roughly shaped like an arrow. As he hunched down that day on the sand and brushed away the seaweed, he saw that it was inscribed with the word "Detroit." The letters were so faded by the elements they could barely be deciphered. Had any beacon for travelers ever journeyed so far?

The strangest part of the story was that the sign ended its wanderings at the point where King would be the one to find it. If anyone ever pointed the way for the motorists of Detroit—from Henry Ford on — it was King. The first horseless carriage on the streets of what was to become the Motor City was his brainchild.

Sitting proudly at the tiller, King was 28 when he drove gingerly out of John Lauer's machine shop at 112 St. Antoine, near Congress, on March 6, 1896. The short stretch of St. Antoine to Jefferson was negotiated without incident.

At Jefferson, King made a rolling right turn. Forthwith, he became the first Detroit motorist to be the subject of criticism.

"Watch out, it'll explode!" shouted one alarmed pedestrian.

"Turn that peanut roaster off before it spooks my horses!" commanded a brewery teamster.

King was unruffled. He steered a zigzag path through Jefferson's tangle of horsecars, surreys, coupes, runabouts and drays. The challenge of traffic exhilarated him.

Once he put on a little speed, King's contraption was accorded more respect. He was driving the world's first four-cylinder, four-cycle automobile engine. This wasn't the place to let it out, but King was sure it could do 25 miles an hour.

The young inventor may not have been seeking attention, but he didn't exactly avoid it. His next turn was north on Woodward Avenue.

Within a block or two, the engine began to backfire. King had a considerable audience when he brought the machine to a shuddering stop in front of the Russell House.

Here occurred two additional events that may be regarded as more or less historic:

For the first time, a Detroit smart aleck shouted "Get a horse!"

The first local horseless carriage expert "got out and got under."

A locomotive engineer expert among the bystanders, proud of his mechanical knowledge, offered assistance. King was glad to get it. But he had a short fuse for a reporter from the Detroit Journal who asked what may well have been the right question at what certainly was the wrong time, as far as King was concerned: "Do you think there is any future in the horseless carriage?"

Soon the mechanical problem was straightened out, and King resumed his ride. He continued out Woodward to Grand Boulevard before deciding to return to base.

Back at the machine shop he found an officer of the bicycle patrol, who hadn't been able to catch up with him on his swath through town, waiting with an ultimatum: If King didn't want to face charges of disturbing the peace, he would have to confine his appearances on the street in the gasoline buggy to the hours of 2 to 4 a.m.

"What about Belle Isle?" King asked. "Nobody is ever on Belle Isle until a lot later than 4 o'clock.

314   "The policemen agreed that King could drive on

Proud of his creation, Charles B. King was photographed with his associate, Oliver E. Barthel, in the first horseless carriage to grace the streets of what was to become the Motor City.

the island as late as 7 o'clock if no one was around to object.

The park in the river became the scene of many pleasant test runs in the dawn's early light. Often King was accompanied by his aide, Oliver E. Barthel, who became a noted automotive engineer. Sometimes Mrs. King came along, and once the passenger was their big collie, Lorna Doone. The pet couldn't be restrained from barking with excitement as they whizzed around the shore road.

Returning across the Belle Isle Bridge, King was reminded that he was not the first member of his family to be a Detroit pioneer of transportation. His grandfather, Louis Davenport, operated the first steam ferry on the Detroit River, the Argo, in 1830. Nervous citizens worried about the Argo blowing up, too.

King's father was an Army officer. Young *315*

Charles was born at Camp Reynolds, on Angel Island in San Francisco Bay. He came to Detroit in 1891, after receiving a master's degree in mechanical engineering from Cornell University.

Working in the city's railroad-car industry, King found time to tinker with inventions on the side. In 1893, he was sent to Chicago to superintend the exhibit of the Russell Car & Foundry Co. at the Columbian Exposition.

He returned with awards for several patents, including a car-coupling device and a pneumatic hammer. He also came back imbued with the horseless carriage bug, having seen a motor-driven quadricycle displayed at the fair by a German inventor.

After the debut of his own machine built in Detroit, King supplied some parts for Henry Ford's first quadricycle, which had its test run three months later. Before 1896 was over he built a small two-cylinder job for Byron J. Carter of Jackson. Carter used it as the prototype of the Carter Car, which became popular in motordom's first decades.

Following Navy service in the Spanish-American War, King designed the first three-point motor suspension for another early auto firm, the Northern Motor Car Co.

In 1907, he designed the first model with the steering wheel on the left side. He patented the automatic spark advance, the center control gear shift, and introduced running boards.

The Charles B. King Co. was organized to put out cars embodying all his innovations. The firm continued production until 1921. His most powerful model was the King-Bugatti, a 16-cylinder, 450-horsepower racing behemoth which set many records.

All this did not satisfy him. Besides possessing the sensitive fingers of a man with deep empathy for metal and wood, King was a mystic and poet at heart.

For a time he was a practicing architect. He was accomplished both as a musician and an artist. Detroit's Scarab Club sometimes displayed his paintings. His etchings were exhibited at the National Gallery of Art in Washington, D.C.

King left Detroit shortly before the United States

entered World War I, to be an engineer in the Signal Corps. After the war his 64 patents made him comfortably well off, and he built the mansion on Long Island Sound, at Larchmont, N.Y.

Nevertheless, Detroit remained in his thoughts. He turned Dolfincour into an automotive museum. He loved to roam the hills and dales in classic cars — you can still see his $500,000 collection of them at Greenfield Village, to which he bequeathed it.

In his later years he was m u c h g i v e n to introspection. On that December day when an unusually high tide cast up masses of driftwood and he picked up the waterlogged arrow, he marveled that when he found it the marker was pointing west by north, towards the city of his youthful exploits.

King set down his ponderings about it in a Christmas letter to old friends in Detroit.

"The course adopted by the marker in its long and fateful journey would be down the Detroit River, across Lake Erie, over Niagara Falls, across Lake Ontario, down the St. Lawrence, through Lachine Rapids, into the Gulf of St. Lawrence, down the Atlantic, past Nova Scotia, entering Long Island Sound and finally to Larchmont.

"However, let us think of the problem the marker had with wind and currents in passing through Lake Erie and Ontario, which could have taken years. And then again, remember the shores of the Gulf of St. Lawrence, the delays on the Atlantic, the further shores of Long Island Sound with their tides, winds and currents, on the way to Larchmont to find its future home.

"That this destination was reached must receive profound thought, with the time and chance elements considered . . . As to the years that covered the venturesome journey and the adventurous experiences, that will be a closed book which one may only surmise. And thus a marker to guide others becomes a marker to guide itself through the turbulence of a Niagara to finally accept the mystery-tide of Dolfincour."

King and Ford came together for the last time two years later, to receive motordom's highest honors at the Automotive Golden Jubilee in Detroit.   *317*

The seagoing arrow still was on King's mind as he philosophized about the pioneer era:

"When we were young," he said, "there was time every day to do great things. Now that life's winds and waters have carried us through so many vicissitudes, each year passes as swiftly as a day did then, but we know that the mystery-tide soon will bring us to rest at last upon a welcoming shore."

King continued to enjoy his classic cars until at 87 he was ruled too old to drive. In the two remaining years of his life, he liked best to take solitary walks along the beach, musing upon the strange and wonderful ways of destiny.

50. Architect of Victory

Wherever you may be in Detroit, you're close to some of the city's legacies from an immigrant boy who came to America at the age of 11.

His monuments cover many acres, for the boy was Albert Kahn, who became the father of modern industrial architecture.

The Fisher Building, the General Motors Building, the Detroit Tank Arsenal, the First National Building, the Detroit Athletic Club, the Public Schools Center, the Kresge Administration Building, Police Headquarters, the New Center Building — all were conceived on Albert Kahn's drawing board.

This article was written in a Kahn structure, The Detroit News Building, and if it had appeared in the Free Press or the old Detroit Times, the same could be said. Kahn designed their buildings, too.

But first of all he was the architect for motordom. He designed more than 1,000 buildings for Ford alone, from the Highland Park plant of yesteryear to the vast Ford Rouge complex of today. He designed for Chrysler for 17 years, and 150 worldwide General Motors plants were his brainchildren.

More than anyone else, Kahn wiped out a milieu of dark sweatshops and firetraps. He replaced them with handsome factories of glass and concrete.

His credo was: "It costs no more to plan for the welfare of the men and to make the plant bright comfortable and good-looking as well as efficient."

Yet all these accomplishments pale before the

Albert Kahn, architect for the automotive industry, planned Detroit's factories to be ready for swift conversion to wartime production needs.

singular niche in history reserved by destiny for the son born to a struggling rabbi in a Westphalian village in Germany in 1869.

The first step toward the future was taken when the rabbi immigrated alone to America, the land of promise. His family waited patiently until he could afford to send for them. Then it fell to the eldest, 11-year-old Albert, to supervise the passage of his mother, himself and five younger brothers and sisters to join the father in Baltimore.

In 1884 the family came to Detroit. Albert was sent to art classes conducted by the city's foremost sculptor, Julius Melchers. Soon his leanings toward architecture became apparent.

It was an era when neophytes in this field trained by working without pay in architects' offices. Melchers, convinced the boy had ability, sent him to the leading Detroit firm of Mason & Rice.

After nine months as office boy, young Kahn was put on the payroll at $30 a month, tracing and drafting. Years later the head of the firm, George D. Mason, said he never knew anyone with such a capacity for work and study.

"Every spare moment of the day and evening — we worked long hours in those days — Albert would spend reading our collection of architectural books," Mason recalled. "Hours meant nothing to him when he was absorbed in his work."

But the promising apprentice suffered from a handicap which could have ended his career before it really got started. He was color-blind. An associate who suspected this reported to Mason, and Kahn was summoned for a test.

Fortunately, he prepared for this contingency by learning the hue of every object in Mason's office. He passed the test with flying — albeit memorized — colors.

At 21, he entered some drawings in a contest conducted by American Architect magazine. He won a traveling scholarship to Europe.

'The only catch to the prize was that I must do 12 articles and 12 sketches on the trip," Kahn related long afterward. "In Europe, I saw so many wonderful things that I was completely bewildered. My sketches proved acceptable, but my articles — whew! After the second one, the editor wrote me, 'Never mind the articles, send more sketches.'"

Early on his Grand Tour, Kahn met Henry Bacon Jr., one of America's finest artists, and later the designer of the Lincoln Memorial in Washington, D.C. The two hit it off well and traveled together for three months. Kahn learned much about drawing from Bacon.

On his return he established an architectural firm of his own on a shoestring. One of his first commissions was to remodel the home of Henry B. Joy, then president of the Packard Motor Car Co. Joy was delighted with the result and Kahn was named to draw plans for a big Packard plant on East Grand Boulevard.

Kahn put everything he had l e a r n e d on his travels into it. His design called for reinforced concrete construction and steel window sash. It was the first of its type in the country.

Henry Ford took note. When he decided to build in Highland Park, he told Kahn what he wanted — not scores of separate buildings in the style then in vogue for manufacturing enterprises, but with all operations under one roof.

Kahn built a plant which became known around the world. It provided the ideal setting for the development of Ford assembly-line precision. Kahn soon became the architect for the industry.

In World War I many automotive leaders went to Washington as "dollar-a-year-men." They spread the word about the speed and efficiency of the Detroit architectural wizard.

Kahn was given government contracts for camps, warehouses, airfields and hangars through the country. His staff designed portable structures for shipment to France to house units of the Army Air Corps.

In all, he designed more than $200 million worth of wartime construction.

After the war he was invited to Russia to help the Soviet Union get on its feet with its first Five-Year Plan. In three years, he prepared a construction program for $500 million worth of factories. Besides building more than 500 plants, he organized technical schools to produce engineers and mechanics to run them, from Kiev, in European Russia, to Yakutsk, in Eastern Siberia.

The Kahn installations proved to be the backbone of the nation's resistance to Nazi invasion in World War II. The defense by the Russians of the model tractor plant which Kahn designed at Stalingrad resulted in a major turning point of the war.

The mention of Stalingrad is a reminder that in the analysis of history, World War II resolved itself essentially into a race — a race between the momentum achieved initially by the Axis powers and the ability of America to translate its industrial might into armament in time to turn the tide.

When the Japanese attack on Pearl Harbor thrust the United States, still largely unprepared, into the fray in 1941, a major question that emerged was:

"How long will it take Detroit to get into wartime production?"

The answer surprised the world. It upset the calculations of Adolph Hitler, who considered America too "mongrelized" to make war efficiently. If Hitler is provided with ample eons on some nether plane to ponder his earthly errors, consideration of one ironic detail may be especially salutary:

The key to the remarkable speed with which Detroit could turn from peace to war was provided by the son of the immigrant rabbi from Germany, a little man scarcely five feet tall who never raised a weapon in his life other than his pencil — Albert Kahn.

On his return home from Russia, Kahn introduced a secret ingredient into the factories he built. Each plant was designed so that it could be converted quickly to war production. Kahn saw to it that truck production lines could be readied with a few changes in conveyor belts to turn out armored cars. Auto engine lines could be transformed into aviation engine lines.

"At dusk, steering gears. At dawn, machine guns." That was the way one of his lightning-change factories worked out.

The aircraft industry repeatedly called upon him. Once aircraft tycoon Glenn L. Martin telephoned Kahn that he had to double his capacity. Could Kahn do it in 2½ months?

The plant Kahn designed for Martin at Baltimore was the size of a couple of football fields. He finished it in 11 weeks, half the time it takes to put up an ordinary house.

"A.K." accomplished it by working at top speed on an absolute minimum of sleep. Sometimes his habits resembled those of Thomas A. Edison; when pressure required working day and night, he would snatch an hour or two of sleep stretched out on a drawing board and then return to the task with fresh energies.

Tributes multiplied with the years. He became a chevalier of the French Legion of Honor and in 1937 received the gold medal of the International Exposition of Arts and Science in Paris. Honorary degrees piled up.

When Architectural Forum acclaimed him as the No. 1 industrial architect in 1938, it noted that the sun never set on his work, adducing Kahn buildings in England, France, Japan, China, Egypt, Mexico Norway — from Scotland and Sweden to South America and Siberia.

But he remained an intrinsically modest man. He worked in shirt-sleeves, pencil over ear, sounding forth instructions to his staff like a string of firecrackers. He worked hard until his death at 73 in 1942.

When the Detroit Institute of Arts saluted his career with a retrospective exhibition in 1970 the title was apt:

"The Legacy of Albert Kahn."

51. 'I Think Mr. Ford is Leaving Us'

He was one of the world's most powerful men, but the only light in his home on the night that he died came from candles and kerosene lamps. The only heat was provided by logs burning in the fireplaces. The telephones were dead.

Swollen from a torrential Easter Sunday rain, the usually placid Rouge River was on a rampage. The water was eight to 10 feet above its normal crest. Never before had it risen so high. The flood had put out of action the power plant for Fair Lane, Henry Ford's mansion on the river's north bank in Dearborn.

Only three persons were in the house on the night of Monday, April 7, 1947. They were Ford himself, his wife, Clara Bryant Ford, and a maid, Rosa Buhler. Ford was 83 and had been in a steady physical decline for three years, but he had insisted that day on seeing the damage caused by the flood.

Ray Dahlinger, his farm superintendent, first drove him to Greenfield Village. The area, where Ford had gathered structures from all over the country that reminded him of the horse-and-buggy America of his youth, was dangerously close to the river, but he was happy to find that no real harm had been done. At Rouge plant he was cheered by finding his giant ore boat, the Henry Ford II, safely in dock from its first spring trip down the Great Lakes.

In midafternoon he rejoined Mrs. Ford at Fair Lane. At dinner he talked over plans for a 100-mile trip with Dahlinger the next day.

325

Ford said that he wanted to see how the village industry centers at Milan and Flat Rock had fared. But talking made him tired. At 9 p.m. he said good night and went to his bedroom.

At about 11:15, Mrs. Ford heard him calling. She hurried to him, as always she did when Henry called. He told her he didn't feel well. His head ached, he said, and his throat was dry.

Mrs. Ford gave him a glass of water. She sent Miss Buhler to alert Robert Rankin, the family chauffeur, in his living quarters over the garage behind the house, to get a message to the family physician. It took Rankin only a few minutes to drive to the nearest workable telephone, half a mile away at the Ford Engineering Laboratories. He called Dr. John G. Mateer, of Henry Ford Hospital in Detroit, and the oldest grandson, Henry Ford II, at his home in Grosse Pointe Farms.

When Miss Buhler returned to the bedroom, she heard Mrs. Ford say, "Henry, speak to me!" Ford's heavy breathing had stopped.

"What do you think of it?" Mrs. Ford asked her. "If only the doctor would come!"

"I think Mr. Ford is leaving us," Miss Buhler said.

Mrs. Ford went to get some warmer clothing. As the maid watched Ford it seemed to her that he tried to fold his hands, as if in prayer, and there was a change in his face. She called to Mrs. Ford. The two women sat on one bed, watching him. Minutes went by and then Miss Buhler got up and listened to the old man's heart.

"I think he has just passed away," she said.

She was right. When Dr. Mateer arrived 20 minutes later, Ford's heart had stopped beating.

Fate had contrived an ironic touch in putting Ford's death in the setting of the same flickering light by which he had come into the world 83 years before. Still, his whole lifetime was marked by irony. He did more to bring about the passing of that earlier era than anyone else, unless it was his friend Thomas A. Edison. But he loved, collected and preserved the artifacts of the old way of life in one of the real passions of his life.

The people who knew Henry Ford best said goodby to him on Wednesday. His body rested on a bier

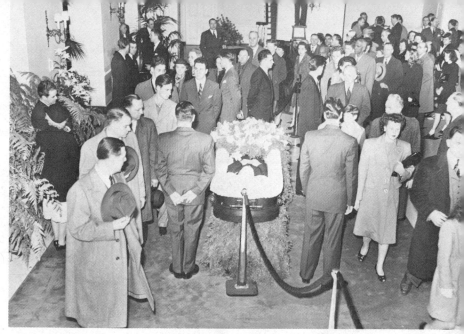

Waiting in line by the tens of thousands, Detroiters patiently filed past the bier of Henry Ford at Greenfield Village, the monument he built to the people's America from which he sprang.

at Greenfield Village. They passed the black casket at the rate of 5,000 an hour, but still the waiting line grew longer with men and women who wanted a last look at Ford's gnarled face.

In the line there was mention of the July in which he was born — the July of Gettysburg, when the struggle of Americans north and south was at the crossroads. And they spoke of Ford as he looked in a more recent July, during World War II on his last public birthday observance. It was a celebration and a testimonial to a man who had lost his only son, and who came out of retirement to work again for an America.

In the line were some who, in past decades, felt that the name of Ford was the personificaiton of America. Born under the eagles of a kaiser or czar, they crossed the seas for a new life under the eagle of freedom — coming with two words of a new tongue to guide them to their goal: "America — Ford."

327

With all seats filled in St. Paul's Episcopal Cathedral, mourners stood in the rain outside through funeral services for Henry Ford, April 10, 1947.

There were men and women in line who had been city children, and who could remember first springtimes in the country, brought to them by the rattling magic of a sturdy Model T.

In many versions, there were stories of the early days of automobiling, when a tall, gaunt stranger in a Ford, who knew all about engines, stopped to help a fellow motorist stranded on the road — and fixed the car himself, on the spot.

One man in line recalled how Ford visited a coal mine that he had just bought in Nuttalsburg, W. Va., and turned from the functionaries in blue suits to talk to the grimy miners. He said Ford asked for a suit of overalls and went down the shaft, to learn that the men worked in corridors so low they could not stand erect. He remembered, too, how quickly Ford modernized the mine.

They spoke of Henry's friendships, of the way he never forgot his friends. John Burroughs — they

thought of the thousands of birdhouses Ford put up

on his home woodland; Thomas A. Edison — they glanced toward the inventor's workshop, enshrined near by.

Some of the Ford stories stressed the adamant side of his nature — some called it, less politely, Henry's stubborn streak. Often quoted was his answer to a suggestion by one of his executives that cars be manufactured in a choice of colors.

Let the customer have the car in any color he wants," agreed Ford, "so long as it's black."

It was remembered how, at a congress of his sales managers, he listened patiently while the men suggested changes to increase sales. Ford heard them out for two hours without saying a word. Then he yawned, stood up and stretched.

"Gentlemen, as far as I can see there is only one trouble with the Ford car," he said. "We can't make them fast enough."

Other stories concerned a contrasting side of his nature, his reverence for all life.

There was the Saturday when he told Dahlinger, on a tour of the Ford farm acreage: "The wheat is ready to cut. Better get into those fields next week."

On Monday morning, a caravan of agricultural vehicles headed out to the wheat fields. Just before work began, however, the wire-wheeled Ford coupe known all over Dearborn as "the chief's" drove up.

"Better hold up a few days," F o r d told Dahlinger.

"But the crop's just right and we're ready to go," answered the farm superintendent.

"I know," said Ford. "But I took a walk here yesterday and saw a lot of meadowlarks. The young ones are still in the nests. Wait until the fledglings will be able to fly away and not get hurt."

It was remembered that when Ford moved into the Dearborn estate he delighted in roaming over the wooded acres to see how the birds and small animals were thriving.

One day his friend Charles Daniel, a former game warden, accompanied him. Driving down an old lane through the property, they came to a point where they could see running water. Nearby, a portion of the streamlet had dried, leaving an isolated pool.

329

"That water will stagnate," Ford said. "I wonder if there are fish in it?"

He leaped out of the car, followed by Daniel. They found half a dozen f i s h trapped in the pool.

"We can't let them die," Ford said.

They drove to the Ford home, obtained two pails, and returned. Scooping up water and fishes, they carried the loads to the running brook, until every marooned fish was rescued.

There were as many stories, it seemed that day, as there were men and women in the line — the almost endless line of friends of Henry Ford.

On Thursday only 600 could get inside St. Paul's Episcopal Cathedral in Detroit for the funeral. But 20,000 stood quietly outside in the rain until the long service ended.

52. Elegy at Elmwood

"Elegy at Elmwood," he might call it . . .

Certainly if poet Thomas Gray, author of "Elegy
Written in a Country Churchyard," were
transported from 18th century England to 20th
century Detroit, he could find inspiration in old
Elmwood Cemetery.

Memorial Day would be the best day for his visit.
The city's first observance of the holiday was held
at Elmwood in 1868. On every May 30 since,it has
been garlanded with fresh flowers, flags and
remembrance.

But the poet would have to come a bit earlier
than "when curfew tolls the knell of parting day."
Elmwood's gates close at 4 p.m.

If he arrived in the early morning hours, passing
the bustle of nearby Eastern Market on the way, it
would underline the deep tranquillity of Elmwood.
You don't have to be a poet, however, to enjoy a
respite "far from the madding crowd" in this
sanctuary less than two miles from Detroit's
downtown skyscrapers.

Even ducks seem to like it. A flock of wild
mallards makes good use of the little lake in the
cemetery every spring.

To the history-minded, Elmwood is a shrine to
Detroit's past. To the mallards, it's just right for a
duckling nursery.

From long experience, they know they can
safeguard their eggs there until new life emerges.
Around the corner from the city's tumult, fledglings
can take swimming lessons in a serene bit of

"It is for us the living"—a tribute to those who fought America's wars on Memorial Day in Elmwood Cemetery.

woodland, along shores lined with tiger lilies, cornflowers and lupine.

Elmwood has pheasants, too, and squirrels are numerous. You can hear birdsong in every season.

But the springtime is best. The stone monuments fit easily into the banks. From the ducks' standpoint, the valley to which they return year after year can't have changed too much since Joseph Parent became the first stroller of record along the waterside.

Parent was an early Detroit gunsmith. Because he liked to come this way to try out a fowling piece — perhaps things in town got hectic even then — the stream here came to be known as Parent's Creek.

It would be ironic if some of Parent's products were among the weapons Chief Pontiac and his tribesmen used in their 1763 siege of Detroit. Parent's Creek got a new name, Bloody Run, when

Indian guns massacred British soldiers at an ambush not far downstream.

Today, Elmwood preserves all that is left of Bloody Run, just as the stones around it preserve the memory of some of Michigan's most famous sons and daughters. The present-day stroller here is apt to be struck by the names he sees on tombstones that long have been familiar on city streets.

Witherell, John R., Sibley.

The stones tell of leaders of Michigan's territorial era. James Witherell was a judge. John R. Williams was adjutant general. Solomon Sibley was first delegate from Wayne County to the Northwest Territory Assembly.

Woodbridge, Brush and Brady—familiar street names all.

William Woodbridge was secretary of Michigan Territory, and later governor. Elijah Brush was territorial treasurer. Gen. Hugh Brady organized the Brady Guards.

Trumbull, the street past Tiger Stadium?

At Elmwood you learn its eponym. was John Trumbull, truly a striped tiger of a man. He would fascinate Thomas Gray.

In his later years, Trumbull was judge of the Connecticut Supreme Court of Errors. (Color it a judicial black.)

In his youth (color it tawny!) he was a firebrand revolutionary poet, author of 1776's biting political satire, "Fingal." In Honorius, a leading character, readers recognized the portrait of Trumbull's law mentor, John Adams.

Trumbull earned his place in Elmwood fairly. His daughter married Gov. Woodbridge, and he spent his last six years as a Detroiter. He lived to be 81.

Name any field and Elmwood has illustrious names to represent it. Discovery? Here is the grave of Douglass Houghton, explorer of Michigan's remotest wilderness.Invention? Here is the stone of William A. Burt, whose solar compass, medal winner at the World's Fair of 1851, enabled surveyors to find the true north even in iron ore country where the magnetic compass was worthless.

It wouldn't be hard to make a fair start at picking a presidential Cabinet in Elmwood. For   *333* secretary of state, there's Lewis Cass, who held office under President James Buchanan in the fatal days when America headed for the Civil War.

Cass also served as secretary of war under President Andrew Jackson. For this portfolio, however, Elmwood has another candidate in Russell A. Alger, who headed the war department under President William McKinley through the Spanish-American conflict of 1898.

Elmwood has the monuments of two Detroiters who served as secretary of the Navy. In addition to Truman H. Newberry, who helped President Theodore Roosevelt send the Great White Fleet around the world, Edwin Denby headed the department under President Warren G. Harding. Denby achieved early fame as a young congressman, when he resigned to enlist in the Army in World War I.

For secretary of the interior, Elmwood offers Zachariah Chandler, whose first contact with his future presidential chief came when Lt. U.S. Grant of the Detroit Barracks slipped on the ice on Chandler's sidewalk.

For "Elegy at Elmwood," it is clear, Thomas Gray would need to revise such lines as:

"Beneath those rugged elms, that yew tree's shade

. . . The rude forefathers of the hamlet sleep."

Detroit's forefathers were anything but rude, and Detroit itself was no hamlet — not even in Joseph Parent's time. By 1845, when the need arose for a new nondenominational burying grounds, the town was bursting at the seams.

Every vessel from the lower lakes brought new settlers to Michigan. Many of them went no farther than the port which was both the metropolis of the region and the state capital.

When the pasture on the Baker farm out Grand River was divided into building lots that summer, they went fast. The response to a subscription drive for funds for a new cemetery also was generous.

It was natural to look for a site in Hamtramck Township east of the city, where a new Catholic cemetery, Mt. Elliott, was located in 1841. The citizens paid $1,850 for 42 wooded acres along

Detroiters who bequeathed a proud heritage to their city are remembered in the quiet that reigns now along the banks of historic Bloody Run in Elmwood Cemetery.

Bloody Run on the farm of George Hunt, adjacent to Mt. Elliott.

Winding drives and sections of irregular s h a p e marked the layout adopted. It was taken from that of Mt. Auburn, in Cambridge, Mass. Elmwood Cemetery was opened Oct. 8, 1846. The next day, subscribers chose their lots at an auction, with prices ranging from $15 to $100.

One of the choicest lots, on a height overlooking a sweeping curve of the stream went to Michigan's favorite son, L e w i s Cass. Elmwood's first interment took place when the body of his eldest daughter Eliza, who died during Detroit's cholera epidemic of 1832, was reburied there.

One of Eliza's surviving sisters, Matilda, married their father's young secretary, Henry Ledyard. When Elmwood was incorporated in 1849 as a nonprofit institution with a self-perpetuating board of six trustees, Ledyard was named one of them. Serving with him were Alexander Fraser, John Owen, Charles O. Trowbridge, Israel Coe and John S. Henness.

Funds from the sale of lots were used to buy more land from the Hunt farm and from that of D.   *335*

The Veiled Lady, sculptured in Rome, survived vicissitudes of storm and shipwreck to bring a message of peace to Elmwood.

C. Whitwood, bringing Elmwood to the 83 acres it still occupies.

Elmwood Avenue was named after the cemetery and borders it on the east. The other boundaries are Lafayette on the south, Waterloo on the north and Mt. Elliott Cemetery on the east.

In 1855, a chapel of quarried limestone was built on the bank of the creek. Of Norman Gothic design, it was to be the scene of strange drama.

But America's greatest drama, the Civil War, came first. It brought marked changes for Elmwood, which through its early years was a civilian cemetery.

Elmwood's most illustrious lot-holder played an important role as the crisis came to a head late in 1860. Secretary of State Cass was 78 years old, but no one in the Cabinet stood taller as the secession of Southern states began. When President

Buchanan failed to send aid to the beleaguered garrison in the forts of Charleston harbor in South Carolina, Cass denounced his chief and resigned. His stirring words electrified the North.

After the bombardment of Fort Sumter a few months later, Cass was a living symbol of unity as he stood shoulder to shoulder with Michigan's Republican leader, Sen. Zachariah Chandler, at a mass meeting in the Campus Martius on April 17, 1861.

The men who m a r c h e d off to war from the Campus that day, and later, earned for Elmwood Cemetery a proud distinction it shares with a scant handful of national shrines. By Act of Congress, the flag is flown both night and day over Elmwood's military plot.

Among the 205 officers and men buried there are members of the 24th Michigan, which suffered the highest casualties of all the 400 northern regiments at Gettysburg. Out of a fighting force of 400, all but 99 were killed or wounded on the battle's first day.

It was the Michigan men's heroic defense of Culp's Hill that paved the way for Gettysburg to become the turning point of the war. The commander of the 12th Corps on the hill that desperate day was Michigan's highest-ranking officer, Gen. Alpheus S. Williams.

B e l l e Isle has an equestrian statue of Gen. Williams, but his grave is in Elmwood. A Detroit attorney who had served in the Mexican War, he was put in charge of all state troops by Gov. Austin Blair. The Detroit Light Guard was mustered in at the mass meeting addressed by Cass and Chandler, and the Sherlock, Brady and Scott Guards followed. Gen. Williams organized an instruction camp at Fort Wayne for later volunteers.

One of the most memorable stories associated with the Civil War dead at Elmwood began when the First Michigan Cavalry was mustered in, 1,150 strong, in September, 1861. In command as it left for the Potomac was 40-year-old Col. Thornton F. Brodhead, who had been postmaster of Detroit.

Col. Brodhead was fatally wounded at the Second Battle of Bull Run. As he lay dying on the battlefield, he wrote a last letter to a brother. The message became the inspiration for one of the war's best loved songs, "The Old Flag Will

Triumph Yet."

He wrote: "I am passing now from earth; but send you love from my dying couch. For all your love and kindness you will be rewarded. I have fought manfully, and now die fearlessly. But the old flag will triumph yet. I had hoped to have lived longer, but now die amid the ring and clangor of battle as I would wish."

Detroit's naval armory near the Belle Isle Bridge was named in 1944 after Col. Brodhead's grandson, Richard Thornton Brodhead. He had a distinguished career of more than 40 years as a Navy officer.

While no city outdid Detroit in loyalty to the flag, Elmwood has the grave of one remarkable citizen who followed the lost cause of the Stars and Bars with devotion. This was Sylvester W. Higgins, the man for whom Higgins Lake in the north central part of the Lower Peninsula in named.

The strange story of his life includes many adventures on many frontiers. He went into the wilds as a protege of Douglass Houghton, and helped to explore and survey remote regions of the Upper Peninsula.

Higgins turned up in 1848 in California as an associate of the unfortunate John Augustus Sutter, whose little paradise at Sutter's Fort was overrun and ruined in the prospectors' rush that followed the nearby discovery of gold.

Restless, Higgins moved on to Texas and became a prosperous cattle rancher. When the Lone Star State joined the Confederacy he enlisted in the cavalry.

He saw hard-riding action in the campaigns of the Southwest. Before the war was over he was colonel of his regiment. But his health was gone. He died of consumption in 1866 in St. Louis. His body was brought back to Elmwood, to the city he still thought of as home.

To balance Elmwood's ledger in the conflict, which those who suffered most called the Brothers' War, it has the grave of a Virginia officer who remained loyal to the Union, Maj. Gen. Philip St. George Cooke.

A Mexican War veteran, Cooke was noted for leading his Mormon battalion on a 2,000-mile trek from Fort Leavenworth in Kansas Territory to Los

Elmwood's chapel had its most memorable day on Easter Sunday, 1898, when spectators filled the slopes around it during services for Margaret Mather, beloved on the stage as Juliet.

Angeles in 1846. En route he raised the first American flag over Fort Tucson.

From 1870 to 1873 C o o k e commanded the Department of the Lakes, with headquarters in Detroit. He found life here so charming that after his retirement he remained as a resident, occupying himself with writing several volumes of lively reminiscences — "Scenes and Adventures in the U.S. Army" and "Conquests of New Mexico and California."

Cooke's adventures read like fiction, but so did the lives of two members of the famed All-Indian Company K Sharpshooters, Joseph Hagler and Nath-Jah-Mi-No-Ling Jacko, who also are buried at Elmwood. Both were from Harsen's Island.

Elmwood never had a color bar. Here are the headstones of the Rev. George DeBaptiste, Dr. Joseph Ferguson and William Lambert, leaders of

339

the colony of freedmen which thrived in Detroit in the years before the Civil War.

The three aided hundreds escaping from bondage in the South who reached the Detroit terminus of the "Underground Railroad," in the big barn of the Finney House at State and Griswold. At night the Detroiters rowed the fugitives across the Detroit River, out of the reach of slave-catchers.

The man who was to become the Great Emancipator, Abraham Lincoln, quoted from Gray's Elegy in 1860 when he was asked to supply material for a campaign biography, likening his own story to "the short and simple annals of the poor." In November, 1863, at Gettysburg, he honored in his own elegy "the brave men, living and dead, who struggled here" whose names would be graven in all the Elmwoods of America.

Don Lochbiler, newspaperman, with *The Detroit News* since 1927, retired as its historical writer in 1973. Also a poet and dramatist, he was the recipient of a New York Theatre Guild prize in 1930. In recognition of his newspaper work, he has received awards from the Common Council of the City of Detroit, the Detroit Historical Society, and the United Press International, in addition to many Michigan newspaper awards.

The book was designed by Richard Kinney and Julie Paul. The text type is Intertypes Imperial designed by Edwin W. Shaar in 1957. The text was set in the plant of *The Detroit News*. The display type is Cooper Black designed by Oswald B. Cooper about 1920. This book was manufactured in the United States of America.